How to Adopt Internationally

A Guide for Agency-Directed and Independent Adoptions

2000-2002 Edition

by

Jean Nelson-Erichsen
L.S.W., M.A., Human Development

Heino Erichsen
M.A., Human Development

Mesa House Publishing
A Division of Two Coyotes, Inc.
Fort Worth, Texas

Cover design by Jim Dodson
Text design by Scott Anderson

Editorial correspondence and requests for permission to reprint should be mailed to Mesa House Publishing, c/o Two Coyotes, Inc., 3202 Greene Avenue, Fort Worth, Texas, 76109. E-mail should be addressed to books@mesahouse.com.

This publication is intended to provide accurate information in regard to the subject matter presented. It is sold with the understanding that the publisher is not engaged in rendering legal, financial, medical, or other professional services.

ISBN: 0-940352-13-3

Printed in the United States of America

Acknowledgments

*W*e would like to thank Jo-Anne Weaver, adoptive parent of a Chinese daughter, who put us in contact with Mesa House Publishing.

Several people were kind enough to supply facts and figures. Maureen Evans of the Joint Council of International Children's Services, Amy Thurston of the National Adoption Information Clearinghouse, the staff at Adoptive Families of America, Dr. William Pierce of the National Council for Adoption, Peter Pfund, Assistant Legal Advisor for Private International Adoption Law at the U.S. Department of State, Mark Leno of the U.S. Department of Agriculture, Lorna Adams, U.S. Immigration and Naturalization Service — Houston office, and Lorraine Lewis of the U.S. Department of State.

A special thank you goes to Jerri Ann Jenista, M.D., who reviewed the medical section and to Sylvia Franzmeier, ACSW, LMSW, ACP, QCSW, who reviewed the sections on the adjustments of adoptive families.

Table of Contents

Sample Forms and Documents

Introduction

When I look back at our first international adoption experience way back in 1973, it seems quaint by today's standards. We took the dearth of information both at home and abroad for granted. "We'll find out when we get there," we reasoned.

Little did we know that the Information Age would change the way we view the world, including international adoption. Most parents today would not proceed with as little information as we had back then. Today's prospective adoptive parents surf the Internet for adoption agencies and make comparisons. They check out the U.S. State Department Web site (http://travel.state.gov/) that publishes adoption procedures country-by-country. They join news groups for emotional support and tidbits from the latest adoption experiences. Their orphan referral is emailed to them and an image of the orphan is attached on gif or jpg files.

However, back when my German-American husband and I adopted twin babies from Colombia, we seemed to be the first parents adopting in South America. Aside from a quick home study and INS filing, we were unable to get much additional information about what would happen on our adoption trip. We had only a rough idea of how long it would take and how much it would cost.

And as for the twins, all we had were their names — Rosana and Tatiana. Such beautiful Latin names. We had no photographs, medical history, or social information. Just before we flew abroad, we received their birth certificates.

We were not too worried about the care and feeding of our infants. At that point, we were seasoned parents. We had two sons, Jörg and Art, who had already graduated high school and a baby boy named Kirk. We had started the process when Kirk was only six months old because we thought it would take a year or more to have a baby girl placed with us. Little did we know that we would soon have three babies!

When we finally laid eyes on our Spanish/Indian twins, we couldn't have been happier. But outside the orphanage, we bumbled along, shocked at the tiny beggar children and baffled by the adoption and visa procedures.

When we left the adoption agency in Bogotá, Colombia, with our new twin daughters in the spring of 1973, the director pressed photographs of eight older children in my husband's hand. We had no idea that we would soon become volunteers for adoption agencies trying to find homes for these "waiting children" who ranged in age from 3 to 6 years old. Back in the United States, prospective adoptive parents fell in love with the photos, and all eight children soon found homes. The new parents might have been slightly better prepared than we were in terms of the process of international adoption, but not all of them were able to contend with postplacement adjustment problems, such as the acting out of neglected, abused, institutionalized children or the acting out of biological children who did not want to share their parents with an exotic newcomer. One of those adoptions disrupted within three months.

Our involvement and knowledge of international adoption continued to grow. Soon we were volunteering for numerous adoption organizations. Adoption agencies referred couples to us for insight and information on international adoption. We spoke to other prospective parents at adoption seminars.

Though it inspired and delighted us to see so many orphaned children from so many different countries finding a home within a loving family, we also came across too many heartbreaking situations that could have been avoided.

Through an adoption support group, we met families who were trying to adopt from Latin America through good-hearted but inexperienced missionaries or greedy, unlicensed, and unschooled facilitators. Time, money, and emotion were spent for naught. The missionaries helped with the adoption, but too often in the end, the child did not qualify for an immigrant orphan visa. The facilitators bribed and bulldozed their way through the adoption system. Unfortunately, the adopters had no recourse when things went wrong. Sometimes the child they longed for did not appear. And sometimes the facilitator vanished with the money.

We also met parents who had adopted children from Asia. Unlike us, they had adopted through established international adoption programs that had developed a procedure to follow. Korea, still recovering from war, had orphanages full of abandoned children. The orphans were brought under guardianships to the United States to approved couples. Unfortunately, most couples adopting from this Asian nation did not have any more information about heritage and culture than the Colombian adopters. They, too, fell in love with a picture and had but a scant bit of social and medical history. Many fell into the same state of disappointment, expecting a quick adjustment, few language barriers, and little pigment.

But for real Asian drama the Baby Lift orphans had every story beat. As Vietnam fell to the communists, panicked parents handed their children to

American officials for quick transport to the United States. Unsure that they would survive themselves, parents were desperate to save their children. Yet, while children of the Baby Lift were being placed in adoptive American homes, some of their parents were making their way toward freedom in Thailand and eventual immigration to the United States. Within a few years, they were holding a green card and a phone, hoping to find their children. Custody suits — the only ones to ever result from an international adoption — followed.

The Baby Lift taught adoption authorities a lesson they never forgot. Refugee children are no longer placed for adoption unless there is documented proof that the child was legally relinquished, orphaned, or abandoned.

Still, it seems that every few years, the media plays on our heartstrings with images and stories of babies languishing in dismal orphanages across the world. And even in this Information Age, not everyone knows that they cannot simply fly abroad to pick up an orphan that they have heard about. The parents are heartbroken and the orphan is stranded when the new family gets to the airport and learns that they cannot bring the child home without an adoption decree and a U.S. orphan visa.

Such was the drama played out in Eastern Europe just a few years ago when televised scenes from Romania's orphanages were broadcast into U.S. living rooms. Good-hearted Americans quickly embarked on a rescue mission. With only the image of a white orphan in mind, they flew to Romania to visit orphanages, pick out a child, and find its parents in order to get them to sign a relinquishment. Sometimes they handed over their coats and jewelry to sweeten the deal. They flew home with their new children and became local celebrities. Unfortunately, not every adoption had a happy ending. Some adoptive parents who had little to go on beyond the vision of rescuing an orphan were not always able to cope with the reality of a needy, institutionalized child. Discussions of attachment disorders and reactive detachment disorders began to seep into the media and newsgroups.

The Romanian government eventually closed access to orphanages by individuals and set up a national Romanian Adoption Committee (RAC). The RAC, in turn, set up a national licensing standard for international adoption agencies. In addition, the RAC requires Romanian nationals who place children for adoption to set up legal foundations for that purpose. The foundations are then required to fund and administrate private foster homes and orphanages. The Romanian government intends to phase out public orphanages as soon as possible. Hopefully, there will never be another situation like there was in Romania.

Despite the occasional stories of sadness and heartbreak, we saw the vast majority of families formed through international adoption — including our own — grow and flourish. Inspired, we began to form a plan for a new international adoption agency that could meet the needs of adoptive families as well as the unique needs of orphans. We founded Los Niños International Adoption Agency in 1981. The same year, we returned to Colombia to renew our relationships with adoption agencies there and to show the twins the orphanage where they had waited for us. While in Colombia, we were introduced to a 9-year-old boy named Omar. He was so cute, bright, and eager to please that we quickly gave in when Kirk, Tatiana, and Rosana insisted that we adopt him. Omar joined our family three months later. Today we are the proud parents and grandparents of a multiracial family. Regardless of whether our children and grandchildren are biological or adopted, they are our most precious treasures.

The number of homeless children has not diminished over the past quarter of a century, even though 12,000-15,000 orphans are adopted by U.S. citizens each year. Unfortunately, the steps required to legally adopt and immigrate foreign orphans are still not common knowledge.

When we wrote the first edition of our book on international adoption more than 20 years ago, our goal was to pave the way for more families by providing solid and practical information. Prior editions have helped thousands of couples and singles to legally adopt and immigrate a child to love. In addition, by the year 2000, the international adoption agency we started in 1981 will have placed more than 2,000 foreign-born children in U.S. homes. The results of international adoption are all around us now in loving homes, schools, and churches. We hope this latest edition of *How to Adopt Internationally* will continue to work the same miracles.

Jean Nelson-Erichsen
Heino Erichsen

CHAPTER 1

Is International Adoption Right For You?

According to the National Adoption Information Clearinghouse, approximately 65,000 nonrelated children are adopted each year by U.S. citizens. This includes international adoptions. Yet, it's estimated that approximately 500,000 women seek to adopt a child. For many couples beginning to explore adoption, the process seems fraught with long waits and stringent requirements. While many older children, sibling groups, and special needs children are available for adoption, there are relatively few healthy, U.S.-born babies compared to the number of people looking to adopt. Because birth control and abortion are accessible to most U.S. citizens, fewer unplanned babies are born. In addition, most unmarried mothers are choosing to keep their babies.

Most adoption support groups advise couples looking to adopt a healthy, U.S.-born, Caucasian baby that the wait will be at least 12-36 months, depending on the agency or attorney selected and the decision of the family to aggressively advertise or to wait for an agency referral. Applicants seeking to adopt an African-American child will usually have a shorter wait.

Yet, transracial adoptions are still surrounded by controversy. Although thousands of Caucasian couples have adopted minority children, most have done so through private agencies. Until recently, many states had laws and policies strongly favoring the placement of children (particularly African-American and Native-American children) with parents of the same race. Unfortunately, this policy resulted in continued foster care for children when same-race parents were not available. A federal law passed in 1996 forbids state public agencies from making same-race placements a priority over timely interracial placements. This law is helping children leave foster care for permanent adoptive homes. According to the most recent statistics from the Department of Health and Human Services, 500,000 children are currently in foster care, but only 110,000 of those have an adoptive placement plan, meaning that the parental rights have been either relinquished or terminated and the child is eligible for adoption by a nonrelated adult.

However, it can still be difficult to adopt a locally born child, whether racially matching or not. Usually, couples and singles adopting through a local social service office will be shown pictures and biographical information on children they could parent well. Applicants then select the child they are most interested in adopting. They, along with other applicants, are then considered for the same child. A social worker assigned to the child, working in cooperation with the rest of the social service staff, selects the adoptive family he or she feels is best for the child. Adoptive parents may have to apply for many different children before they are finally matched with a child. On the bright side, many individuals who might not be accepted by a private agency are accepted at county social service offices. Foster parents, parents over fifty, parents with large families, and those with low incomes are eligible as adoptive parents through public social service agencies.

The procedure at private adoption agencies is quite different. When prospective adoptive parents work with a private agency, the birth mothers, under the supervision of social workers, choose a family from their pictures and profiles. Not surprisingly, birth mothers tend to choose people that they themselves would have wanted as parents. Young, attractive couples with an active lifestyle and an upper-middle income have the best chance of being chosen. Terms of "openness" regarding disclosure of information about the biological mother are negotiated at this time. The costs involved are similar to that of an international adoption.

To cope with the high demand for babies, private U.S. adoption agencies have established strict rules in an attempt to be fair to the adoptive parents. Childless couples take first priority. Some agencies may even require that the couple be infertile. Twenty-five- to thirty-five-year-old adopters without physical disabilities are considered to be ideal. Single parents are not accepted at many agencies. If the adoption agency is religiously affiliated, preference may be shown on the basis of religion. (As noted in Chapter 3, adoption agencies will often waive their requirements when potential clients have found a U.S.-based international agency or foreign source that will accept them as parents.)

Those who have become disillusioned with this process, who do not meet the requirements for a U.S. adoption, who believe in ZPG (zero population growth), or who simply have a strong desire to adopt a foreign child often turn to international adoption. The number of foreign-born orphans adopted by U.S. citizens rose from 9,356 in 1988 to 15,774 in 1998.

In addition to shorter waits and less stringent requirements, there are many other advantages to international adoption. One main advantage is that there is no competition for a child. Once you have been approved by the adoption agency and the Immigration and Naturalization Service (INS) and you have prepared documents for a foreign court, a child will be selected and referred to you. The U.S.-based international adoption agency's representative

COPING WITH THE INTERNATIONAL ADOPTION PROCESS: HOW ARE YOU LIKELY TO HANDLE IT?

Adopting abroad means pleasing a lot of entities. Your state welfare department, your local adoption agency, the Immigration and Naturalization Service (INS), and the presiding judge each have an interest in your capabilities as an adoptive parent. Each entity needs assurance that the adoption will endure.

Each of these entities will give you a list of documents that they require in order to approve your home study, to approve your advance petition to classify an orphan as an immediate relative, and to grant a final adoption decree. If you readopt your foreign-born child in your state of residence, you will also have to meet the requirements of the court in your county.

At this point, you might ask yourself, "Why do I have to measure up to someone's idea of the perfect parent when all I want is to bring a child into my life? Biological parents don't have to go through this!"

Of course, biological parents are not necessarily good at parenting. Most of them would benefit from the type of training you will be receiving. To work successfully with an adoption agency, you will fare best if you are naturally kind, open, trusting, understanding, and flexible in dealing with unforeseen problems. You must be helpful and cooperative during this long and complicated process. In the past, you have probably had to put your trust in other professionals to reach your goals. If you can tell that forming this kind of relationship with your adoption agency is going to be difficult, think about the fact that successful parenthood requires the same kinds of traits.

Here's a summary of some personalities commonly seen in the adoption process. It may help you understand your strengths and weaknesses in coping with the adoption process.

Dreamers: These are sensitive, intuitive people who feel driven to help others. They do not fear the unknown and are willing to explore new pathways. They involve themselves in causes to help humanity. They volunteer to help their agency and make contributions after they have adopted. Dreamers are popular with everyone because they are articulate, loving, and so persuasive that they are able to bring out the best in everyone around them.

Behavior: The Dreamer looks at international adoption in terms of the big picture and does not bother with the details. Unfortunately, they can set themselves up for disappointment if they are not realistic about the requirements or about the child of their dreams. However, dreamers make good ambassadors on their adoption trips. If they travel with a group and find a problem abroad, they quickly act as mediators to help find solutions.

Tips for Dreamers: Make certain that your ideas about the adoption process, your dreams of the child, and your perceptions of the trip abroad are realistic. Talk to the agency director in person and visit with other families who have recently adopted before you apply. Be certain that you are not under any illusions or assumptions. Your dream of a child must match the reality of an institutionalized child — in appearance and behavior. Reread all of the information you have been given by your agency to make certain that you know what will happen in each step of the process.

Organizers: Stable and conservative, organizers are always well prepared. They are always on time, dependable, reliable, and make their environments orderly and structured. Organizers have strong opinions. They uphold policies, procedures, and rules. They support established social norms and traditions. They take on a lot of responsibilities and like to take care of others, which is one of the best reasons for why they are adopting a child.

Behavior: Organizers send perfectly prepared documents to their adoption agency in record time. They answer the questions in their international parenting courses thoroughly. They are likely to advise their adoption agency on how to improve their delivery of services. The organizer's biggest problem is in trying to accept some of the vagaries of international adoption regarding waits and schedules. They need to know on a regular basis how they stand in the waiting pool. Once they have been assigned a child, they want a schedule of events for each day they are abroad, even though these appointments are not usually finalized until they are abroad. They become frustrated and tend to become outraged when changes occur.

Tips for Organizers: Make an outline or a flow chart of the sequential adoption steps you have already accomplished. Ask pertinent questions of the adoption agency staff to track your progress. If you are suddenly told something in the process has changed, think about how your cooperation is helping your family, the staff at the agency, and especially your future child. Get a copy of *The Adoptive Parent Preparation System* published by the Joint Council on Adoption to complete your preparation. Envision a clear picture of the end result, when you are back home with your child in your arms.

Risk Takers: Risk Takers are resourceful and practical. They have great problem-solving skills and thrive in a crisis as well as in situations where the outcome is unknown. They make friends easily because they are charming, witty, and exciting. Risk takers live for today and dislike having to live by a time clock or a schedule.

Behavior: The Risk Taker is not very well organized when it comes to documentation. They tend to skim their agency's written directions and instructions rather than studying them. However, they are practical. They need to know their status in the waiting pool at all times. They love to discuss, to argue, and to rework their adoption plans. The wait for the referral of a child is extremely frustrating to them. They want to dispense with all the red tape and just go!

Tips for Risk Takers: Rewrite your adoption plans. Discuss alternatives to your original plan with your adoption agency staff whenever you feel the need to do so. They will help you readdress each issue. Would another country be more suitable? What positive activities can you latch on to during your wait for a referral and a court date? Reward yourself each time you progress through a step. Once you are satisfied with your adoption plan, at least for the time being, complete your international adoptive parenting training. Then look at the tips given to the Organizers.

Thinkers: These are the folks everyone calls "workaholics" because they live for the pursuit of information and self-improvement. They look at international adoption in terms of the big picture, such as international treaties and demographic changes. They come up with a lot of theories. Adopting a child brings out their playful side and gives them a reason to loosen up. They think big — although not necessarily realistically. Their calls to the adoption agency are logical and quick. They mostly want to know where to find objective information.

Behaviors: Thinkers are analytical and examine cause and effect. They are concerned about how international adoptions are viewed in Third World "sending countries." They think about the social change affected by international families in First World "receiving countries." They are frustrated at the dearth of information provided by adoption agencies. Thinkers want books, social studies, and research.

Tips for Thinkers: Your adoption agency may not have enough material or manpower to satisfy the scope of your intellectual needs. University social science libraries; the National Council for Adoption (NCFA); the Joint Council on International Children's Services (JCIC); Adoption Medical News newsletter; and the Internet will provide all of the information currently available. Two documents you may wish to obtain from NCFA or JCIC are the Inter-country Adoption Act and the Hague Convention on the Protection of Children and Cooperation in Respect of Inter-country Adoption.

will locate a child based on the age, gender, ethnicity, etc. that you requested. Another compelling reason for adopting legally abroad is the fact that the stringent requirements concerning the documentation of a child's status as an orphan by both the U.S. and child-placing governments make custody suits by foreign birth parents virtually unheard of. Everyone in America remembers the outcome of the Baby Jessica case, and most courts still seem inclined to rule in favor of the birth parent's rights rather than the child's rights.

Most importantly, international adoption opens a whole new dimension in your life. Suddenly, you view your child's homeland as yours as well. You pay more attention to news of that part of the world. Your foray into another country and culture becomes a hot news item, too. Word travels fast. New acquaintances of that ethnic group and others are eager to celebrate your family's diversity. Just as suddenly, your adopted child gathers a caring flock of adults and children who become your friends as well.

As the Pulitzer Prize winning journalist, Charles Krauthammer recently wrote, "Fertility rates in the United States are barely at replacement level. In 40 years, there would not be enough working young people to pay pensions for the old were it not for immigration. Immigrants are the magic cure — the American cure — for the birth dearth."

Immigrant orphans are doubly magic. They evoke social change. Infants and children bridge American social divisions of color, culture, and nationality. After more than a quarter of a century of watching international adoption statistics, I've seen a generation of children grow up and take positions in society as responsible citizens.

Our family has extended far beyond the confines of a white middle-class community. We benefited from the companionship of children and adults of other ethnicities and nationalities we otherwise might not have met. Heino and I both feel that the time, money, and energy we expended to raise our family and to establish Los Niños International Adoption Center has been worth every minute and every penny. Sometimes our house and our office are like a joyful mini United Nations. Our lives have been enriched beyond all measure.

It's a special blessing to see these happy infants, children, and teenagers so confident and secure within the circle of a loving family.

EVALUATING MOTIVES FOR ADOPTION

Despite all of the advantages, international adoption is not for everyone. As with a biological birth or any other adoption, the parent and child are entering a life-long relationship. Adopting a foreign child means that your family will become intercultural and perhaps interracial. Furthermore, your family will remain changed for all future generations as your child grows up, forms friendships, dates, marries (perhaps a different minority), and begins a family of his or her own.

Before even beginning the process of international adoption, potential adopters need to examine their motives and carefully consider the challenges of adopting and raising a foreign-born child.

A skilled social worker can lead prospective adopters to decide whether or not their abilities and motives are sufficient for a long-term transracial relationship. For example, one of the first questions a social worker might ask ("Why do you want to adopt a foreign child?") may bring forth a straight-forward answer, an around-the-bush answer, an angry retort, or even a shocked or baffled silence.

One of the most frequent responses to the question is, "We are an infertile couple." More than half of all international adoption candidates are unable to bear a child. New technologies encourage would-be parents to continue their treatments for many years. Sometimes a woman doesn't consider adoption until she is in her late thirties or early forties. Unfortunately, at that point she is over the age limit to adopt an infant from some foreign countries.

A social worker interviewing an infertile couple may want to discuss how the couple feels about their inability to produce children. Are they angry or resentful that they must seek help? Authorities on the subject of infertility believe that infertile parents are not able to cope well with parenthood until they learn to handle the emotional stress of infertility and to resolve their dreams of producing children.

Some other common responses to the question "Why do you want to adopt a foreign child?" are listed below:

We prefer to put our money toward adopting a child rather than spending it on high-tech infertility treatments.

We don't want to get involved with local birth mothers.

We've had several adoptive placements fall through.

We're worried about possible repercussions with the open adoptions that are common in domestic placements.

We don't meet the age, length of marriage, religious, or other requirements of U.S. adoption agencies.

We don't want to wait two to three years for a baby.

We prefer to adopt rather than produce a child in an already overpopulated world.

We believe in ZPG (zero population growth) philosophy: produce two children and adopt the rest.

I am still nursing my toddler; I want to adopt a tiny baby to nurse.

*We want to adopt from _____ (country) because there is
less prejudice toward people of that nationality than toward other
nationalities in our locality.*

*I am single. Local adoption agencies will not place a U.S.-born
baby with me.*

I have a medical problem that prevents another pregnancy.

Our family has all boys, no girls; or all girls, no boys.

*We are capable of dealing with medical disabilities. We would
like to adopt a handicapped child.*

I have a history of stillbirths and miscarriages.

Most of these responses exhibit a responsible sincerity, and few seem
likely to end in failure. Whereas the responses listed below may be given in
all sincerity, their potential for failure is higher.

*We want to adopt a child orphaned in Bosnia because of the war; in
Honduras because of the hurricane; in Mexico because of the earth-
quake; and so on. (Every child deserves a parent and should not have
to feel grateful for being saved. In addition, children orphaned or made
homeless by disaster are not necessarily available for adoption.)*

*We want to try to get pregnant and adopt at the same time. Then we'll
go with whatever happens first. (This is irresponsible. Both choices are
highly stressful. The couple needs to decide. To turn down the referral
of an orphan because of a pregnancy can delay the orphan's placement
with a different family for many months.)*

*One of us was medically sterilized through a vasectomy or tubal
ligation.*

*We want a child to enhance our marriage. (OK, if they don't mean
to save the marriage.)*

*We want a child of every race. (Child collectors? Liberals out to prove
their viewpoints?)*

*Our child died. (Counseling is needed to be certain the parents do not
expect an identical replacement for the dead child.)*

*We want an older child because we hate the loss of sleep and the mess
connected with baby care.*

We want a playmate for our only child. (The children may not be able to get along with each other for a year or more.)

We want an older child, handicapped child, or sibling group unlikely to be adopted by anyone else. (Do parents expect gratitude and recognition?)

Some of the most important questions, however, cannot be answered with any degree of certainty: Will the child feel that there is something wrong with him because his mother rejected him? Will the parents and child grow to love each other? Will racial prejudice appear only after the child joins the family? Will the family stay together throughout the child's growing-up years? Adopters must learn to know themselves before they create a family in the hope of living happily ever after.

Adoptive parents must be able to acknowledge that their foreign-born children will always have a unique situation. Coping with the fact that they have another set of parents somewhere and that they are racially and/or culturally different from you can be difficult during childhood and adolescence. Counseling and/or family therapy are sometimes necessary. Adoptees end up explaining their adoptive status throughout their lives, even as adults.

Most foreign adoptions within our experience have been successful placements. However, children older than two, handicapped children, and sibling groups present a greater challenge to a harmonious family adjustment. The most successful placements of children more than two years old occur when the parents fulfill the child's needs without expecting anything in return. These parents adopt knowing that the child may not be able to love or trust them for many years. If you are applying for a child more than two years of age, remember that he or she already has a personality, memories, habits, and probably a different language.

AN OVERVIEW OF THIS BOOK

In addition to examining individual motives, potential adopters need to have a clear understanding of the international adoption process itself and the legal requirements, expenses, and potential bureaucratic headaches that can be part of the process. This book is designed to do that by first giving an overview of the international adoption process (Chapter 3) and then providing the information for a step-by-step approach to conducting a successful international adoption (Chapters 4-15) should you decide to pursue this route. Samples of most of the documents needed for an international adoption are included at the end of the chapter in which they are discussed.

The last half of the book is a Compendium of the adoption laws and requirements for most countries participating in international adoption. For each country listed, the Compendium includes a summary of the adoption laws for that country, the central authority in charge of adoption, the address and phone number for the U.S. visa issuing post, and, if available, the number of orphans immigrated into the United States from that country. In addition, the Compendium also includes basic information on geography, demography, language, currency, and major religions.

How to Adopt Internationally also includes an Appendix and a Bibliography. The Appendix includes a collection of resources and contacts that may be helpful during the adoption process, including information on adoptive parent support groups; addresses and phone numbers for district offices of the INS; and contact information for state licensing agencies that supervise adoption agencies. Although care was taken to include the most recent information available, phone numbers, addresses, fees for filing INS forms, etc., change frequently. You can find updated information for many of these items on the Internet. We include Web site addresses along with other information when possible.

The Bibliography includes a list of recommended books on cross-cultural, interracial, and special needs adoption; magazines and newsletters of adoptive parent groups; information on travel and foreign languages; and other resources that may be helpful as you research and pursue an international adoption.

Finally, the book includes a Glossary of common terms used in the international adoption process as well as an Index to the content of the book.

CHAPTER 2

A Parent's Journal

Before moving on to the more practical proceedings of international adoption, we've provided an excerpt highlighting the personal journal of one set of adoptive parents. This brief selection provides a glimpse of how foreign children and their adoptive families begin to adjust to one another and illustrates a few of the unexpected joys and bureaucratic mishaps that are common in international adoption.

Jan and Bob Ostrum, both teachers, decided to adopt rather than to produce more children in our overpopulated world. The Ostrums chose Colombia because they had a knowledge of the language and an appreciation for the culture. Jan's journal is printed here in a condensed version.

As the Ostrums' experience illustrates, there are major differences in children and how they react to an adoptive placement. Some things reported by the Ostrums appear to be related to culture. Some may be the child's temperament. Others may be related to family changes. Adoptive parents are stuck with the job of trying to separate one from the other in a child who may not have the language or emotional or developmental maturity to express his or her feelings.

Adoption is the aftermath of a tragedy. Every child who is adopted has lost a mother, a father, and other familial ties. Abandonment, relinquishment, and death are all perceived as final separations. Many social service professionals believe that even the tiniest infant feels this loss and experiences grief. These emotions affect the way that each adopted child adjusts to his or her new life in an adoptive family.

Adoption can change a child's behavior. A child's needs are intensified. He or she may be anxious and demanding and may push his new parents to prove over and over again that they will provide care and protection.

THE OSTRUMS' JOURNAL

April 10: Bob sends our adoption application airmail, registered special delivery, to Colombia!

April 28: Surprised by a phone call from Bogotá as I plant our first vegetable garden. So astounded when told that Bob and I have a boy, four, and a girl, two, that I forget to ask for children's names or whether they are siblings! I, of course, say yes, we will accept them. Directress wants to know when we can come down. Says the children are of medium complexion and that's it. Bob isn't home. He's pitching at a baseball game. I call and have him paged. He says, "I have to go somewhere and think about this." We are both still unbelieving.

April 30: I tell my supervisor and the staff. Everyone is so happy for us!

May 1: Receive birth certificates in the mail. Boy, Clamaco Perez. Girl, Carmen Perez. We like the name Carmen, not sure about Clamaco. We both like Maco. Take papers to the International Institute for translations. We're excited and thrilled.

June 18: Much has happened since May. Just a few days before we received notice of our approval from Immigration (INS), we got a letter from Bogotá telling us not to come down until they notified us. We called that night to find out why, but the directress told us to call the next day. Bob called. The directress said she couldn't remember; she would write us.

June 20: It was a depressing day; the day we were supposed to have left for Colombia.
We've done so much to prepare for the children. We painted their upstairs room and decorated one wall with pictures of a giraffe, a hippo, and a lion. We bought a swimming pool. Our friends gave us a party and showered us with gifts for the children. We were so busy and excited during our preparations in May. I feel lazy now but unable to enjoy my freedom and leisure before we begin our family.

July 13: Postman delivers letter from Bogotá telling us the children have *el sarampion* (the measles). The orphanage is quarantined. Our departure date is more unsure than ever.

July 24: A letter with Colombian stamps informs us that Clamaco has been reclaimed by relatives. Thankfully, they have a Felipe for us. What a beautiful name. But we haven't received Felipe's birth documents, which were mailed to us. What a mess. Now we're back to where we were in April.

July 25: Seems unbelievable, but Carmen and Felipe are no longer. Bob called Bogotá to confirm Felipe's addition and, lo and behold, we have two different children, still a girl and a boy, two and four. Orphanage will send the birth documents special delivery.

July 30: Played tennis this morning. Just as I park in front of our house so does a U.S. Mail car. Special delivery. Birth documents for Angelita and Manuel. I spend the evening translating and typing. [Jan used the translated copy of the birth documents for the first two children assigned to them.]

July 31: I carry the documents to the [Minnesota] Department of Public Welfare office near the Capitol building in Saint Paul.

August 1: I take them to the Immigration office. Thinking of flying to Bogotá this Sunday. So scary and exciting. Two beautiful children coming home with us, changing all our lives forever.

August 4: Four-hour layover in Miami. Full of all sorts of feelings about our adventure: fear, anticipation, regret, expectations.

August 5: We arrive in Bogotá. Surprised to see many people watching us land. Must be the Sunday afternoon entertainment. (Actually, the relatives and friends waiting for the Colombian passengers.)

August 6: Arrive at the adoption agency very nervous, not knowing what to expect, realizing this is one of the most important events in our lives. Wait about fifteen minutes for our children. Bob is very, very nervous. We hear the kids coming down the hall. Angelita shyly enters and comes right to me. Manuel enters hesitantly a few seconds later and comes right to Bob. I can't voice my feelings of disappointment at that moment; both children are very fat.

Anyway, *los niños* (the children) are dressed really cute, blue plaid bib shorts for Manuel and skirt with suspenders for Angelita. Bob is relieved to know the children were expecting us. We are left alone, and the children sit stiffly on our laps. Angelita looks up at us shyly; Manuel looks up at us fearfully. We give Angelita a Raggedy Ann doll and Manuel a truck. We play for about an hour. The children won't speak with us except once when we ask Angelita her name. She says it so forcefully and assertively we are very surprised.

11:30 a.m.: Manuel toddles out of the room. I don't know why. I carry him back. He's screaming and crying. The maids ask him what is wrong. Manuel wants to eat — our first clue that Manuel feels very strongly about food. While the children eat, we speak with the directress. She tells us to get pictures taken of the children and to be back by 5:00 p.m. to sign the custody contract, then the kids will be ours. That doesn't sound so good. We are prepared to have the children on the evening of the second day, but not the first. We leave the orphanage to get photos taken. A surprising little one-room place.

Manuel starts screaming his head off. But when our little angel smiles to have her picture taken, then what can he do?

After that we go the embassy doctor. He is also a surprise. A distinguished-looking fellow who does a cursory exam. We mention that Manual recently had surgery for a rectal obstruction. The doctor doesn't care; he allows us to write "NO" to the question on the U.S. State Department form that asks about recent operations.

We taxi back to the hotel and order food from room service. We don't order for the *gamines* thinking they weren't hungry yet. Wrong! The *niños* eat quite a bit. When Bob leaves the room, Manuel follows me around, demanding, *"Deme pan!"* ("Give me bread!"). He is amazingly persistent. Later we leave the hotel to pick up the photos and return to the orphanage. Bob and I feel almost relieved when the directress says we do not have enough photos, and we will have to return tomorrow to acquire custody of the children. The day had seemed long and trying. The *niños* don't seem to mind being back home. As we talk to the directress, the children start talking and playing freely together for the first time. It's so nice they can communicate and relax together.

We feel exhausted and have a quiet evening together. There had been so much tension; not knowing how the children would respond to us, not knowing the language well, and meeting time deadlines. Bob was immediately affectionate and warm with the children. I didn't feel affection, but it was silly to think I would immediately.

August 7: Pick up the photos and go to the orphanage. Sign custody contract. Our children do not seem as scared of us. We feel more relaxed, too.

Back at the hotel and bedded down for the night, we all sleep poorly. Manuel is tossing and calling out all night; both kids seem to always be uncovered.

August 8: What a delightful day! Finally have a chance to enjoy the children and get to know them a little. It's a holiday. President Lopez's inauguration.

Big scare this morning. Manuel spit up all his eggs. The waiter says we shouldn't give him so much food.

Return to our room and read the children a story. Manuel has a temper tantrum, which we ignore. Seeing him quiet down is a small triumph for us. We really feel like we're becoming parents. I feel so much closer to the children now than I did yesterday. When they wake up, we go shopping. Angelita and Manuel both get new shoes. The children are so proud when they think they look nice. Manuel has a little temper tantrum again when he can't have any candy. He's learning he can't have everything he wants; it's a nice feeling to know we're overcoming that. Angelita is just like a little angel.

We give them a bath. Manuel doesn't try it until Angelita does. We give them soap dishes, and they use them for a water fight. It's the first time they laugh so spontaneously and so much. After that, Angelita and Manuel loosen up and play freely with their toys. I'm so glad I brought matchbox cars. Then we read them a children's book. (I read; Bob does the sound effects.) We put them to bed feeling like real parents, so happy to have children.

August 9: Manuel did it again. We only ordered oatmeal and bread, but it was too much for Manuel. He spit it up while Angelita quietly polished off all of hers. It scares us. Glad we have an appointment with a pediatrician this afternoon. It takes Manuel about an hour to eat, and it's one hour of nerves for us, wondering if he'll make it. After eating we go to crowded embassy and hear good news: as soon as we get Angelita and Manuel's passports, we can fly home. Back to hotel for naps. No temper tantrum from Manuel this time, just a frown, a pout, and no kiss. Our stalwart Angelita goes right to bed.

After naps we visit pediatrician. He says Angelita and Manuel could be brother and sister. Our children are from southern Colombia (indicated by skin problems) and both have worms and malnutrition. Fat is actually bloating caused by malnutrition; with good nutrition it soon disappears. Angelita's facial scars will eventually heal and become less noticeable. She is probably 4½ to 5 years old.

Manuel is around four, stunted from malnutrition and an intestinal problem. Testicles are undescended. Vomiting is probably due to new diet. Doctor writes prescriptions for worms.

Bedtime: Slight tantrum from Manuel when it's time to put away toys, but he comes around when it's time for the dulce (candy), actually worm medicine. Both jump into bed by themselves. Bob and I enjoy sharing our time with the children more each day.

August 10: Lawyer says passport will not be ready for four more days. Disappointing. Visit Plaza de Bolivar and Museo del Oro, a museum housing solid gold Chibcha Indian artworks. Always so many people on the streets. No one takes care of their vehicles. City seems always stinky and dirty.

August 11: No stomach problems for Manuel. Angelita is so good-natured, giggly, and happy. Bought souvenirs. Angelita delighted with her ruana. Wants to know if she can wear it *mañana* (tomorrow). Manuel makes such funny faces. He has rosy gopher cheeks. Expectant eyes when about to eat; cow-eyed when wanting something. Angie tells Carlos, our waiter, that she wants Mama to help her.

August 13: Tour Zipaquira, a salt mine with a great cathedral deep inside. *Los niños* play all day long. We notice Angelita gives in to all Manuel's demands. Kids repeat English words: cow, sheep, tree, bath. Manuel has a speech problem; not sure if it's a lisp or an impediment. Both seem happy and secure.

Tan bueno! (So good!) is Angelita's favorite phrase. *Deme manzana* (Give me an apple) is Manuel's.

August 14: Absolutely the worst day as far as tension and worry go. Passports are to be picked up at orphanage at noon and delivered to embassy at 1:00. We don't count on two-hour lunch/siesta at orphanage. Embassy clerk says she will issue visas if we bring passports to the embassy by 3:00.

Rush to bank to get money for visas. Speed to orphanage. Kids miss their nap. Manuel has temper tantrum. We're so racked with emotion we feel like pounding him. Bob takes hopping, stamping, shrieking Manuel out to wait in the taxi while I assure directress I'll phone in our flight number if they will please give us the passports immediately. Request refused.

Rush to embassy, then to lawyer for his bill, to hotel for flight number, back to lawyer, back to embassy, back to orphanage, dash to embassy again. I notice passports have Oothoudt as last name, not ours. Then Bob reads custody contract and sees Isabel, not Angelita. Bob nearly has a nervous breakdown. Caramba!

Tomorrow we will repeat the race from office to office in Bogotá's congestion of cars, people, trucks, burros, buses, and bicycles. It will be very nice to get home again.

CHAPTER 3

Understanding International Adoption: An Overview

Should you decide to adopt internationally, it is in your best interest and that of your future child to learn the adoption procedures both in the United States and abroad. You will be handling much of the paperwork in cooperation with your U.S. social worker and your international agency or attorney. Your function is that of expediter. Endless delays can be avoided if you take responsibility for the paperwork shuffle; always know who has your papers, why they have them, and what happens next. While most adoption agencies, here and abroad, have years of experience in handling foreign adoptions, a few foreign adoption sources cited in the Compendium are not yet familiar with foreign adoptions; in fact, the same is true for some of the private and public agencies in the United States. And yet, some of them may be involved in processing your paperwork. The more you know about the process, the more likely it is that your experience will go smoothly.

One of the best ways to become familiar with the adoption process itself and to understand the issues facing both the parents and children of international adoption is to attend orientations or educational seminars. These are typically sponsored by private, licensed adoption agencies to provide potential adopters with information on how a home study is conducted and to give an overview of the U.S. immigration and foreign adoption process. Adoptive parent support groups may also sponsor seminars and usually invite all of the adoption agencies to participate. (See Appendix for a list of adoptive parent support groups.) At seminars for international adoption, postadoptive parents usually bring their children and speak about their experiences. Prospective adoptive parents find out about seminars by word of mouth, by keeping in contact with local agencies, and through public service announcements on television, radio, and newspapers. Attend as many seminars as possible before selecting an agency. Information more specific to you and your personal situ-

STEP 1

Learn all you can about international adoption from available resources. Attend orientations and seminars hosted by adoptive parent organizations and private adoption agencies.

ation may require an individual consultation. International adoption professionals with degrees in social work or human development can give you the attention you need to make an informed decision.

THE INTERNET AND ADOPTION:
A WORLD OF INFORMATION BUT USER BEWARE

I adore the Internet. Need a state department or INS form? Find it and print it. Heading to Moscow? Travel information is at the touch of your fingertip. Need to know your status in the waiting pool at your adoption agency? Visit their ListServe or email your agency contact.

Yes, the Internet can be a wonderful place, but the naive user can easily be led astray. Unfortunately, it's just as easy to find misinformation on the Internet as it is to find information. To help provide some direction, we've tried to include the Internet addresses for helpful Web sites throughout the book. Of course, you'll find many other helpful resources on the Internet as well, but these sites are a good place to begin your research. In fact, you might even start now by taking a look at the Web sites of some organizations dedicated to helping individuals learn more about international adoption.

http://www.jcics.org (Joint Council on International Children's Services)

http://www.ncfa-usa.org (National Council for Adoption)

http://eeadopt.org (Eastern European Adoption Coalition)

http://frua.org (Families for Russian and Ukrainian Adoption, including neighboring countries)

http://catalog.com/fwcfc (Families with Children From China)

http://www.fcvn.org (Families with Children from Vietnam)

In addition to misinformation, the Internet also opens the door to a variety of ethical dilemmas. One frequently questioned issue is the photo listing of waiting children. A waiting child is defined as one who is school age, handicapped, or whose sibling group or race has hampered placement into an adoptive home. Some countries, such as Bolivia and Russia, will not allow U.S. agencies to photo list their children because of critical stories calling it "baby-selling."

Although the issue of photo listing has been blown out of proportion, the use of this medium to find families for orphans can create serious problems. However, most problems that result from photo listings are due to a lack of knowledge regarding social and legal issues. Some prospective adoptive parents impulsively search for an orphan before they have completed the preliminary steps of INS clearance, home study approval, and the compilation of supporting documents. In turn, overeager or inexperienced adoption facilitators may be so anxious to make a placement that they refer a child to parents who are neither approved nor prepared to adopt internationally. Such scenarios are adoption disruptions waiting to happen! An important part of the home study process is designed to help people understand their own capabilities and motives regarding an adopted child so the agency can make an appropriate referral.

Another potential problem arises in some adoption newsgroups. Newsgroups are typically created by volunteer, postadoptive parents to provide support and information to others going through the adoption process. Their words of encouragement and responses to general adoption questions have been a blessed relief to countless prospective adoptive parents. Unfortunately, many also use newsgroups to post hostile and erratic messages berating the INS, foreign governments, or U.S. agencies for not rubber stamping them through the process. One of the biggest dangers in posting such messages is that they can just as easily be read by officials in foreign countries! In addition, some of the more specific questions posed to newsgroups — particularly those regarding state and INS procedures or child-placement policies — are best directed to the adoption agency handling the case. The requirements and procedures for a foreign adoption can change quickly. Your agency is the best source of information for staying on top of these changes.

In addition, begin learning all you can about international adoption from other sources, such as books, newsletters, magazines, videos, the Internet, and adoptive parent groups. The typical adoption candidate has access to the Internet and orders books on adoption, parenting, and the country he or she is planning to adopt from on-line. A list of recommended publications is found in the Bibliography. The National Adoption Information Clearinghouse (NAIC) also offers a series of publications on various aspects of the international adoption process. Many of these publications are free. Write or call the NAIC at

330 C Street, S.W.
Washington, DC 20447
Tel: 888-251-0075 (toll-free)
Web site: www.calib.com/naic

International adoptions occur in eight major stages:

1. Preliminary Home State Approval (Chapter 5)

2. Preliminary INS Approval (Chapter 6)

3. Application to a Foreign Adoption Source (Chapter 7)

4. Receiving Referral of the Child (Chapter 8)

5. Filing the Orphan Petition (Chapter 9)

6. Travel Abroad (Chapter 10)

7. Emigration, Immigration (Chapter 12)

8. Postplacement Procedures (Chapter 14)

Twenty-three steps are dealt with, from agency registration to U.S. naturalization or citizenship (see Table 3-1). These steps are highlighted, beginning in this chapter and ending in Chapter 14.

TABLE 3-1   STEPS IN THE INTERNATIONAL ADOPTION PROCESS

Step 1   Learn all you can about international adoption from available resources. Attend orientations and seminars hosted by adoptive parent organizations and private adoption agencies.

Step 2   Collect agency information.

Step 3   Choose an international adoption agency.

Step 4   Choose the agency that will conduct your home study (if different from your international adoption agency).

Step 5   Initiate home study by applying to appropriate agency.

Step 6   Obtain documents required for home study.

Step 7   Prepare documentation required for Form I-600A (Application for Advance Processing).

Step 8   File Form I-600A (Application for Advance Processing).

Step 9   Apply for a passport.

Step 10   Select an adoption program in a foreign country.

Step 11   Obtain documents required for your foreign dossier.

Step 12   Obtain translations for documents in your foreign dossier.

Step 13   Obtain notarization, verification (or apostille), and authentication of documents in your dossier.

Step 14   Prepare for the referral of your child.

Step 15   Obtain visa or tourist card (if necessary) for travel to your child's country.

Step 16   File Form I-600 (Orphan Petition) if this is to be filed in the United States. (This is usually filed abroad if the adoption is finalized in the child's country and both parents travel to meet the child.)

Step 17   Prepare for your adoption trip.

Step 18   Meet your child.

Step 19   Obtain the guardianship or final adoption decree.

Step 20   Apply for the orphan visa and file Form I-600 (Orphan Petition) if this was not filed earlier.

Step 21   Participate in postplacement supervision.

Step 22   Readopt your child in your state of residence.

Step 23   File for U.S. citizenship for your child.

It is best to follow the steps in the order they appear, whenever possible. Based on our experience and that of the many adoptive parents we have guided, prospective U.S. adopters who try to alter this approach will encounter serious difficulties along the way.

REQUIREMENTS FOR ADOPTIVE PARENTS

In reviewing the Compendium at the back of this book, most prospective adoptive parents are pleased to see that the adoption requirements of many foreign adoption agencies are less stringent than those of local adoption agencies in the United States. At most U.S.-based international agencies, single persons and couples married one year or more, between the ages of twenty-five and fifty-five, with or without children, of all races and religious affiliations, as well as persons who were previously divorced can find adoption programs in countries to accept their applications. Prospective adoptive parents must be in the middle to upper income bracket, able to expedite documents, and able to travel abroad if required.

However, prospective adoptive parents must also meet the requirements of the Immigration and Naturalization Service (INS). The INS requires that at least one spouse be a citizen of the United States. The INS does not approve welfare recipients, unmarried heterosexual or homosexual couples, or persons who have been convicted of a felony.

AGENCY-INITIATED AND PARENT-INITIATED ADOPTIONS

There are two major types of legal foreign adoptions: agency-initiated adoptions and parent-initiated adoptions (also known as direct or independent adoptions).

In an agency-initiated foreign adoption, prospective parents work with a U.S.-based international adoption agency, which handles paperwork and communications and assigns a child to a client through a child-placing agreement or contract with a foreign source. This is the most common type of international adoption. Upon the assignment of a child, the foreign child-placing entity sends the U.S.-based agency copies of the mother's release or the decree of abandonment and the child's birth certificate. The U.S. agency, in turn, presents these documents to the adoptive parents. In addition, the foreign source will send medical and biographical information and a picture and/or video of the child for the U.S. agency to share with you. Once the adoptive parents have accepted the referral, the U.S. agency coordinates their adoption trip. The agency and its bilingual representatives take responsibility for assisting you with the child, your lodging, and obtaining the final adoption decree and the child's passport and exit visas. They will also provide the documents required for the orphan visa by the American Consulate. (A more detailed description of the different types of agency-initiated adoptions is given in Chapter 7.)

Parents do not have to travel to some countries. For example, Korea arranges proxy adoptions and allows for escorts to bring the child to you. The U.S. adoption agency is the guardian of the child until you adopt about six months later. Guatemala also permits adoption by proxy; when the final decree is issued, the child can be brought to you.

This type of escort service has a down side. The most obvious problem is that the child becomes a part of your family sight unseen. Parents usually have very little idea about the behavior of these children until they are in their new home. The other problem with escorting is that it takes longer to arrange than it would if you traveled there yourself, and it is not substantially cheaper.

In a parent-initiated adoption (also known as an independent or direct adoption), prospective parents obtain a home study from a licensed adoption agency or social worker. After this point, they are on their own as far as filing with the INS and preparing a dossier of documents for the court abroad. The adoptive parents are solely responsible for selecting and securing a foreign lawyer or agency who will, in turn, refer a child to them.

The foreign agency, government staff, or lawyer arranges for the adoption hearing in court and tells the adoptive parents when to take their adoption trip. After that, the parents are again on their own. They must take full responsibility for the child as well as obtaining the proper documentation for the child's adoption, passport, and orphan visa.

While independent international adoptions are certainly possible, the risks are much higher than in agency adoptions, which are regulated by the state. In addition, many foreign countries do not allow independent adoptions. According to the National Adoption Information Clearinghouse, the risks of an independent adoption include involvement in the black market; loss of confidentiality; infringements upon the child's privacy; inadequate medical information; the possibility of outright fraud; and the lack of proper documentation of the child's status as an orphan.

The safest way to adopt a foreign child is to involve a licensed adoption agency or social worker (if individually licensed) in your state of residence and adopt the child through an international adoption agency or public welfare department abroad.

Over the years, we have heard of many sad cases in which a missionary or foreign lawyer, rather than an international agency abroad, assigned a couple a child but was unable to obtain the birth documents needed for a legal international adoption. The prospective adoptive parents send money overseas for years in the hope that the child can be legally freed for adoption. We usually meet them when they have given up hope and want to start over with an agency-initiated adoption.

TYPES OF U.S. ADOPTION AGENCIES

The safest way to adopt a foreign child is to involve an experienced, licensed, and accredited adoption agency. Licensed U.S. adoption agencies fall into three general categories: public adoption agencies; private, local adoption agencies; and U.S.-based international adoption agencies. (All U.S.-based international agencies are private.) In addition, some states also license individual social workers to conduct home studies and supervise adoptive placements. Understanding the functions of and differences between these types of agencies will help in your understanding of the adoption process.

Although no special standards have yet been established for international adoption agencies, all adoption agencies in the United States are mandated and licensed by the state. In the future, under the Hague Convention, national accreditation will be required. (A discussion of the Hague Convention can be found later in this chapter.) Lawyers, facilitators, or other professionals involved in an independent adoption, but not working with an adoption agency, are not regulated by the state.

Public Adoption Agencies

Public adoption agencies are funded by your tax dollars. They are set up to provide social services to children in their counties. Public adoption agencies maintain the cases of children in foster care who have been removed from their parental home due to abuse or neglect. If the parents terminate their parental rights, the children are placed in adoptive homes. There is very little cost to prospective parents adopting children through a public adoption agency. However, because of their ever-growing case loads, these agencies seldom have time to conduct home studies for international adoptions.

Private Adoption Agencies

Private adoption agencies are funded in many different ways. If they specialize in placing children from the public adoption agencies, they are usually funded by the state. If they specialize in handicapped children or locally born infants, they usually rely on client fees. However, many of them receive funding through a church or synagogue affiliation, the United Way, Independent Charities of America, Children's Charities of America, and so on.

Most local, private adoption agencies will usually perform casework and a home study for foreign adoptions, even though they will not be able to refer a child for adoption. Such agencies, which include nonprofit, licensed private, church-funded, or community organization-funded placement agencies, charge fees or need donations of anywhere from $2,000 to $4,000 for pre- and postadoptive services. Each agency has its own set of requirements for applicants. If the agency is church-funded, it may require church membership in that denomination. (Many private agencies may waive their own requirements if the adopter has found an international agency or foreign source that will accept him or her as an adoptive parent.)

U.S.-Based International Adoption Agencies

U.S.-based international adoption agencies have child-placing contracts with foreign government child welfare departments, adoption agencies, liaisons, or attorneys in foreign countries. U.S.-based international agencies handle the foreign application, coordinate the referral of the adoptive child, and coordinate state, foreign, and emigration/immigration procedures. In addition, such agencies do the casework and perform the home study and postplacement supervision for residents of the state where the agency is licensed. (If an applicant lives in another state, a locally licensed private agency or licensed, certified social worker must conduct the home study and postplacement supervision.)

When traveling for an adoption, a liaison of the international agency will meet you at the airport and assist you throughout the process in the child's country of origin. In foreign countries where adoption sources permit proxy adoptions or guardianships, international agencies may arrange to escort the assigned child to the United States if laws permit this. International agencies usually charge fees or need donations.

Social Workers and Certified Adoption Investigators

Social workers are the largest professional group providing mental and social health services. Every state has different standards for social workers, but the minimum is usually a bachelor's or master's degree in social work (BSW or MSW, respectively) and certification with the state board. State certification includes credentials such as a Certified Social Worker (CSW) or an individual with a master's degree, an Advanced Clinical Practitioner (ACP). To keep their licenses current, social workers are required to continue their education and must submit proof of this on an annual basis.

Some states license individual social workers to conduct home studies and supervise adoptive placements. Prospective adoptive parents will need to get in touch with their district INS office to see if it will accept a study written by a social worker independent of an agency.

The advantage to using an independent, certified social worker over an agency might be that they are less expensive and possibly speedier. If the social worker is networking with an international adoption agency, there should not be any problems. Otherwise, adoptive parents may discover that their home study is not accepted by the INS or government abroad. U.S.-based international adoption agencies have a full-time or part-time social worker with a master's degree who reviews the home study to be certain that it is in compliance with the requirements of the state, the INS, and the foreign country prior to signing it. Another disadvantage to using an independent social worker is that most don't have access to the current international adoption situation or the cross-cultural educational and parenting resources of a large adoption agency. Many child-placing countries also want the additional endorsement of an agency on the formal agreement to provide postplacement supervision and reports.

U.S. SAFEGUARDS FOR FOREIGN ADOPTED CHILDREN

Any adoption can be a legally complicated affair, but in international adoptions the typical issues are compounded by U.S. immigration requirements, the legal requirements of the country from which the child is originating, and the requirements of the state in which the child will ultimately live.

Immigration and Naturalization Service (INS) laws are strict. Adopters must have documents to prove their identities, whom they are married to, whom they are no longer married to, and how much money they have to support a family. INS will not approve advance applications for the orphan petition until the adopters get FBI clearances to prove they have no criminal records. U.S. immigration laws are designed to prevent criminal activities by foreign and U.S. citizens who are involved in the adoption process. Without a doubt, unscrupulous persons with criminal intent would import large numbers of children if they could.

A number of legal and procedural safeguards have been enacted by the federal and state governments to ensure the success of foreign adoptions by U.S. citizens.

On the federal level these actions include:

• *A home study performed by a licensed agency or a licensed social worker in the adopter's home state.*

• *INS orphan immigration petition requirements.*

• *FBI check of every preadoptive parent.*

• *Good practice, intercountry adoption guidelines established by the U.S. Departments of Health, Education, and Welfare.*

• *U.S. citizenship for every legally immigrated orphan.*

Those actions on the state level are as follows:

• *Postplacement visits by a licensed social worker.*

• *Social worker's recommendation for readoption.*

• *Issuance of a new birth certificate (in most states).*

ICPC

Also, be aware that the Interstate Compact for Children (ICPC) regulates certain kinds of placements, such as guardianships from countries that do not issue final adoption decrees (India, Korea, and the Philippines, for example). In this case, if an agency, parent group, or individual in one state causes a foreign child's placement in another state, ICPC forms must be filed. The ICPC was never intended for use in intercountry adoptions, only for child placements between U.S. states. In many ways, the ICPC illustrates the almost *ad hoc* evolution of laws and regulations governing international adoption in the United States.

In his article, "Transnational Adoption of Children,"[1] Richard R. Carlson describes the international adoption process as it has evolved, identifies in the existing process, and proposes legislative reform.

Here, he describes some of the difficulties and frustrations in foreign adoptions:

"Transnational adoption is an increasingly important facet of immigration and adoption in the United States. However, transnational adoption

---

[1] Richard Carlson, "Transnational Adoption of Children," *The University of Tulsa Law Journal,* Volume 23, No. 3, 1988.

*has received surprisingly little attention from lawmakers and legal
scholars. Congress has enacted legislation facilitating the immigration
of prospective adoptive children, but has not endeavored any substantial
regulation of the adoption process. A few states have enacted special
legislation dealing with transnational adoptions, but most states continue
to rely on the same legislation that was enacted primarily for adoption of
locally born children."*

*"The adoption of a foreign-born child, however, can raise difficult legal
problems that are rare or unknown in the adoption of American-born
children. These problems arise partly from the difficulty of reconciling
foreign and domestic law and partly from the failure of American
lawmakers to develop a rational allocation of authority among foreign,
federal, and state officials."*

*"Despite the early views of Congress that large-scale transnational
adoption was a temporary phenomenon, transnational adoption has not
only grown over the past forty years, but is likely to continue for the
foreseeable future. Transnational adoption is both an important solution
to the shortage of adoptable children in the United States and the
shortage of adoptive parents in many developing nations. Greater
attention must now be focused on the unique problems of transnational
adoption in order that the process will not be jeopardized by poorly
formed rules and standards at the immigration phase and overly
restrictive rules at the state adoption [or readoption] phase."*

THE HAGUE CONVENTION

An international convention known as the Hague Conference on Private
International Law was concluded in May of 1993. At the conclusion of this last
session, the final text of an international treaty (known as the Convention on
Protection of Children and Cooperation in Respect of Intercountry Adoption)
was passed. The intent of this treaty is to set standards and procedures
designed to protect the interests of the children being adopted as well as those
of the birth parents and the adoptive parents. The standards set forth in the final
version of the Convention will apply to all adoptions between countries that
have ratified the Convention. However, the treaty does not prohibit countries
party to the Convention from setting additional requirements and standards for
children leaving their country.

By the fall of 1999, twenty-six countries had ratified the
Convention. (See Table 3-2.) Nine countries had joined by acceding to the
Convention and thirteen countries (including the United States) had
signed the Convention but had not yet ratified it. By signing the Convention,
the country expresses, in principle, its intention to ratify. However, the signature
does not, in any way, oblige a state to take further action (towards ratification

TABLE 3-2 Status of Countries Signing and Ratifying the Hague Convention

More up-to-date information on countries that have signed or ratified the Hague Convention can be found on the Hague Conference's Web site at http://www.hcch.net/e/status/adoshte.html.

Country	Signature	Ratification, Acceptance, Approval, or Accession*	Entry into Force
Andorra	01/03/97	A—01/03/97	01/05/97
Australia	08/25/98	R—08/25/98	12/01/98
Austria	12/18/98	R—05/19/99	09/01/99
Belarus	12/10/97		
Belgium	01/27/99		
Brazil	05/25/93	R—03/10/99	07/01/99
Burkino Faso	04/14/94	R—01/11/96	05/01/96
Burundi	10/15/98	A—10/15/98	02/01/99
Canada	04/12/94	R—12/19/96	04/01/97
Chili	07/13/99	R—07/13/99	11/01/99
Colombia	09/01/93	R—07/13/98	11/01/98
Costa Rica	03/25/93	R—10/30/95	02/01/96
Cyprus	11/17/94	R—02/20/95	06/01/95
Denmark	07/02/97	R—07/02/97	11/01/97
Ecuador	05/03/94	R—09/07/95	01/01/96
El Salvador	11/02/96	R—11/17/98	03/01/99
Finland	04/14/94	R—03/27/97	07/01/97
France	04/05/95	R—06/30/98	10/01/98
Georgia	04/09/99	R—04/09/99	08/01/99
Germany	11/07/97		
Ireland	06/19/96		
Israel	11/02/93	R—02/03/99	06/01/99
Italy	12/11/95		
Lithuania	04/29/98	A—04/29/98	08/01/98
Luxemburg	06/06/95		
Mauritius	09/28/98	A—09/28/98	11/01/99
Mexico	05/25/93	R—09/14/94	01/05/95
Moldova	04/10/98	A—04/10/98	08/01/98
Monaco	06/29/99	A—06/29/99	01/15/2000
Netherlands	12/05/93	R—06/26/98	10/01/98
New Zealand	09/18/98	A—09/18/98	01/19/99
Norway	05/20/96	R—05/25/97	01/01/98
Panama	06/15/99	R—09/29/99	01/01/2000
Paraguay	05/13/98	R—05/13/98	09/01/98
Peru	11/16/94	R—09/14/95	01/01/96
Philippines	07/17/95	R—07/02/96	11/01/96
Poland	06/12/95	R—06/12/95	10/01/95
Portugal	08/26/99		
Romania	05/29/93	R—12/28/94	05/01/95
Slovakia	06/01/99		
Spain	03/27/95	R—07/11/95	11/01/95
Sri Lanka	05/24/95	R—01/23/95	05/01/95
Sweden	10/10/96	R—05/28/97	09/01/97
Switzerland	01/16/95		
United Kingdom	01/12/94		
Uruguay	09/01/93		
United States	03/31/94		
Venezuela	01/10/97	R—01/10/97	05/01/97

* An R designates ratification, while an A designates accession

or not). More up-to-date information on those countries that have ratified, signed, or acceded to the Convention can be found on the Hague Conference's Web site: http://www.hcch.net/e/status/adoshte.html.

Ratifying the Hague Convention will require the establishment of a central authority for U.S. international adoptions. Currently, the United States has no national adoption law; each state has its own laws regulating adoption. The United States is in the process of creating implementation legislation for the Convention — one in a series of steps toward ratification. The first bill, an administration bill of the White House, Health and Human Services, State Department and the Attorney General's Office was given to Congress in June of 1998. However, it was never dealt with and expired with the 105th Congress in December of 1998. In March of 1999, a bipartisan bill (S-682, the Inter-Country Adoption Act) was introduced in the U.S. Senate by Senator Jesse Helms, Republican, North Carolina, and Senator Mary Landrieu, Democrat, Louisiana. The House introduced its own version, (H.R. 2909) later in the same year.

Several items in the latter bill were not in the first. Accreditation of agencies was to be supervised by the Department of Health and Human Services, but Helm's bill designates the Department of State to take this role. The number of entities who will be appointed as accrediting bodies differs in both bills as do the requirements for accreditation. Hearings will be set to compromise on these items.

In addition, for the first time, there will be procedures for American children leaving the country for adoption by foreigners. Records on this phenomenon have not been kept by the INS or the State Department in the past.

Whether ratifying the Convention will help or hinder U.S. citizens adopting abroad will remain to be seen. With the ratification of the Hague Convention by the United States, approval from the central authorities in this country and the country abroad may be required for each adoption case. However, without ratification by the United States, we will lose our clout in international adoption.

CHAPTER 4

Choosing the Right Agency

STEP 2

Collect agency information.

In the years following World War II, when U.S. citizens were first trying to adopt abroad, it was difficult to find a local agency to conduct pre- and postadoption services. The first U.S.-based international agency was Holt International Adoption Services of Eugene, Oregon, which was founded in the 1950s. That agency made arrangements with private agencies in various states to provide services to Korean orphans being placed through Holt. However, prospective adoptive parents who did not fit the requirements for Holt because of their age, length of marriage, or religious beliefs had a difficult time finding alternatives.

International adoption nowadays is a completely different story. So many agencies exist and so much information is available that potential parents are overwhelmed.

Most potential adoptive parents find an international adoption agency by word-of-mouth, through recommendation by their local adoption agency or parent group, by researching all available books on the subject, and by searching the Internet and requesting literature and additional information from agency Web sites. In addition, adoption information and referral services have popped up in many states to help adoptive parents find the most suitable agency for their needs. Annual adoption conferences are held in many states. This gives preadoptive parents the chance to talk to all the agencies, both local and out of state, and to take home their literature. Most local agencies hold their own seminars or orientations to present an overview of their services.

Several excellent directories of agencies are also available. Two sources for this kind of information are the *Report on Foreign Adoption* and *The Adoption Directory*, which list the names, addresses, and telephone numbers of U.S.-based international agencies that process guardianships and adoptions in other countries. Information on both of these publications is found in the Bibliography.

Other resources include your state licensing specialists who supervise adoption agencies, Adoptive Families of America, National Council for Adoption, the Joint Council on International Children's Services, and the North American Council on Adoptable Children. The Appendix includes contact information for each of these organizations.

Los Niños International Adoption Center (LNI) provides adoption services to residents in Texas and to residents of states where LNI networks with other licensed adoption agencies. Many other U.S.-based international adoption agencies also network with private adoption agencies in other states.

CHOOSING AN INTERNATIONAL ADOPTION AGENCY

Once you have gathered information on the agency or agencies you are interested in contacting, you may wish to prepare a list of questions for each one. That done, you can ask the questions not covered in the literature by phone, e-mail, or in person. Since some agencies work with several different countries, the answers to questions regarding requirements, waits, and fees may differ according to country. In addition, each agency should be able to provide you with names and telephone numbers of postadoptive parents who enjoy discussing their adoption experiences. What follows is a sample of some helpful questions for evaluating an international adoption agency.

International Agency Administration

Q: Is your agency accredited, or have you applied for accreditation?

Q: Is your agency licensed and nonprofit? Which government body licenses you?

Q: Who directs the agency, human service professionals, business administrators, or lawyers?

Q: How many years have you been placing children?

Q: May I have a copy of your policies and the contracts for adoptive parents?

Q: Who helps me prepare a dossier of documents for the child-placing authorities?

Q: What types of education and support services do you provide before, during, and after the placement of a child?

Q: Are you licensed or approved by the foreign governments in countries where you have programs?

Q: Do you have bilingual staff abroad to obtain the referral of a child and to assist the adoptive parents while they are there?

Q: May I have names of people who have recently adopted from _____ (country)?

Placement Procedures

Q: How many children did you place last year?

Q: What are the ages and nationalities of the children you place?

Q: What is their general state of health?

Requirements for Adoptive Parents

Q: What are your requirements for adoptive parents, relating to age, income, religion, marital status, living arrangements, length of marriage, divorce, state of health, or records of a legal misdemeanor?

Q: What is your policy regarding single applicants?

Q: Which countries do you think might accept my application?

The Referral of a Child

Q: After my dossier is completed, how long is the wait for a girl/boy of ___ years of age from _____ (country)?

Q: When I am referred a child, what kind of information will I receive?

Q: What happens if I don't feel I can accept this referral?

Q: Once I accept the referral, how long will it be until I can travel to _____ (country) to immigrate the child? Will that be one trip or two?

Q: How long will I need to stay abroad? If I choose a country where the child will be escorted, how long does it take for the child to be brought to me?

Q: What happens if the child becomes too ill to be adopted before or during my stay? What happens if I decide I don't wish to adopt that particular child?

Q: What happens if we can't adjust to this new child?

Expenses

Q: What is the total cost for an adoption from _____ (country)?

ESTIMATING THE COSTS OF AN INTERNATIONAL ADOPTION

The costs of an international adoption vary greatly depending on the agency you use, the range of services provided, the country from which you adopt your child, the cost of travel, present exchange rates for the U.S. dollar, and a host of other factors. The average cost for an international adoption in 1999 was between $12,000 and $25,000, which included agency fees, dossier and immigration processing fees, and court costs. This estimate does not include the cost of travel, foster care, or medical care.

The only way to get a firm handle on what an adoption will cost is to keep track with a sheet of estimated expenses (see nearby table). Whatever the figure you arrive at, the amount will be trifling in comparison to the costs of actually raising the child. The U.S. Department of Agriculture estimates that it will cost $224,000 for the average two-income couple to raise a child born in 1999 to age 17. This does not include college.

Although an international adoption agency should be able to provide exact figures for costs such as the agency's international processing fee and the

---

TABLE 4-1   ESTIMATING ADOPTION EXPENSES

The fees listed below are estimates only and will vary according to the agency you work with, the country you adopt from, and your individual situation. We've made these estimates based on the fees charged by adoption agencies with which we are familiar. To determine your approximate cost, select only the expenses that apply to your individual case or choice of country. Most countries have a widely varying rate of inflation that is generally much higher than in the United States, as well as fluctuating exchange rates.

PREADOPTION U.S. AGENCY FEE

Registration with agency ....$50 to $600

Home study fee ....$600 to $2,500
(Assumes international agency also conducts home study.)

Agency fee for services ....$3,000 to $6,000
(Some agencies do not list this fee separately, but combine it with the program fee.)

Preplacement checklist update ....$150 to $300

OTHER ADOPTION-RELATED EXPENSES INCURRED IN THE UNITED STATES

INS filing fee for Orphan Applications $405
(There is no filing fee for the Orphan Petition if done in the same year as the application.)

Fingerprinting $25
      (Fee applies to each member of family over age 18.)

Certified copies of birth, marriage, and divorce certificates ....$10 to $60
      (Fees range from $5-$10 per document.)

Notarization and verification fees ....$400 (average)
      (Varies according to state and number of documents.
      Most states charge $10 per document.)

Translations of documents ....$500 (average)
      (Averages $300-$1,000 when done in the United States.
      If done overseas, costs vary and are often included in the program fees.)

Authentication of documents by the foreign consulate ....$800 (average)
      (Ranges from $600 to $1,500.)

Program fee for child...$3,000 to $30,000
      (If agency fee for services is separate.)

TRAVEL-RELATED COSTS

One round-trip ticket per person traveling ....$600 to $2,000
      (Varies tremendously depending on country traveling to,
      time of year you are traveling, and type of ticket you buy.)

One-way ticket for child to United States..$200 to $900
      (Tickets may be as low as $200 for infants and children up to age two.
      Tickets for children age three and older generally cost about ninety percent of the adult fare.)

Food and lodging...$50 to $150 (per day)
      (Varies depending on whether stay is in a major city,
      an average hotel, or with a family.)

U.S. consular service Orphan Visa fee $325

Orphan's photos for passport and visa...$25 to $35

Orphan's passport ....$25 to $100

POSTPLACEMENT EXPENSES

Postplacement supervision...$800 to 2,500
      (Varies according to agency and whether international agency
      or network local agency conducts supervision. Also varies
      according to the number of supervision contacts required.)

Legal fees for readoption...Fees vary
      (Legal fees may vary tremendously. Call a lawyer in your state for an estimate.
      If you are conducting a pro se adoption, you will only be responsible for court fees.)

U.S. Citizenship filing fee...$125

*POSSIBILITIES FOR ADDITIONAL COSTS:
Other less common costs that may come into consideration, depending on the country and the type of program you choose, include the costs of foster care for the child, escort fee for bringing the child to the United States if you do not travel overseas, fees for transferring INS paperwork if you change foreign programs, fees for professional handling of documentation, fees for obtaining visas (required for China, Russia, Vietnam, Bolivia), etc.

---

foreign program fee, other costs such as document preparation and travel may vary considerably according to the adoptive parents' individual situation and the country from which they are adopting. For example, a single or a couple in Pennsylvania who adopt through a U.S.-based international agency in Texas will know ahead of time what the pre- and postadoption fees will be for their adoption agency in Pennsylvania. However, the costs of obtaining their certified documents and getting them translated, notarized, and verified will differ, since a typical single will have fewer documents than a married couple who were both previously divorced.

One of the most expensive parts of many adoptions is travel. The costs of air travel, hotels, food, and transportation within the country will vary according to the part of the world you are traveling to and the exchange rate at the time of your trip. Miscellaneous expenses such as fees for photos and the medical examination required for the orphan visa will also vary. A good, up-to-date guidebook will help you estimate most of your travel expenses. The guidebook will also provide information about tipping and whether or not small gifts are expected by officials.

One of the easiest ways to calculate travel expenses is to talk to several adoptive parents who have recently returned from their adoption trip. However, since we all have different spending and saving habits, you may find a difference of several thousand dollars. Some folks spend hundreds of dollars to phone home every day, or even include the cost of expensive souvenirs in their accounts of travel and adoption expenses.

While international adoption is costly, the fees can be paid over a series of months. Payments are due in increments as you move through the process. Be sure you know what all of the fees will be (excluding travel) before you begin the process. Some people finance their international adoption by applying and qualifying for an unsecured loan.

UNDERSTANDING ACCREDITATION

As mentioned in Chapter 3, the safest way to adopt a foreign child is to involve an experienced, licensed, and accredited adoption agency. The accreditation process provides for an independent, in-depth examination of the agency's operation, including personnel and safety, administration of adoption programs, and fiscal management. In order to be accredited, an agency must also be licensed by the state in which it is headquartered and must hold nonprofit status.

Accreditation ensures that the agency has written a service plan for

- *each adoptive parent, which identifies, refers, and arranges the adoption of a child and follows up when they return home.*

- *each child, to assure that the placement will be beneficial.*

In addition, accreditation also proves that the agency has

- *met rigorous standards concerning the referral of appropriate children.*

- *paid attention to the quality and consistency of the services delivered.*

- *developed a systematic method for evaluating its services.*

- *prepared for an annual audit that proves it is accountable for the management of its finances.*

- *joined a group of other agencies in the Council of Accreditation committed to high ethical and legal standards.*

- *created a procedure to follow if clients are displeased with the service they have received.*

- *implemented a strategy for making improvements.*

The Council of Accreditation is located at 120 Wall Street, 11th Floor, New York, NY, 10005. You can reach the council by phone at 212-797-3000, by fax at 212-797-1428, or by email at coanet@aol.com. More accrediting bodies are slated for appointment in the future.

EVALUATING YOUR OPTIONS

STEP 3

Choose an international adoption agency.

Choosing an adoption agency is an act of faith. The agency assumes a lot of responsibility toward coordinating an adoption. Trust is the key word. And a lot of paperwork.

Warning signs that may make you decide against using a certain agency boil down to communication, administration, and finances. Was your initial phone call, fax, or e-mail requesting information during business hours responded to within five working days? If not, the agency may be understaffed or overextended. Are the administrators experienced enough in international adoption to be able to solve all the complex problems that arise? Does the agency work in more than one country? If a foreign country changes its adoption requirements and you no longer qualify, will they help you to apply in a different country? Does the agency have sufficient financial reserves to cover losses due to major changes in a foreign adoption program and the resultant loss of income?

Other factors to consider are expenses and the extent of service provided. Not surprisingly, the more work an agency does for the adoptive parent, the higher the agency fee is likely to be. For example, some agencies assist the adoptive parents in filing with the INS as well as preparing the dossier of original documents for the foreign court, while other agencies show the adoptive parents how to do it themselves. Either the international agency or its networking agency must be licensed in the state where you reside in order to handle the documentation for you. Generally there is a separate fee for this service that can range from $3,000 to $7,000.

TABLE 4-2 INTERCOUNTRY ADOPTIONS 1993-1998

	1993	1994	1995	1996	1997	1998
ALL COUNTRIES	7,348	8,200	9,384	11,316	13,621	15,774
EUROPE	1,521	2,370	2,660	3,568	5,176	5,660
Belarus	33	7	7	36	49	2
Bulgaria	126	101	108	157	148	151
Georgia	1	15	58	90	21	6
Hungary	54	36	27	51	72	34
Kazakhstan	15	29	20	3	26	54
Latvia	17	35	59	83	108	76
Lithuania	23	93	102	80	78	72
Moldova	2	4	41	42	43	46
Poland	70	100	32	66	78	77
Romania	88	197	260	554	621	406
Russian Federation	695	1,324	1,684	2,328	3,816	4,491
Ukraine	248	163	5	10	59	180
Other Europe	149	266	257	68	57	65
ASIA	3,163	3,687	4,843	6,100	6,483	7,827
Cambodia	1	3	10	30	66	249
China, total	388	809	2,098	3,363	3,637	4,263
Mainland	330	748	2,049	3,313	3,597	4,206
Taiwan	31	34	23	21	19	30
Hong Kong	27	27	26	29	21	27
India	342	390	368	381	349	478
Japan	59	51	61	38	45	39
Korea (South)	1,765	1,757	1,570	1,580	1,654	1,829

	1993	1994	1995	1996	1997	1998
Philippines	358	320	293	228	163	200
Thailand	65	45	50	53	63	84
Vietnam	105	228	316	354	425	603
Other Asia	80	84	77	73	81	82
AFRICA	59	83	104	89	182	172
Ethiopia	29	44	66	39	82	96
Liberia	0	1	3	3	38	9
Other Africa	30	38	35	47	62	67
OCEANIA	1	8	9	4	4	4
NORTH AMERICA	1,133	847	764	750	1,228	1,456
Canada	7	1	3	5	1	0
Mexico	97	95	91	89	152	168
Caribbean	150	130	115	135	200	314
Dominican Republic	39	17	13	15	19	140
Haiti	49	62	50	69	142	121
Jamaica	48	34	36	39	31	38
Other Caribbean	14	17	16	12	8	15
CENTRAL AMERICA	878	621	555	521	875	976
Belize	5	2	6	7	3	4
Costa Rica	48	28	19	20	22	7
El Salvador	97	39	30	19	5	13
Guatemala	512	431	436	420	788	911
Honduras	183	76	27	28	26	7
Nicaragua	9	18	10	16	13	16
Panama	24	27	27	11	18	16
OTHER NORTH AMERICA	1	0	0	0	0	0
SOUTH AMERICA	1,471	1,205	1,004	805	548	655
Bolivia	123	42	21	35	77	73
Brazil	178	150	134	101	91	103
Chile	61	77	86	62	41	26
Colombia	416	342	338	258	233	351
Ecuador	42	42	70	52	43	55
Paraguay	405	497	332	261	33	7
Peru	230	37	15	17	14	26
OTHER SOUTH AMERICA	16	18	8	19	16	14

Sources: Immigration and Naturalization Service and U.S. Department of State

Your choice of an international agency will also be driven by the country or countries you are most interested in adopting from, as well as whether you qualify in terms of age, length of marriage, and so on. No agency has adoption agreements with every country in which it is possible to adopt.

It's best to have more than one country in mind when selecting an agency. Choose an agency with several foreign programs that interest you. For example, a lot of potential parents decide to adopt from a particular country because they have met an adoptive family or seen a television show on adopting in that country. This has been particularly true of Romania, Russia, and China, where the media has given the orphans a lot of coverage. The couple's next step is to contact an agency with a program in that country. However, if that agency only has one viable program and that country changes its requirements or puts a moratorium on adoptions, the couple may be left without other options.

The determination of some couples to adopt from a particular country can sometimes get in the way of good sense if they do not fit the age restrictions, length of marriage, and so on. If the prospective parents are unusually persistent, they will call every agency in America until they find one that will take them as clients, not fully realizing that they could be turned down at the end of the process by a judge who reviews that country's national adoption law before granting a final adoption decree.

WORKING WITH THE INTERNATIONAL AGENCY

While prospective parents expect to be guided and kept informed, agencies have certain expectations, as well. They expect the potential parents to read their contracts, handbooks, and program packets of directions before calling for help. They also trust that the documents required from the prospective parents will be sent to the agency in a timely fashion. Responsible agencies expect that prospective parents will fully participate in the agency's training for international adoptive parenting. They also expect that prospective parents will be prepared to take an adoption trip abroad on short notice. More importantly, the agencies abroad have the expectation that the adoptive parent has applied to only one foreign child-placing entity.

You may be required to sign a contract that specifies the services performed by the international agency. It should cover the illness or death of a child awaiting adoption, as well as relatives reclaiming the child and adoption disruptions. Waiting pool policies and a postplacement supervisory agreement are usually outlined, as is the addition of a child to the adopting family during the waiting period by pregnancy or adoption through another agency. A reimbursement schedule for international processing and foreign program fees should be included, usually with a disclaimer such as one posted in the International Concerns Committee for Children (ICCC) Report on Foreign Adoption:

"Due to circumstances beyond the control of any agency, the possibility exists that the adoption process could be discontinued by foreign nations, governmental action, or judicial decrees beyond the control of the agency. You must further understand that it is necessary to advance funds to accomplish agency objectives and that the portion of those funds already utilized very possibly cannot be recovered in the event of such discontinuance. You need also to understand that in spite of information to the contrary, the child, when received, might have some undiagnosed physical or mental problem or might develop such a problem at a later date. You need to know, finally, that despite agency efforts to work with competent and honest lawyers, their actions are beyond agency control. This is by no means meant to scare you, but to tell you the simple facts about intercountry adoptions."

CHAPTER 5

Obtaining State Approval: The First Steps

Once you have learned as much as you can about the international adoption experience, attended as many educational seminars as possible, talked to prospective parents and visited with adoptive parents and their children, and thoroughly evaluated the agencies you are interested in working with, you are ready for the next formal step in the adoption process: registering with the licensed agency or certified social worker that will conduct your home study and any postplacement supervision required.

If the U.S.-based international agency you plan to use to adopt your child is located and licensed in your state, it will be the one to conduct your home study. When the potential adoptive parents live in a state where the international agency is not licensed, they will need to find another agency or a certified social worker to conduct the home study. Thus, in some cases, you will actually need to formally apply with two agencies: a local agency that is close enough to your residence to conduct your home study and an international agency that will connect you with a child overseas. Fortunately, because most international adoption agencies use a network of local agencies across the United States, finding a local agency to do your home study is usually not difficult. To make certain that the staff is qualified and that the agency is committed to high ethical and legal standards, ask about the agency's accreditation standards.

The agency conducting your home study must have a countywide or statewide license, but it does not necessarily need to have an office in your city. Many agencies utilize social workers in other cities and counties on a contract basis in order to provide services for a wider area. You will have a long relationship with the agency you choose since the agency will follow up to monitor your family's adjustment for six months or more following the child's placement.

STEP 4

Choose the agency that will conduct your home study (if different from your international adoption agency).

THE HOME STUDY

The INS mandates that all states require a home study by a licensed social worker or adoption agency in the adopter's home state before a child is adopted abroad or is brought into the United States for adoption. The home study must follow the requirements of the state licensing department for child-placing agencies. INS requirements must also be included. You will need an adoption agency or social worker to conduct a home study even if you plan to enter into an independent or parent-initiated adoption.

A home study usually consists of an orientation meeting, the application, a private interview, a home visit, and group discussions led by a social worker. Data gathered at the study meetings is summarized by the social worker in a document that becomes the official home study. The home study may take anywhere from six weeks to six months depending on individual circumstances.

Home studies deal with the dynamics of the individual adopter, the marriage, the challenges of transracial and cross-cultural adoptions, and the subsequent adjustments of parent and child. Social workers are professionally trained to help prospective adopters explore the many facets of adoption and to help them make the best possible decisions for the family they are planning. The social worker and the prospective adoptive parents must explore and discuss the types of children available and their ability to parent such a child or children. The minimum and maximum age, the number of siblings, gender, race, and possible handicapping conditions must be agreed upon in the social worker's closing recommendation. This study process ends when a mutually agreed upon decision is reached either to proceed toward adoption or to withdraw the application.

APPLYING TO YOUR LOCAL AGENCY

STEP 5

Initiate home study by applying to appropriate agency.

Every adoption agency has an application form that must be filled out before the home study begins. If you have a serious disease or disability, a history of mental illness, a history of alcohol or drug abuse, or a criminal record, discuss your problem with the director of the agency before registering. You may be requested to provide a letter of recommendation from a psychiatrist, counselor, or probation officer before you register. Many agencies also request that you fill out a form indicating your level of acceptance of certain medical conditions in the child you wish to adopt. (See sample list of handicapping conditions of waiting children at the end of this chapter.) This list ranges from conditions as minor as a lisp or small scar to much more serious health issues. Adopting parents who want a generally healthy child may answer "no" to all listed conditions or may decline to fill out the form.

You may also be required to sign a home study contract, which outlines the agency's responsibilities and your own. If, for some reason, your agency or social worker does not offer a home study contract, you might request one. The home study sessions and the conditions necessary for approval are set forth in the contract. Most contracts or agreements will state the conditions under which some or all of the fees you pay will be refunded.

Before you commit to any agency, you should know exactly what services this agency will perform and what its fees will be. Call or contact the agency by e-mail to request literature explaining the agency's requirements for adoptive parents, fees, policies, length of licensure, and accreditation.

Two separate entities are involved in licensing adoption agencies and social workers. Social workers are licensed in their state by the State Board of Social Worker Examiners. The board issues a directory of social workers each year. Adoption agencies are licensed by the licensing division of their state adoption unit. There is a unit in each county. State adoption units go by different names. In Texas, it is the Department of Protective and Regulatory Services. To ensure that you are registering with a qualified adoption agency or social worker, check with the appropriate licensing agency. (Note: In most states, a home study conducted by an agency is required; however, in some states, such as New York, Iowa, Florida, Louisiana, and Texas, a licensed social worker may conduct the study instead.)

In addition, before you commit to having an agency conduct your home study, you should know the answers to the following questions:

What does your home study consist of?

Who will conduct it?

How soon will the social worker contact me after I apply?

What credentials does the social worker have and how much experience does he or she have in foreign adoptions?

How long will it take for approval?

Why would someone not be approved?

What happens after the home study?

OBTAINING DOCUMENTS FOR THE HOME STUDY

Once you have registered with an agency to conduct your home study, you should begin to collect the documents needed to meet your home study requirements and the requirements of other federal and foreign agencies that will be involved in your adoption. Many of the documents assembled for your home study will also later be used to prepare a dossier (or collection of

STEP 6

Obtain documents
required for home study.

documents) for the foreign court or central authority.

You will be collecting a combination of certified and original documents. A certified document is an official document issued by the state or county, as opposed to a document issued by a hospital for a birth or a document issued by a church for a marriage. Original documents are individually generated. Job letters, health certificates, police clearances, letters of reference, and your home study are all considered original documents.

Each prospective adoptive parent must obtain the following documents before the home study can be approved. (You can initiate the home study before you have all of the documents.)

Required Documents

1. Certified birth certificates for each member of the family. Order three for each spouse (one for the foreign dossier, one for the passport, and one for the INS) and one for each child already in your home.

Certified birth certificates can be ordered from the Bureau of Vital Statistics in the state where you were born. If you need help finding this office, contact directory assistance in the capital city of the state where you were born. Obtaining certified birth certificates takes about four weeks by mail or two hours in person, unless you use express mail services.

If you are a naturalized citizen, use your naturalization certificate for evidence at the INS office and passport office. Use a certified copy of your birth certificate for the formal adoption dossier. This can be accomplished through the consul of your native country, who will authenticate a photocopy of your original. If you are from a country that does not have a consul here (i.e., Cuba), you may request the consul of the country from which you are adopting to handle this step. If you do not have a birth certificate, ask INS for Form G-342. An alternative is to photocopy your certificate of citizenship and get it notarized.

2. Certified marriage license. Order two (one for the foreign dossier and one for INS).

Certified marriage licenses are available from the County Clerk in the county where you were married. These usually cost between $3.00 and $10.00. This takes one week by mail or two days if you call ahead and pick it up. Tell them the month, day, and year of the marriage, the names of both parties, and your return address.

3. Certified death certificate, if applicable, of former spouses. Order two of each (one for the foreign dossier and one for INS). Certified death certificates are available from the Bureau of Vital Statistics in the state where the death occurred.

4. Divorce decree, if applicable. Order two of each (one for the foreign dossier and one for INS). If both you and your spouse are divorced, you will each need two copies of both divorce decrees. Divorce decrees are available from the Clerk of Court in the county in which the divorce occurred.

5. Job letter from your employer stating your length of employment and annual salary. (You need one letter for each applicant.) If you are self-employed, a public accountant may prepare the statement. In either case, address the letters with "To Whom It May Concern."

6. A statement of net worth written by you or your accountant. (See sample net worth statement at the end of this chapter.)

7. Copies of your health and life insurance policies. You need only the page showing the company name, beneficiary, and amount. A photocopy will usually suffice. (Note: Not all states require this.)

8. Medical examination forms for all household members signed by the family physician. (See sample health form at the end of this chapter.) The date of the exam must be included on the form. The medical examination form is valid for one year from the date of the exam.

9. Photocopies of your federal income tax returns (first and second page only) for the last three years. On the side of the form, type the following statement: "I certify that this is a true copy of the original."

10. Form I-171H (Notice of Favorable Determination Concerning Application for Advance Processing of Orphan Petition). Form I-171H is received after Form I-600A (Application for Advance Processing of Orphan Petition) is filed. Details for filing Form I-600A appear in Chapter 6. The I-171H is not required for home study approval; however, a copy must be presented to your agency before a child is assigned.

11. For all household members over age 18, a letter from your local police department stating that the individual has no criminal record. (See sample police clearance form at the end of this chapter.) You will usually need a separate letter for each applicant. Try to get the signature of the Chief of Police notarized at the same time. Ask at the police station for information on doing this.

12. Letters of reference from at least three people (not related) who are acquainted with you and your family. These letters should come from professionals or community leaders if at all possible. (See sample format for letters of reference at the end of this chapter.) Try to obtain letters of reference from people in your locality. Then, the same notary public, Secretary of State, and foreign consul can be used to sign, stamp, verify, and authenticate all or at least most of your documents.

13. Child abuse clearances and criminal clearances for each member of the family over age 18. These documents are obtained by your social worker through your state welfare system while the home study is in progress.

14. Pictures of applicants in front of their home and individual close-ups (or passport pictures). You should also include photos of existing children. You need at least three sets of photos. Pose in business attire. Jeans, shorts, swimsuits, and bare feet will not make a favorable impression, since your dossier should be presented with as much dignity as possible. (See sample photos at the end of this chapter.)

Submit photocopies of your documents to the agency conducting your home study. You must retain the originals for your foreign dossier. Documents not usually required abroad are birth certificates and medical forms on children already in your family and insurance policies.

Documents for the foreign dossier may need notarization or apostilles, verification, and authentication, depending on the country you adopt from. (Some adoptive parents notarize each of the original documents as they are gathered.) Chapter 7 explains the process for ensuring that your documents are appropriately endorsed. Try to get all of your original documents generated in the same state. This way, you may need only one notary public to sign all of your documents. This also makes them easier to verify or apostille.

SAMPLE GUIDELINES FOR A TYPICAL HOME STUDY

Most U.S.-based international agencies have a specific guide for social workers conducting the home study as well as the postplacement supervisory reports. Your international agency will inform you if your local agency or social worker needs to follow a specific format.

Since many foreign adoption agencies will ask to see a translated copy of the home study, adopters should ask their social worker to make the home study as brief as possible. In most cases, ten to twelve pages are adequate.

What follows is an example of a set of home study interview guidelines used by the administering agency or social worker. Prepared by Los Niños International Adoption Center, this particular home study guide incorporates Texas minimum standards, the INS regulations cited in Form I-600A, and the requirements of several of the more active child-sending countries, such as Colombia, China, and Russia. Although the home study guidelines of other agencies may vary somewhat, you can expect that all of these topics will be brought up at some point in the home study process.

In addition, the social worker will also conduct an environmental evaluation of your house to be sure the home would be safe for a baby or child. (See sample environmental health checklist at the end of this chapter.)

THIS GUIDE IS FOR THE EXCLUSIVE USE OF LOS NINOS AND NETWORKING AGENCIES

Revised from the Federal Register/Vol. 59, No. 146
Re: INS Regulations 9/30/94
Texas Minimum Standards 5/10/94

PREPARING THE HOME STUDY & DOCUMENTS
A Guide for Social Workers
© 1999 Los Niños International Adoption Center

A rewrite or addendum will be requested if this guide is not followed.
Please use your agency letterhead

Prospective candidates must be a legally married couple or a single person. Couples who cohabit cannot legally adopt abroad.

HOME STUDY
Quote: *"This study is approved for the sole us of LNI foreign adoption programs."*

Name of prospective adoptive parent(s)
Address (street, city, state and zip)
Home and work telephone numbers
Email addresses

Quote if accurate: *"Prior to approval, I obtained criminal and child abuse clearances, and a complete set of supporting documents was presented for my review."*

HOME STUDY APPROVED:_____(Date)
Contacts (INS and LNI standards require these separate interviews and dates:)
- (Date) First consultation or orientation
- (Date) An individual interview with each applicant
- (Date) Interviews with school-age children or other persons living with family
- (Date) At least one visit to the home with all present
- (Date) At least one interview with adult children living at home who are over age 18
- (Date) Interview either by phone or in person with each adult/child no longer residing in the home

Home Study for Second or Subsequent Adoption
- All contacts listed above, including individual interviews, must be conducted and documented
- Date of the first adoption must be cited
- Approval date of the first home study must be indicated
- All categories must be reviewed

You may write "No Changes" if there have not been any changes since the first home study, providing that they were covered and documented in the first study. However, categories of "Child Desired," "Police Clearance," "Child Abuse Clearance," and "Recommendation" must be covered in the second study.

- Include a section on the child presently in the home and how the parents' life changed when that child arrived
- In regard to studies where "No Changes" are stated, the first study must be attached to the second study

TOPICS TO BE COVERED IN THE HOME STUDY

Child Desired

- Knowledge of types of children available, flexibility, level of acceptance
- Indicate the number of siblings, minimum and maximum ages, gender, health, whether low birth weight or correctable/non-correctable handicaps are acceptable, and the race or ethnicity, such as: Asian, Asian/Anglo, Asian/Hispanic, Asian/Black, Hispanic, Hispanic/Anglo, Hispanic/Black, Caucasian, Black, Caucasian/Black, Caucasian/Gypsy, or Caucasian/Turkish

  DO NOT SPECIFY THE COUNTRY SINCE THE INTERNATIONAL ADOPTION SITUATION OFTEN CHANGES

Motivation and Readiness to Adopt

- Evolution of decision to adopt and reason for choosing international adoption
- Length of time spent considering adoption
- Infertility — diagnosis and attempts at treatment, if applicable
- Efforts to prepare for an adoption
- Summary of worker's preadoption counseling

Quote if accurate: "*I advised and discussed with (Name) the process, expenses, medical risks, difficulties, and delays associated with international adoption; the requirements of the Immigration and Naturalization Service; and the adoption laws of the state. I also explained the need to read the LNI Handbook and the text How to Adopt Internationally and follow LNI's systematic approach in order to become knowledgeable on cross-cultural parenting.*"

- Mention whether they have been previously rejected for adoption or the subject of an unfavorable home study
- Explain whether they are trying to become pregnant or are adopting through another source
- Inform them that if they do become pregnant or they receive a child from another agency before LNI assigns them a child, the adoption plan must be put on hold for six months; when the adoption process is resumed, an update to their home study must be conducted
- Mention whether they will travel abroad for the legal process to adopt and to immigrate their child or children

Knowledge of the Foreign Adoption Process

- Attitude toward the prospect of a child from a different ethnicity, race,

culture, and nation
- Understanding of reasons children from foreign countries become available for adoption and willingness to accept an orphaned, abandoned, or relinquished child
- Acceptance of risks and unknowns in foreign adoption

Adoptive Mother
- Worker's description of applicant's appearance, including weight and height
- Date and place of birth (state the word "verified" by birth certificate). Names and address(es) of her parents, their occupation, health, marital status, marital relationship, and each parent's support/nurturing and decision-making abilities
- Siblings' names, sex, order of birth, education, occupation, marital status, children, location, and past and current relationships with each sibling
- Relevant extended family and current contacts, growing-up years, economic circumstances, family lifestyle, and work and play activities
- Type of discipline and/or punishment received and the feelings about it
- Any history as a victim of emotional, physical, and/or sexual abuse or neglect and how this experience was resolved
- Any history of drug or alcohol abuse and the resolution of this experience
- Major family values, friendships and social life, feelings about parents (include information about absent parent, if appropriate), and expectations by parents
- Feelings about childhood including both the happiest and most traumatic memories, what they would change about their parents and their childhood, feelings about themselves, and key factors contributing to sense of self, i.e., significant persons and events, frustrations and successes, ways stress is handled and ways negative feelings are expressed

Adoptive Father
- Same as for adoptive mother

Previous Relationships or Marriages
- History and termination of significant relationships and marriages, reason the relationships ended, how the relationships ended, date and place of divorce(s) (state the word "verified" by divorce decree)
- Children from previous relationships/marriages, parental visitation, and child support

Present Marriage
- Length and nature of courtship, date and place of marriage (state the word "verified" by marriage license)
- Factors that attracted spouses to one another
- Marital lifestyle, roles, and decision-making processes
- Areas of pride in one another and sexual relationship
- Primary areas of stress and/or disagreement
- Method for resolving differences
- Areas that they hope to improve upon
- Separations or threats of divorce

- Participation in marriage counseling — dates, duration, resolutions
- Address the quality of marital and family relationships in relation to the family's ability to provide an adoptive home

Singles and Couples with Children
- Feelings about themselves as parents
- Their decision-making processes regarding child raising, their agreements and disagreements about parental discipline and how they are resolved, and their support for one another as parents
- Issues of possessiveness or control
- Reasons they decided to adopt when they already have a child
- Understanding adjustment difficulties for the child or children already in the home

Single Parents
- Significant relationships with both men and women, including sexual relationships
- Attitude toward marriage
- Identify their support system

Current Children (This includes adults over age 18. Include those in the home, college age children, children of previous marriages, and their whereabouts.)
- Name, sex, date of birth, psychological and social adjustment, personality, schooling and academic performance, hobbies, and nature of relationship with each parent
- Sibling relationship, both strengths and weaknesses
- Attitude toward the adoption of a sibling(s)—include issues relating to birth order and role changes

Others in the Home (Include grandparents, exchange students, part and full-time help.)
- Name, age, relation, duration of stay in the home, physical and financial dependency
- Reasons for a single applicant sharing the home with a non-family member
- Interaction with family members
- Attitude toward the adoption
- Indicate whether or not other adults reside in the home

Extended Family
- Interaction and relationship with family members, neighbors, church, and community
- Extended families' attitudes toward the adoption plan and any opposition

Attitude Toward Discipline and Child-Rearing
- Philosophy
- Understanding child development stages
- Methods of disciplining children, including those already in the home
- Discuss LNI Discipline Policy and obtain signatures
- Child care experience if they have no children

- Ability to understand and manage a child's behaviors associated with separation and loss
- Expectations of their adoptive child
- Ability to assess and identify a child's needs to promote self-esteem
- Willingness to obtain professional advice, if needed
- Capability to prepare an older child to live independently

Understanding the Child's Needs Regarding the Birth Family
- Understanding the dynamics of child abuse and neglect
- Responsiveness to children who may have been subjected to abuse, neglect, separation, and loss of their biological family
- Ability to communicate and help their child with being adopted
- Sensitivity and feelings about the child's birth family and understanding the reasons why the birth mother made an adoption plan
- Acceptance of the adoptive child's feelings about their birth family and their abilities to help the child deal with these feelings
- Capability to help build continuity in the child's life, such as keeping a memory/life book
- Ability to support a child's search for birth family

Interracial, Cross-Cultural Parenting Issues
- Understanding the beliefs, behavior, customs, diet, language, and other practices of the culture from which they wish to adopt a child
- Plans for learning about the child's cultural background and cross-cultural parenting
- Strategies for maintaining the child's heritage and identity and incorporating it into their lifestyle
- Commitment to provide the child with positive racial and cultural experiences and information
- Tolerance and ability to deal appropriately with personal questions, ambiguity, or disapproval from others
- Acknowledgment that their foreign-born child may choose friends of every race and nationality and could marry someone from a completely different cultural group and that adopting interracially will make their family interracial forever, impacting all family members

Child Care Plan
- Immediate plans for an adjustment period following the arrival of a child, taking advantage of the Family Leave Act if both parents are employed, and long range plans

Employment, Education, and Economic Situation
- Current job, title, description, future prospects, job satisfaction, work schedule, salary (state the word "verified" by job letter) and bonuses
- Education
- Other sources of income, including the type and amount of savings, checking, and investments
- Verify policies and insurance coverage (health and life) of all household members including children to be placed

- Stocks and bonds — value
- Outstanding debts — amount and monthly payments
- Home value, mortgage balance, and monthly payment
- Evidence used to verify source and amount of income and financial resources, i.e.1040s, job letter, etc.

Quote if accurate: *"The applicants have sufficient money management ability to provide for a child until that child reaches adulthood."*

Interests, Hobbies, and Use of Leisure Time
- A statement regarding their philosophy toward society
- Activities they enjoy together and separately
- Social contacts — significant friends of other nationalities, races, religions

Religion
- Formal membership, extent of practice of faith, role of religion in the life of each family member, religious training of current children, plans for religious membership and training of adopted child

Physical and Mental Health
- Significant history of disease, handicaps, illnesses, and general level of current health, prognosis, and life expectancy (cite medical report)
- Method of dealing with health limitations and effect on other family members
- Counseling (A copy of an evaluation or report addressing what transpired, results of treatment, and any restrictions must be attached for our file.)
- Hospitalizations
- Current medications

Quote for each applicant if accurate: *"Name_____is in good health and appears to be able to raise the child to adulthood."*
- A statement must be made regarding each applicant's personality, maturity level, ability to handle stress, logical thinking, and overall judgment

Quote if accurate: *"There is no evidence of psychopathology."*

Home Environment and Community
- Description of home — adequacy of space both inside and out
- Discussion of yard area, landscaping, and fencing (if any)
- Rate the housekeeping standards
- Community resources and racial make-up of neighborhood and ethnic attitudes for accepting children from another culture
- Discuss basic care and safety issues with applicant — all medications and poisonous liquids must be kept out of the reach of children or locked in a storage area
- Address any trampoline safety issues, if appropriate
- Discuss firearm safety issues. State whether firearms are or are not present. If they are, be certain that all necessary precautions are taken. LNI requires firearms and ammunition must be kept separate from each other and in locked compartments at all times.

- Discuss water hazards near the property including how to protect the child. LNI requires family swimming pools to have a pool alarm or a lockable fence around the perimeter of the pool.
- Record the number and placement of smoke and fire alarms. All homes must be equipped with at least one working fire extinguisher.
- Inspect the home and property using the LNI Environmental Checklist
- If the home and property pass your inspection, write a statement that the above precautions are taking place and that the physical environment inside and outside the home are safe and appropriate for the care of the child
- If the parents plan to move or if they live abroad but plan to raise the child in the United States, include a description of the house where they will reside, if this is known

Police and Child Abuse Clearances (Must be completed for all household members age 18 and over, including children away at school.)
- Ask each applicant if they have ever been arrested and state their answer
- Write that the letter of clearance from the local police verifies that, "(Name) has no criminal record"
- Ask each applicant whether they have ever been accused or charged with child abuse or neglect and state their answer
- Document that the Child Abuse Registry has been checked and state "(Name) does not have a criminal record of child abuse"
- Document if your state does not provide child abuse clearances for prospective adoptive parents registered with private, licensed, nonprofit adoption agencies
- Explain the circumstances of any offenses, the trial and outcome, and the attitude of the offender toward incident
- Ask if there is any history of substance abuse, sexual or child abuse, or domestic violence, even if it did not result in an arrest or conviction and include their response

Adults must disclose any record of arrest no matter what the disposition, no matter how minor, no matter how long ago, and no matter if they were told that it was expunged. (Failure to do so may result in a denial of the application.)

- Ask the prospective parent if the record of their arrest can be expunged. They may need to consult an attorney for this. If the offense cannot be expunged, LNI may not be able to approve them for adoption.

Will and Guardianship Plan (In event of untimely death of adoptive parents.)
- Names, addresses, relationship to adoptive parents, and their commitment to the child

References
- State the number of references received and summarize briefly, using direct quotes regarding the applicant's qualities as relating to adoptive parenting
- References from attending physicians — relatives or therapists cannot be accepted

Conclusion
- Fitness of couple or single for adoption in general; summarize their strengths
- Adequacy of couple or single for foreign adoption
- Capabilities of couple or single to raise the child/children they requested

   Discuss whether the applicant can accept and can cope with a child whose birth parents' history may show physical or mental illness, alcohol and/or drug abuse/usage, a criminal history, or that they may have been accused of neglect or physically and/or sexually abusing the child

   Mention the strengths of the prospective parent who expresses interest in a child with special needs and/or handicaps, or emotional or behavioral problems

   Explain the problems of an abandoned child with no background information

- State what the couple or single can or cannot accept

Approval and Recommendation
- A recommendation of the couple or single for the adoption of a child/children. The statement must include age, gender, number of siblings, race, and state of health. If the child desired is handicapped or has special needs, a recommendation must include the prospective parent's willingness and ability to provide proper care for such an child

Quote if accurate: *"I certify that the family (name) has met all of the preadoption requirements of their state."*

Quote if accurate: *"(Name of agency or social worker's name) agrees to provide postplacement supervision according to the requirements of LNI, the state, and the foreign country, including any required follow-up reports to the child's agency, orphanage, or other source. If necessary, I/we will refer family to outside sources of support and assistance for the well-being of the entire family unit and in particular the adopted child/children."*

Written and Submitted By:

_____

(Include credentials)

Signature of Supervisor:

_____

Attachments to the Home Study
- Discipline policy
- Environmental checklist
- Service plans (one for child and one for prospective parents)

- Copy of client's child abuse clearance
- Agreement with international adoption requirements
- Copy of license or certification of social worker or copy of license of supervisor of social worker
- Copy of the agency license
- Copy of accreditation certificate

AFTER THE HOME STUDY

Immediately upon the approval of your home study by the supervisor of social work, copies of the home study, supporting documents, and Form I-600A should be filed at INS. Do not forward these documents to the INS until you have formally applied to a U.S.-based international agency. Chapter 6 explains the process for filing Form I-600A.

Updating the Home Study

A home study is valid for six to 18 months depending on state law. A home study update must be written if the home study has expired, or if you have moved or experienced some other major life change. If you move out of state, you must register with an agency there to update your study according to their state requirements. INS fingerprint charts and petitions must also be updated and/or transferred to your new local INS office.

Each home study topic must be covered in the update. If a topic remains the same, "No changes" may be written below the topic heading. Dates on preceding documents 5 through 11 expire after six to 18 months. These items must be updated during the time the home study update is in progress.

Handicapping Conditions of Waiting Children

Indicate your level of acceptance of a child who has the following problems:

	Indicate		
NEWBORNS	YES	NO	MAYBE
A. Low Apgar score, prognosis uncertain	☐	☐	☐
B. Birth mother on drugs or alcohol, prognosis uncertain	☐	☐	☐

CHILDREN

1.
A. Slight limp ☐ ☐ ☐
B. Leg braces ☐ ☐ ☐
C. Missing limb ☐ ☐ ☐
D. Is in a wheel chair ☐ ☐ ☐
E. Is paraplegic ☐ ☐ ☐
F. Is quadriplegic ☐ ☐ ☐
G. Cerebral Palsy ☐ ☐ ☐
H. Cystic Fibrosis ☐ ☐ ☐

2.
A. Seizure disorder that is controlled by medication ☐ ☐ ☐
B. Seizure disorder not controlled but child has infrequent seizures ☐ ☐ ☐
C. Seizure disorder not controlled and has frequent seizures ☐ ☐ ☐

3.
A. A blood disorder that requires blood transfusions every 3 months ☐ ☐ ☐
B. Blood disorder that requires hospitalization once a month ☐ ☐ ☐
C. Blood disorder resulting in a limited lifespan ☐ ☐ ☐

4.
A. Heart murmur, activity not curtailed ☐ ☐ ☐
B. Heart murmur, vigorous activity curtailed ☐ ☐ ☐
C. May require open heart surgery at a later date but at placement needs only to be watched ☐ ☐ ☐
D. Definitely will require open heart surgery ☐ ☐ ☐
E. Will require more than one open heart surgery ☐ ☐ ☐

5.
A. Sight in both eyes but vision is limited and special glasses needed ☐ ☐ ☐
B. Sight in one eye only ☐ ☐ ☐
C. Blind but surgery may give partial sight ☐ ☐ ☐
D. Blind and will never have sight

6.
A. Hearing problem with only partial hearing and surgery may help ☐ ☐ ☐
B. Hearing problem with partial hearing but surgery will not help ☐ ☐ ☐
C. Hearing in only one ear ☐ ☐ ☐
D. No hearing, deaf and does not speak ☐ ☐ ☐

7.
A. Deformed hand ☐ ☐ ☐
B. Deformed arm ☐ ☐ ☐
C. Deformed leg ☐ ☐ ☐
D. Deformed face ☐ ☐ ☐
E. Two deformed arms ☐ ☐ ☐
F. Two deformed legs ☐ ☐ ☐

Handicapping Conditions of Waiting Children

	YES	NO	MAYBE
8. A. In special education	☐	☐	☐
B. In EMR	☐	☐	☐
C. In TMR	☐	☐	☐
D. Retarded and will always need supervision, such as sheltered home	☐	☐	☐
E. Downs syndrome	☐	☐	☐
9. A. Hyperactive	☐	☐	☐
B. Hyperactive, requires medication but functions relatively normal	☐	☐	☐
C. Hyperactive, requires medication and some kind of special classroom setting	☐	☐	☐
10. A. Emotionally damaged, very withdrawn and will require therapy for an extensive period of time	☐	☐	☐
B. So emotionally damaged he/she is very abusive toward other people; a child who is abusive to animals	☐	☐	☐
C. Emotionally damaged; he/she is very abusive toward his/her person, such as pulling out hair, pinching himself/herself	☐	☐	☐
11. A. Stutters	☐	☐	☐
B. Lisp	☐	☐	☐
C. Speech at age 6 is very hard to understand	☐	☐	☐
D. Will always have trouble speaking and being understood	☐	☐	☐
12. A. Hare lip	☐	☐	☐
B. Cleft palate	☐	☐	☐
C. Both hare lip and cleft palate	☐	☐	☐
13. A. Had one parent who is schizophrenic	☐	☐	☐
B. Had two parents who are schizophrenic	☐	☐	☐
C. Schizophrenic, but medication helps	☐	☐	☐
14. A. Sickle Cell carrier	☐	☐	☐
B. Sickle Cell Anemia but relatively controlled	☐	☐	☐
C. Sickle Cell Anemia with frequent episodes	☐	☐	☐
15. A. Burn scars	☐	☐	☐
B. Slight	☐	☐	☐
C. Extensive, needing surgery	☐	☐	☐
16. A. Birth marks	☐	☐	☐
B. Small	☐	☐	☐
C. Large or extensive	☐	☐	☐

Statement of Net Worth

NAME(S): _____

ADDRESS: _____

_____

Home Telephone Number: (   )   –

ASSETS

Cash on hand & in banks $ _____

Investments   _____

Savings accounts   _____

Cash surrender value
  of life insurance   _____

Other Stocks & Bonds   _____

Real Estate: _____

1. _____   _____

2. _____   _____

Automobile   _____

Trucks, boats, planes   _____

Personal property   _____

TOTAL ASSETS $ _____

LIABILITIES & NET WORTH

Mortgages & real estate notes $ _____

Notes payable   _____

Credit card (balances):

_____   _____

_____   _____

_____   _____

Loans (balances): _____   _____

_____   _____

_____   _____

_____   _____

_____   _____

TOTAL LIABILITIES $ _____

NET WORTH* $ _____

(*Net Worth is the difference between Assets & Liabilities)

Date _____   Signature _____

Date _____   Signature _____

SUBSCRIBED AND SWORN to before me on the _____

day of 199__ . To which witness my hand and seal of office. _____

Notary Public in and for the State of _____ , county of _____

My commission expires:. _____ .

Medical Statement

Medical Statement for Adoptive Applicant
and all Household Members
Page 1 of 2

Name (Last, First, Middle):	Date of Birth:

Address (Street, City, State & Zip):

1. Have you had treatment for a serious or chronic illness? ☐ Yes ☐ No
   Have you been hospitalized in the past five years? ☐ Yes ☐ No
   Have you ever received, or been advised to seek, mental health services? ☐ Yes ☐ No
   Have you ever received, or been advised to seek, treatment for alcohol/substance abuse? ☐ Yes ☐ No
   Have you ever had a communicable disease? ☐ Yes ☐ No

   If the answer to any of these questions is yes, please explain:
   _____
   _____
   _____

2. Do you have or have you had any of the following? (Check all that apply.)

   ☐ Arthritis _____   ☐ Heart Disease _____
   ☐ Asthma _____   ☐ Hypertension _____
   ☐ Cancer _____   ☐ Kidney Disease _____
   ☐ Epilepsy _____   ☐ Tuberculosis _____
   ☐ Diabetes _____   ☐ Ulcers _____

   If any are checked, please explain: _____
   _____

3. Is there a history of other hereditary disease? ☐ Yes ☐ No
   If yes, please explain: _____
   _____

AUTHORIZATION FOR RELEASE OF INFORMATION

I hereby affirm that I have completed this form to the best of my ability, and that the information provided is true and correct. I further authorize the physician completing the reverse side of this form to release any information he/she may have concerning my physical or mental health to:

Name/Address of Agency: _____

Signature of Applicant:	Date:

COMPLETION OF THIS FORM IS REQUIRED FOR THE AGENCY TO PROCEED WITH YOUR APPLICATION.

Subscribed and sworn to before me on the _____ day of _____, 19___ to which witness my hand and seal of office.

Notary Public in and for the State of _____, County of _____.

My Commission Expires: _____

Medical Statement

Medical Statement for Adoptive Applicant
and all Household Members
Page 2 of 2

(This side of form to be completed by a licensed physician.)

Date you last completed a physical examination of this individual:		Date you last treated this individual:	
Do you provide medical services to this individual:	❑ Regularly	❑ Occasionally	❑ First Time

Please respond to each of the following to the best of your knowledge:

1. Does this individual suffer from an illness, including a communicable disease, that would be detrimental to the care of a adoptive child placed in his/her home? ❑ Yes ❑ No

2. Are there any chronic or serious disorders for which this individual has received treatment? ❑ Yes ❑ No

3. Is this individual currently taking medication? ❑ Yes ❑ No

4. Is this individual experiencing any physical, behavioral or emotional problems that would be detrimental to an adoptive child placed in his/her home? ❑ Yes ❑ No

5. Have you ever referred this individual to other medical services , mental health services or treatment for alcohol/substance abuse? ❑ Yes ❑ No

   If the answer to any of the above questions is YES, please explain: _____

   _____

   _____

6. In your opinion, does the individual have the normal life expectancy?_____

7. Physical Examination:

Weight:		Blood Pressure:		Pulse:	
Height:		Temperature:		Lungs:	
Heart:		Abdomen:		Nervous System:	

8. Laboratory Tests:

HIV:		Urinalysis:	
Hep B:		Tine or Mantoux:	
Hep C:		CBC:	

9. Any recommendations for medical care? _____

Please state your professional opinion regarding this individual's suitability as an adoptive parent from the standpoint of health, considering the individual's medical history as given on the reverse side of this form and from knowledge you have of the individual. _____

_____

_____

_____

Physician's Signature:	Date:	Name of Physician (Print or Type):
Physician's Work Address:	Physician's Work Phone Number: ( ) -	Physician's State License Number:

Police Clearance

NOTE: This form is not accepted by all police departments. If your local police department does not accept this form, request a letter of clearance on the department's letterhead.

Dear Sir/Madam:

Our adoption agency requires that all applicants have a record check. Please check this information through the NCIC and, (for Texas residents) the TCIC. In some localities, neither police nor sheriff offices can produce fingerprint charts. In this event please return the chart to our clients.

MALE APPLICANT: _____ Date of Birth: _____

Social Security No.: _____ Place of Birth: _____

Present Address: _____

Father's Full Name: _____

Mother's Full Name: _____

FEMALE APPLICANT: _____ Date of Birth: _____

Social Security No.: _____ Place of Birth: _____

Present Address: _____

Father's Full Name: _____

Mother's Full Name: _____

RELEASE OF INFORMATION PERMISSION: I willingly give my permission for the above information to be checked and released in full to _____ (agency name) at _____ _____ (agency address).

MALE APPLICANT: _____ Date: _____

FEMALE APPLICANT: _____ Date: _____

TO BE FILLED OUT BY LAW OFFICER

TO WHOM IT MAY CONCERN: The subject has been checked by our department. Records were also checked through TCIC/NCIC and were found to be clear.

The record of this male subject is: _____
_____

The record of this female subject is: _____
_____

Signature of law officer: _____

    SUBSCRIBED AND SWORN to before me this _____ **day of** _____ **, 199 __ .**

_____

Notary Public in and for the State of _____ **, County of** _____

My commission expires: _____ **.**

Letter of Reference

Try to obtain letters of reference from people in your locality. Then the same notary public, Secretary of State (verification), and foreign consul (authentication) can be used to stamp and sign all or at least most of your documents.

Photocopy three copies of this form for the persons you have selected to write your letters. Ask them to give you the letter for your formal adoption dossier.

TO: _____

FROM: _____

DATE: _____

RE: Letter of Reference: A letter must be typed and signed before a notary.

We have applied to _____ (agency) for assistance with our adoption plans. We hope that you will be able to write a letter of reference for us, and return it to us by _____ (date). Following are seven categories which the agency wishes you to consider and to include in a letter of reference.

1. How long have you known us and in what capacity?

2. Have you observed us around children? Under what circumstances?

3. Do you believe we can easily handle the problems that could arise when an adopted and/or foreign child enters our home?

4. Have we discussed our adoption plans with you? How do you feel about our plans?

5. How do you think an adopted and/or foreign child will be accepted in our community?

6. Do you believe we manage our money responsibly?

7. How would you rate our homemaking and property upkeep?
   We will appreciate any additional comments and/or information you would like to include.

Sample Photos for Home Study

Environmental Health Checklist

	YES	NO	N/A
1. Home is clean and maintained in good repair	☐	☐	☐
2. Furnishings and equipment used by an ill child are cleaned with soap and water	☐	☐	☐
3. Sheets and pillowcases are washed before use by another child	☐	☐	☐
4. Yard is free of hazards to children	☐	☐	☐
5. Rooms are adequately ventilated and without objectionable odors	☐	☐	☐
6. Windows and doors used for ventilation are screened	☐	☐	☐
7. Plumbing appears in good repair. Home is free of water stains or other indications of water leaks	☐	☐	☐
8. Home has hot and cold water available	☐	☐	☐
9. Glasses are used by only one child between washings	☐	☐	☐
10. Outside area is free of indication of sewage overflow or related problems	☐	☐	☐
11. Home uses a public water supply. NOTE: Where a private well is used, the Texas Department of Health Resources or the local health department may be requested to provide assistance in regard to standards and sampling	☐	☐	☐
12. Home uses a public sewage disposal system. NOTE: If problems are observed with private sewage disposal systems, assistance may be requested to provide assistance in regard to standards and sampling	☐	☐	☐
13. Adequate number of garbage containers available	☐	☐	☐
14. Garbage containers have tight fitting lids	☐	☐	☐
15. Garbage containers designed for reuse are kept clean	☐	☐	☐
16. Garbage is collected from the premises at least once a week	☐	☐	☐
17. Garbage is disposed of in a sanitary manner if collection is not available	☐	☐	☐
18. Yard is well drained and there is no standing water	☐	☐	☐
19. Premises are free of garbage and rubbish	☐	☐	☐
20. Steps have been taken to keep the premises free of insects (flies, mosquitoes, cockroaches) and rodents.	☐	☐	☐
21. Label instructions on rat and pest poisons are followed	☐	☐	☐
22. Pesticides and other poisons are kept in areas not accessible to children	☐	☐	☐
23. Food is prepared, stored, refrigerated, and served under safe and sanitary conditions	☐	☐	☐
24. Food is obtained from approved sources in labeled containers	☐	☐	☐
25. Eating and cooking utensils are properly washed	☐	☐	☐
26. Food preparation area is cleaned after each use	☐	☐	☐
27. Eating and cooking utensils are stored on clean surfaces	☐	☐	☐
28. Medication is stored separately from food	☐	☐	☐
29. Animals are vaccinated for rabies and other diseases as recommended	☐	☐	☐
30. Bathrooms are located inside home	☐	☐	☐
31. A minimum of one toilet, lavatory, bathtub, or shower is available	☐	☐	☐
32. Each child is provided with own clean towel or single use towels are available	☐	☐	☐
33. Adequate soap and toilet paper are available	☐	☐	☐
34. Bathroom floors, walls cabinets and work surfaces are clean and easily cleanable	☐	☐	☐
35. Plumbing facilities are in good working condition	☐	☐	☐

Comments:

_____   _____   _____
Signature   Title   Date

CHAPTER 6

Preliminary INS Approval

Although adoption or readoption procedures are defined by the laws of the county of the state in which you reside, the federal government has an interest in the fact that your child is entering the United States legally. You will be dealing with two different departments of the U.S. government: the Department of Justice, Immigration and Naturalization Service (INS), which processes orphan visa petitions and applications for citizenship, and the Department of State (U.S. Consular Service office abroad), which issues the orphan's U.S. visa.

Once you are sure you are going to adopt internationally, you should begin advance placement for INS by filing Form I-600A (Application for Advance Processing of Orphan Petition) and supporting documents. With advance filing, INS processes paperwork on the adoptive parents first, so that later it is only necessary to process the child's paperwork. This helps to keep the approval procedures moving as fast as possible.

This chapter will cover advance filing of Form I-600A. More detailed information on working with the INS and finalizing the immigration of your adoptive child will be covered in Chapters 9 and 12. Unfortunately, the INS does not have a standard procedure for filing Form I-600A; each INS office has its own procedure. For example, Texas has four INS offices and they all have their own procedures. What follows, however, are the general instructions common to many of the offices.

A United States citizen who plans to adopt a foreign orphan but does not yet have a specific child in mind can have the immigration paperwork done much faster by advance processing. Even though you may not yet know what child you will adopt or even what country you will adopt from, advance filing will help expedite INS clearance when you are ready to bring your child home.

Advance processing can also be applied in the following case: the child is known, the prospective adoptive parents are traveling to a country where there is no INS office, and the petitioners wish to file an orphan petition at a U.S. consulate or embassy in the country where the child resides.

Until you obtain citizenship for your child — an event that usually occurs more than six months after your child enters the United States — he or she is classified as a permanent resident, but is legally an alien. If you try to have your child enter the United States under a nonimmigrant student or visitor visa, changing his or her status from a nonimmigrant to a permanent resident and finally to a U.S. citizen can be difficult, time-consuming, and expensive.

PREPARING THE NECESSARY DOCUMENTATION FOR FILING

STEP 7

Prepare documentation required for Form I-600A (Application for Advance Processing).

U.S. Immigration and Naturalization Service (INS) forms may be ordered ahead of time by calling your District INS office and requesting the packet of forms to immigrate an orphan as an immediate relative. This package should include Form I-600A (Application for Advance Processing of Orphan Petition); Form I-600 (Petition to Classify Orphan as an Immediate Relative); Form I-864 (Affidavit of Support); and Form I-864A (Contract Between Sponsor and Household Member). You can also go to http://www.ins.usdoj.gov/graphics/index.htm and download these forms from the Internet. Keep Form I-600 in your files. You will need it after a child has been assigned to you. (Filing Form I-600 is covered in Chapter 9.)

Required Documents

To utilize advance processing, only two items are needed initially: Form I-600A and the filing fee. The rest of the items listed below can be filed when the home study is approved.

INS does not require notarization of documents.

1. Form I-600A (Application for Advance Processing of Orphan Petition). Both spouses must sign the form. (See sample form at the end of this chapter.)

2. Home study, which covers criteria set forth in Form I-600A. (If your home study is not yet complete, include a statement in your cover letter noting that you will forward the completed home study as soon as final approval is obtained.)

3. Birth certificate, or other proof of birth and citizenship (such as a baptismal certificate), or an original naturalization certificate, or an up-to-date U.S. passport. You need one birth certificate for each applicant, as well as for any other adult or child residing in the home.

4. Form I-864 (Affidavit of Support) and Form I-864A (Contract Between Sponsor and Household Member). Copies of your federal tax returns for the past three years must accompany the affidavit. These forms will be filed abroad unless parents are not traveling to complete the adoption, in which case they will be filed in the United States. (Samples of forms I-864 and I-864A can be found at the end of the chapter.)

5. Marriage certificate, if applicable.

6. Divorce decree and death certificates of former spouses, if applicable.

7. Evidence that your state's preadoption requirements have been met, such as a statement to that effect in the home study, or a Consent and Approval form, if required by your state. (See sample Consent and Approval form at the end of this chapter.) U.S. Consular service offices abroad are usually not aware of the adoption laws in each of the fifty U.S. states. They may require proof that you have met the preadoption requirements of your state and that your home study is valid there. (See first page of home study guide.) Information on how to establish that these requirements have been met may be obtained from public and private adoption agencies.

8. A copy of the license of your local adoption agency (required by some INS offices).

9. A copy of the license or certification of your social worker (required by some INS offices).

FILING FORM I-600A

As soon as you initiate your home study, you should file the completed Form I-600A. If you don't know all the details about the proposed adoption, write "unknown at this time" in the appropriate blank. Include a cover letter with your name, daytime telephone number, and address. Most INS offices will let you file Form I-600A and the fee before the home study is approved, in order to save time. The rest of the documents may be forwarded when the home study is complete.

It's best to file Form I-600A in person. Consult the Appendix to find the INS office nearest you. Otherwise, send the signed, original Form I-600A, plus two copies, and a money order for $405.00 by certified mail or Federal Express. Be sure to request a return receipt. Cash and personal checks are not always accepted.

Some INS offices will let you send copies of the home study and other required documents. Others will accept copies after they see the originals. Do not leave the original home study with the INS unless you have more than one copy. You will need the original home study for your foreign

STEP 8

File Form I-600A (Application for Advance Processing).

dossier.

When you file Form I-600A, ask for the name of the adoption officer, so you will be able to call about your clearance later on. The INS will start a file on your case that they will maintain throughout the child's U.S. orphan visa application and U.S. citizenship.

Be certain to photocopy one full set of documents, including Form I-600A, to hand-carry abroad. In the event that your child is ready to immigrate before the U.S. Consulate receives your file of the above documents sent by diplomatic pouch, you may be able to obtain the visa with your set of copies, in addition to a copy of Form I-171H (Notice of Favorable Determination), which is described later in the chapter.

Instead of sending your file by diplomatic pouch, INS may expedite the process and send "Visa Cable 37" instead. This message indicates that your INS office has issued approval of your Form I-600A and supporting documentation and it also shows that you have met your state's pre-approval requirements (the home study). In emergency situations, INS may fax the information contained in "Visa Cable 37."

Fingerprinting

In order to be cleared by the INS, every household member over age 18 must be fingerprinted. At the same time that you submit Form I-600A and the $405.00 money order for the filing fee, submit another separate money order to cover the fees for fingerprinting ($25.00 for each individual to be fingerprinted). If you are mailing Form I-600A, indicate in your cover letter the number of family members who need to be fingerprinted.

The INS has designated Application Support Centers to handle the fingerprint forms for adoption cases. After INS receives your application, the INS will send you an appointment letter with the time and address of your fingerprinting appointment at the nearest Application Support Center. Please read the instructions in the appointment letter and bring it with you when you go to your fingerprinting appointment. (A sample fingerprint chart appears at the end of this chapter.)

APPROVAL OF FORM I-600A

INS must decide from the facts listed in the home study whether the prospective adoptive parent is able to take care of one or more orphans properly, depending on the number of children being adopted. Form I-171H (Notice of Favorable Determination Concerning Application for Advance Processing of Orphan Petition) is sent to you if you appear to qualify for further processing. This notice will also state the date of the determination and the location of the filing of the petition (A sample of Form I-171H is included at the end of this chapter.)

You must send a copy of Form I-171H to your U.S.-based international agency immediately upon receipt. The agency cannot refer an orphan to you without it.

INS does not permit convicted felons to adopt. A misdemeanor that appears on your records must be discussed with the adoption agency if you failed to mention it on your application. Depending upon the nature of the misdemeanor, the agency may request documentation from you and proceed, or they may close your case.

A Notice of Favorable Determination does not guarantee that the orphan petition (Form I-600) will be approved. An orphan petition may still be denied because the child does not qualify as an orphan or for other proper cause.

Filing to approval of Form I-600A takes about 30-60 days and sometimes even longer.

Unfavorable Determination

When there is unfavorable information about the prospective adoptive parent(s) and INS concludes that proper care could not be given to a child or children in that case, INS makes an unfavorable determination. You are advised of the reasons for the unfavorable determination and of the right to appeal the decision.

Updating Form I-600A

Form I-600A is valid for 18 months. If an orphan has not immigrated before then, a new application, updated home study and documents, and new fingerprint charts must be filed again, and another $405.00 fee must be paid, as well as an additional $25.00 for each member of the family to be fingerprinted.

OBTAINING YOUR PASSPORT

Once your dossier is complete and your child is assigned, you will need to be ready to go abroad on short notice. Since it can take three to four weeks to receive your passport in the mail and you will need your passport to apply for a visa or tourist card (which may take a number of weeks depending on the country), you should apply for your passport early in the adoption process. In addition, in some countries, a photocopy of your passport is required for the dossier of documents.

Passport numbers are often demanded in foreign courts as another means of identification; each spouse should apply for a passport, even if only one plans to travel.

The passport application form can be picked up at your local post office.

STEP 9

Apply for passport.

To acquire a passport, you will need this form, two 2" X 2" color photos, and a certified copy of your birth certificate. You can get one-day service on passport photos at many places, such as business centers, photocopy stores, and the American Automobile Association (AAA). Passports are valid for ten years.

One-day service for passports can also be found in most major cities. You will need to present proof that you have a ticket or a travel itinerary. Call ahead for information about this service and office hours.

Form I-600A

Application for Advance Processing of Orphan Petition, Page 1 of 2

U.S. Department of Justice
Immigration and Naturalization Service

OMB No. 1115-0049
Application for Advance Processing
of Orphan Petition [8CFR 204.1(b)(3)]

Please do not write in this block.

It has been determined that the
☐ Married ☐ Unmarried
prospective petitioner will furnish proper care to a
beneficiary orphan if admitted to the United Sates.

There
☐ are ☐ are not
preadoptive requirements in the state of the child's
proposed residence.

The following is a description of the preadoption requirements,
if any, of the state of the child's proposed residence:

The preadoption requirements, if any,
☐ have been met. ☐ have not been met.

Fee Stamp

DATE OF FAVORABLE
DETERMINATION

DD

DISTRICT

File number of petitioner, if applicable

Please type or print legibly in ink.

Application is made by the named prospective petitioner for advance processing of an orphan petition.

BLOCK I - Information About Prospective Petitioner

1. My name is: (Last) (First) (Middle)

2. Other names used (including maiden name if appropriate):

3. I reside in the U.S. at: (C/O if appropriate) (Apt. No.)

   (Number and street) (Town or city) (State) (ZIP Code)

4. Address abroad (if any): (Number and street) (Apt. No.)

   (Town or city) (Province) (Country)

5. I was born on: (Month) (Day) (Year)

   In: (Town or City) (State or Province) (Country)

6. My phone number is: (Include Area Code)

7. My marital status is:
   ☐ Married
   ☐ Widowed
   ☐ Divorced
   ☐ Single
   ☐ I have never been married.
   ☐ I have been previously married _____ time(s).

8. If you are now married, give the following information:

   Date and place of present marriage

   Name of present spouse (include maiden name of wife)

   Date of birth of spouse | Place of birth of spouse

   Number of prior marriages of spouse

   My spouse resides ☐ With me ☐ Apart from me
   (provide address below)

   (Apt. No.) (No. and street) (City) (State) (Country)

9. I am a citizen of the United States through:
   ☐ Birth ☐ Parents ☐ Naturalization ☐ Marriage
   If acquired through naturalization, give name under which naturalized,
   number of naturalization certificate, and date and place of naturalization:

   If not, submit evidence of citizenship. See Instruction 2.a(2).
   If acquired through parentage or marriage, have you obtained a
   certificate in your own name based on that acquisition?
   ☐ No ☐ Yes
   Have you or any person through whom you claimed citizenship ever lost
   United States citizenship?
   ☐ No ☐ Yes (If yes, attach detailed explanation.)

Continue on reverse.

Received	Trans. In	Ret'd Trans. Out	Completed

Form I-600A (Rev. 8/25/89) Y

Form I-600A

Application for Advance Processing of Orphan Petition, Page 2 of 2

BLOCK II - General Information

10. Name and address of organization or individual assisting you in locating or identifying an orphan

(Name) _____

(Address) _____

11. Do you plan to travel abroad to locate or adopt a child?
    ☐ Yes ☐ No

12. Does your spouse, if any, plan to travel abroad to locate or adopt a child?
    ☐ Yes ☐ No

13. If the answer to question 11 or 12 is "yes", give the following information:
    a. Your date of intended departure _____
    b. Your spouse's date of intended departure _____
    c. City, province _____

14.. Will the child come to the United States for adoption after compliance with the preadoption requirements, if any, of the state of proposed residence?
    ☐ Yes ☐ No

15. If the answer to question 14 is "no", will the child be adopted abroad after having been personally seen and observed by you and your spouse, if married?
    ☐ Yes ☐ No

16. Where do you wish to file your orphan petition?
    The service office located at _____

    The American Consulate or Embassy at _____

17. Do you plan to adopt more than one child?
    ☐ Yes ☐ No
    If "Yes", how many children do you plan to adopt? _____

Certification of Prospective Petitioner

I certify under penalty of perjury under the laws of the United States of America that the foregoing is true and correct and that I will care for an orphan/orphans properly if admitted to the United States.

(Signature of Prospective Petitioner) _____

Executed on (Date) _____

Certification of Married Prospective Petitioner's Spouse

I certify under penalty of perjury under the laws of the United States of America that the foregoing is true and correct and that my spouse and I will care for an orphan/orphans properly if admitted to the United States.

(Signature of Prospective Petitioner) _____

Executed on (Date) _____

Signature of Person Preparing Form if Other Than Petitioner

I declare that this document was prepared by me at the request of the prospective petitioner and is based on all information of which I have any knowledge.

(Signature) _____

Address _____

Executed on (Date) _____

Form I-864

Affidavit of Support, Page 1 of 3

U.S. Department of Justice Immigration and Naturalization Service	OMB #1115-0214 **Affidavit of Support Under Section 213A of the Act**

START HERE - Please Type or Print

Part 1. Information on Sponsor (You)

Last Name	First Name	Middle Name

Mailing Address *(Street Number and Name)*	Apt/Suite Number

City	State or Province

Country	ZIP/Postal Code	Telephone Number ( )

Place of Residence if different from above *(Street Number and Name)*	Apt/Suite Number

City	State or Province

Country	ZIP/Postal Code	Telephone Number ( )

Date of Birth *(Month, Day, Year)*	Place of Birth *(City, State, Country)*	Are you a U.S. Citizen? ☐ Yes ☐ No

Social Security Number	A-Number *(If any)*

FOR AGENCY USE ONLY

This Affidavit   Receipt

[ ] Meets

[ ] Does not meet

Requirements of Section 213A

Officer's Signature

Location

Date

Part 2. Basis for Filing Affidavit of Support

I am filing this affidavit of support because *(check one)*:

a. ☐ I filed/am filing the alien relative petition.

b. ☐ I filed/am filing an alien worker petition on behalf of the intending immigrant, who is related to me as my _____ .
(relationship)

c. ☐ I have ownership interest of at least 5% of _____
(name of entity which filed visa petition)
which filed an alien worker petition on behalf of the intending immigrant, who is related to me as my _____ .
(relationship)

d. ☐ I am a joint sponsor willing to accept the legal obligations with any other sponsor(s).

Part 3. Information on the Immigrant(s) You Are Sponsoring

Last Name	First Name	Middle Name

Date of Birth *(Month, Day, Year)*	Sex: ☐ Male ☐ Female	Social Security Number *(If any)*

Country of Citizenship	A-Number *(If any)*

Current Address *(Street Number and Name)*	Apt/Suite Number	City

State/Province	Country	ZIP/Postal Code	Telephone Number ( )

List any spouse and/or children immigrating with the immigrant named above in this Part: *(Use additional sheet of paper if necessary.)*

Name	Relationship to Sponsored Immigrant			Date of Birth			A-Number *(If any)*	Social Security Number *(If any)*
	Spouse	Son	Daughter	Mo.	Day	Yr.		

Form I-864 (1/21/98)Y

Form I-864

Affidavit of Support, Page 2 of 3

Part 4. Eligibility to Sponsor

To be a sponsor you must be a U.S. citizen or national or a lawful permanent resident. If you are not the petitioning relative, you must provide proof of status. To prove status, U.S. citizens or nationals must attach a copy of a document proving status, such as a U.S. passport, birth certificate, or certificate of naturalization, and lawful permanent residents must attach a copy of both sides of their Alien Registration Card (Form I-551).

The determination of your eligibility to sponsor an immigrant will be based on an evaluation of your demonstrated ability to maintain an annual income at or above 125 percent of the Federal poverty line (100 percent if you are a petitioner sponsoring your spouse or child and you are on active duty in the U.S. Armed Forces). The assessment of your ability to maintain an adequate income will include your current employment, household size, and household income as shown on the Federal income tax returns for the 3 most recent tax years. Assets that are readily converted to cash and that can be made available for the support of sponsored immigrants if necessary, including any such assets of the immigrant(s) you are sponsoring, may also be considered.

The greatest weight in determining eligibility will be placed on current employment and household income. If a petitioner is unable to demonstrate ability to meet the stated income and asset requirements, a joint sponsor who *can* meet the income and asset requirements is needed. Failure to provide adequate evidence of income and/or assets or an affidavit of support completed by a joint sponsor will result in denial of the immigrant's application for an immigrant visa or adjustment to permanent resident status.

A. Sponsor's Employment

I am: 1. ☐ Employed by _____ *(Provide evidence of employment)*
Annual salary $ _____ *or* hourly wage $ _____ *(for____ hours per week)*
2. ☐ Self employed _____ *(Name of business)*
Nature of employment or business _____

3. ☐ Unemployed or retired since _____

B. Use of Benefits

Have you or anyone related to you by birth, marriage, or adoption living in your household or listed as a dependent on your most recent income tax return received any type of means-tested public benefit in the past 3 years?
☐Yes ☐ No (*If yes, provide details, including programs and dates, on a separate sheet of paper)*

C. Sponsor's Household Size   **Number**

1. Number of persons (related to you by birth, marriage, or adoption) living in your residence, including yourself. *(Do NOT include persons being sponsored in this affidavit.)*
2. Number of immigrants being sponsored in this affidavit *(Include all persons in Part 3.)* _____
3. Number of immigrants **NOT** living in your household whom you are still obligated to support under a previously signed affidavit of support using Form I-864. _____
4. Number of persons who are otherwise dependent on you, as claimed in your tax return for the most recent tax year. _____
5. Total household size. *(Add lines 1 through 4.)*   **Total** _____

List persons below who are included in lines 1 or 3 for whom you previously have submitted INS Form I-864, *if your support obligation has not terminated.*
(If additional space is needed, use additional paper)

Name	A-Number	Date Affidavit of Support Signed	Relationship

Form I-864

Affidavit of Support, Page 3 of 3

Part 4. Eligibility to Sponsor   *(Continued)*

D. Sponsor's Annual Household Income

Enter total unadjusted income from your Federal income tax return for the most recent tax year below. If you last filed a joint income tax return but are using only your *own* income to qualify, list total earnings from your W-2 Forms, or, *if* necessary to reach the required income for your household size, include income from other sources listed on your tax return. If your *individual* income does not meet the income requirement for your household size, you may also list total income for anyone related to you by birth, marriage, or adoption currently living with you in your residence if they have lived in your residence for the previous 6 months, or any person shown as a dependent on your Federal income tax return for the most recent tax year, even if not living in the household. For their income to be considered, household members or dependents must be willing to make their income available for support of the sponsored immigrant(s) and to complete and sign Form I-864A, Contract Between Sponsor and Household Member. A sponsored immigrant/household member only need   complete Form I-864A if his or her income will be used to determine your ability to support a spouse and/or children immigrating with him or her.

You must attach evidence of current employment and copies of income tax returns as filed with the IRS for the most recent 3 tax years for yourself and all persons whose income is listed below. See ™Required Evidence⌡ in Instructions. Income from all 3 years will be considered in determining your ability to support the immigrant(s) you are sponsoring.

- ☐ I filed a single/separate tax return for the most recent tax year.
- ☐ I filed a joint return for the most recent tax year which includes only my own income.
- ☐ I filed a joint return for the most recent tax year which includes income for my spouse and myself.
    - ☐ I am submitting documentation of my individual income (Forms W-2 and 1099).
    - ☐ I am qualifying using my spouse's income; my spouse is submitting a Form I-864A.

Indicate most recent tax year
_____
(tax year)

Sponsor's individual income $ _____

or

Sponsor and spouse's combined income $ _____
*(If joint tax return filed; spouse must submit
Form I-864A.)*

Income of other qualifying persons.
*(List names; include spouse if applicable.
 Each person must complete Form I-864A.)*

_____ $ _____

_____ $ _____

_____ $ _____

Total Household Income $ _____

Explain on separate sheet of paper if you or any of the above listed individuals are submitting Federal income tax returns for fewer than 3 years, or if other explanation of income, employment, or evidence is necessary.

E. Determination of Eligibility Based on Income

1. ☐ I am subject to the 125 percent of poverty line requirement for sponsors.
   ☐ I am subject to the 100 percent of poverty line requirement for sponsors on active duty in the U.S. Armed Forces sponsoring their spouse or child**.**
2. Sponsor's total household size, from Part 4.C., line 5 _____.
3. Minimum income requirement from the Poverty Guidelines chart for the year of _____ is $ _____
   for this household size.   *(year)*

If you are currently employed and your household income for your household size is equal to or greater than the applicable poverty line requirement (from line E.3.), you do not need to list assets (Parts 4.F. and 5) or have a joint sponsor (Part 6) unless you are requested to do so by a Consular or Immigration Officer. You may skip to Part 7, Use of the Affidavit of Support to Overcome Public Charge Ground of Admissibility. **Otherwise, you should continue with Part 4.F.**

Form I-864A

Contract Between Sponsor and Household Member, Page 1 of 2

Part 1. Information on Sponsor's Household Member or Sponsored Immigrant/Household Member

Last Name	First Name	Middle Name

Date of Birth *(Month, Day, Year)*	Social Security Number *(Mandatory for non-citizens; voluntary for U.S. citizens)*	A-Number *(If any)*

Address *(Street Number and Name)*	Apt Number	City	State/Province	ZIP/Postal Code

Telephone Number ( )	Relationship to Sponsor:_____ I am: ☐ The sponsor's household member. *(Complete Part 3.)* ☐ The sponsored immigrant/household member. *(Complete Part 4.)*	Length of residence with sponsor (_____ years, _____ months)

Part 2. Sponsor's Promise

I, THE SPONSOR, _____, in consideration of the household member's promise to support the
(Print name of sponsor)

sponsored immigrant(s) and to be jointly and severally liable for any obligations I incur under the affidavit of support,
promise to complete and file an affidavit of support on behalf of the following_____sponsored immigrant(s):
(Indicate number)

Name of Sponsored Immigrant *(First, Middle, Last)*	Date of Birth *(Month, Day, Year)*	Social Security Number *(If any)*	A-Number *(If any)*

Part 3. Household Member's Promise

I, THE HOUSEHOLD MEMBER, _____, in consideration of the sponsor's
(Print name of household member)
promise to complete and file the affidavit of support on behalf of the sponsored immigrant(s):

1) Promise to provide any and all financial support necessary to assist the sponsor in maintaining the sponsored immigrant(s) at or above the minimum income provided for in section 213A(a)(1)(A) of the Act (not less than 125 percent of the Federal poverty line) during the period in which the affidavit of support is enforceable;

2) Agree to be jointly and severally liable for payment of any and all obligations owed by the sponsor under the affidavit of support to the sponsored immigrant(s), to any agency of the Federal Government, to any agency of a State or local government, or to any private entity;

3) Agree to submit to the personal jurisdiction of any court of the United States or of any State, territory, or possession of the United States if the court has subject matter jurisdiction of a civil lawsuit to enforce this contract or the affidavit of support; and

4) Certify under penalty of perjury under the laws of the United States that all the information provided on this form is true and correct to the best of my knowledge and belief and that the income tax returns I submitted in support of the sponsor's affidavit are true copies of the returns filed with the Internal Revenue Service.

Form I-864A

Contract Between Sponsor and Household Member, Page 2 of 2

Part 4. Sponsored Immigrant/Household Member's Promise

I, THE SPONSORED IMMIGRANT/HOUSEHOLD MEMBER, _____

(Print name of sponsored immigrant)

in consideration of the sponsor's promise to complete and file the affidavit of support on behalf of the sponsored immigrant(s) accompanying me:

1) Promise to provide any and all financial support necessary to assist the sponsor in maintaining any sponsored immigrant(s) immigrating with me at or above the minimum income provided for in section 213A(a)(1)(A) of the Act (not less than 125 percent of the Federal poverty line) during the period in which the affidavit of support is enforceable;

2) Agree to be jointly and severally liable for payment of any and all obligations owed by the sponsor under the affidavit of support to any sponsored immigrant(s) immigrating with me, to any agency of the Federal Government, to any agency of a State or local government, or to any private entity;

3) Agree to submit to the personal jurisdiction of any court of the United States or of any State, territory, or possession of the United States if the court has subject matter jurisdiction of a civil lawsuit to enforce this contract or the affidavit of support; and

4) Certify under penalty of perjury under the laws of the United States that all the information provided on this form is true and correct to the best of my knowledge and belief and that the income tax returns I submitted in support of the sponsor's affidavit of support are true copies of the returns filed with the Internal Revenue Service.

Part 5. Sponsor's Signature

_____   Date: _____

Sponsor's Signature

Subscribed and sworn to *(or affirmed)* before me this _____ day of _____, _____

(Month)   *(Year)*

at _____ . My commission expires on _____ .

_____   _____

Signature of Notary Public or Officer Administering Oath   *Title*

Part 6. Household Member's or Sponsored Immigrant/Household Member's Signature

_____   Date: _____

Household Member's or Sponsored Immigrant/Household Member's Signature

Subscribed and sworn to *(or affirmed)* before me this _____ day of _____, _____

(Month)   *(Year)*

at _____ . My commission expires on _____ .

_____   _____

Signature of Notary Public or Officer Administering Oath   *Title*

Form I-864A (1/21/98)Y **Page 3**

Consent and Approval

This letter verifies that prospective adoptive parent(s)_____

of this address: _____

has/have met the preadoption requirements of their state of residence.

A home study, conducted by a certified social worker, which meets the standards of their state of residence, has been completed and approved. Supporting documents provided by the prospective adoptive parents validate the data therein.

I hereby grant consent and approval of an adoptive placement for the aforementioned person(s).

_____   _____
Date   Supervisor of Adoptions (agency name)

SUBSCRIBED AND SWORN to before me on the _____ day of _____ , 199__,
to which witness my hand and seal of office.

Form FD-258

Fingerprint Chart

APPLICANT	LEAVE BLANK	TYPE OR PRINT ALL INFORMATION IN BLACK		FBI	LEAVE BLANK

LAST NAME **NAME**   FIRST NAME   MIDDLE NAME

SIGNATURE OF PERSON FINGERPRINTED

ALIASES AKA   O R I

NBINSORPZ
USINS
LINCOLN, NB

RESIDENCE OF PERSON FINGERPRINTED

DATE OF BIRTH DOB   Month   Day   Year

CITIZENSHIP CTZ   SEX | RACE | HGT. | WGT. | EYES | HAIR | PLACE OF BIRTH POB

DATE   SIGNATURE OF OFFICIAL TAKING FINGERPRINTS

YOUR NO. OCA

LEAVE BLANK

EMPLOYER AND ADDRESS

FBI NO. FBI

ARMED FORCES NO. MNU   CLASS _____

REASON FINGERPRINTED

SOCIAL SECURITY NO. SOC   REF. _____

MISCELLANEOUS NO. MNU

1. R. THUMB	2. R. INDEX	3. R. MIDDLE	4. R. RING	5. R. LITTLE

6. L. THUMB	7. L. INDEX	8. L. MIDDLE	9. L. RING	10. L. LITTLE

LEFT FOUR FINGERS TAKEN SIMULTANEOUSLY	L. THUMB	R. THUMB	RIGHT FOUR FINGERS TAKEN SIMULTANEOUSLY

Form I-171H

Notice of Approval

United States Department of Justice

Immigration and Naturalization Service
509 NORTH SAM HOUSTON PARKWAY EAST
HOUSTON, TEXAS 77060

Name and Address of Prospective Petitioner

Name of prospective petitioner	
Name of spouse, if married	
Date application filed	Date of completion of Advance processing

NOTICE OF FAVORABLE DETERMINATION CONCERNING APPLICATION
FOR ADVANCE PROCESSING OF ORPHAN PETITION

IT HAS BEEN DETERMINED THAT YOU ARE ABLE TO FURNISH PROPER CARE TO AN ORPHAN OR ORPHANS AS DEFINED BY SECTION 101(b) (1) (F) OF THE IMMIGRATION AND NATIONALITY ACT. A SEPARATE ORPHAN PETITION, FORM I-600, MUST BE FILED IN BEHALF OF EACH CHILD WITH DOCUMENTARY EVIDENCE AS DESCRIBED IN INSTRUCTIONS 2c, 2d, 2e, 2f, 2g, AND 2h OF THAT FORM. A FORM OR FORMS FOR YOUR USE ARE ENCLOSED. NO FEE WILL BE REQUIRED WITH FORM I-600 IF YOU FILE ONLY ONE FORM I-600 WITHIN ONE YEAR FROM THE DATE OF COMPLETION OF ALL ADVANCE PROCESSING. IF YOU DO NOT FILE FORM I-600 WITHIN ONE YEAR FROM THE DATE OF COMPLETION OF YOUR ADVANCE PROCESSING APPLICATION, YOUR APPLICATION WILL BE CONSIDERED ABANDONED. ANY FURTHER PROCEEDINGS WILL REQUIRE THE FILING OF A NEW ADVANCE PROCESSING APPLICATION OR AN ORPHAN PETITION.

Form I-600 should be filed at the Service office or American consulate or embassy where your advance processing application is being retained or has been forwarded as indicated by an "X" mark below:

1. ☐ YOUR ADVANCE PROCESSING APPLICATION IS BEING RETAINED AT THIS OFFICE.

2. ☐ YOUR ADVANCE PROCESSING APPLICATION HAS BEEN FORWARDED TO OUR SERVICE OFFICE
AT_____ .

3. ☐ YOUR ADVANCE PROCESSING APPLICATION HAS BEEN FORWARDED TO THE AMERICAN CONSULATE OR
EMBASSY AT_____ .

In addition, please note the following:

☐ Any original documents submitted in support of your application are returned to you.

☐ Your home study is returned to you.

THIS DETERMINATION DOES NOT GUARANTEE THAT THE ORPHAN PETITION(S) WHICH YOU FILE WILL BE APPROVED. AN ORPHAN PETITION MAY BE DENIED BECAUSE THE CHILD DOES NOT QUALIFY FOR CLASSIFICATION AS AN ORPHAN OR FOR OTHER PROPER CAUSE. DENIAL OF AN ORPHAN PETITION, HOWEVER, MAY BE APPEALED.

Form I-171H
(12-15-82)

CHAPTER 7

Application to a Foreign Source

STEP 10

Select an adoption program in a foreign country.

If you have not already done so, now is the time to make a decision on the country from which you would like to adopt. After your home study is approved and you have completed your preliminary INS paperwork, assess the current international adoption situation with your international adoption agency. Requirements for adoptive parents, the age and ethnicity of the children available, the length of wait until the assignment of a child, the number of trips required, the length of your stay abroad, program fees, and numbers of children being assigned monthly by each adoption program are all factors you should consider. If you are having difficulty making a decision, consult the agency staff or director, or seek further information from an adoptive parent support group.

METHODS OF ADOPTION REQUIRED BY FOREIGN COUNTRIES

A final important factor to consider before choosing a country program is the legal means by which an adoption is facilitated. This is determined by the child's country of origin. One of six different methods may be used to meet the various legal requirements of foreign countries. (See the adoption law summary for each country listed in the Compendium.)

For example, a power of attorney form is used in most countries to initiate adoption procedures prior to the arrival of the adoptive parents. An attorney acts on behalf of the prospective parents. This saves the adopters from spending time abroad at all the appointments with government officials and court hearings and waiting there for legal custody. Power of attorney forms are also used in some countries for a guardianship or a final adoption by proxy.

They are also utilized in certain countries for authorized escorts to immigrate children to their new parents. (A sample of a power of attorney form can be found at the end of this chapter.)

Advantages and disadvantages are inherent in each of the six methods. Adoptive parents may choose one country over another simply because they prefer the power of attorney method to avoid making one long stay or two short trips abroad. Other couples might decide that they prefer to adopt in a country where they can go to see the child immediately after the referral and to be involved in all the adoption proceedings. Adoption by proxy carries more risk for the adoptive parents, since they have not observed the child prior to his or her final adoption and/or immigration. There are more cases of disrupted adoptions in this method, since the families are not always pleased with the child that is delivered. The child does not meet their expectations, and they cannot overcome their disappointment.

Method 1: U.S. parents plan to assign a power of attorney to a foreign adoption agency or attorney who initiates the adoption. The parents present themselves later in the foreign country to complete the remaining adoption procedures. This is the most common method used and is found in both agency-initiated and parent-initiated adoptions.

If you are conducting a parent-initiated adoption and the country you are adopting from uses a power of attorney, request the power of attorney form and custody contract as soon as the adoption source has agreed to place a child with you. Power of attorney procedures can be quite time consuming. From the time you receive the forms, it takes from two to eight weeks for them to be signed, authenticated, and returned unless air courier services are used instead of airmail.

Method 2: Proxy adoptions or proxy permanent guardianships are also initiated by a foreign adoption agency or attorney who has been given power of attorney by preadoptive parents. The assigned child is escorted to his or her adoptive family by a person designated by the foreign child-placing entity. INS requires that the adoptive parents must readopt in their state of residence.

This method is mainly used in agency-initiated adoptions, especially by countries such as India. The country, in turn, has child-placing agreements with U.S. adoption agencies. In this case, the child remains under the managing conservatorship of the U.S. adoption agency until the child is legally adopted in the child's new country of residence. Guatemala is one of the few countries that grant a final adoption decree by proxy. The children in these cases are immigrated and escorted by an individual authorized by the U.S. adoption agency or the adoptive parents.

Method 3: The orphan emigrates the foreign country under a permanent guardianship agreement, usually with the adoptive parents or an authorized escort. Some countries consummate the adoption six to twelve months later.

The prospective adoptive parents must promise to adopt the child in their state of residence in order to comply with INS regulations.

Method 4: Formal final adoption decree preceded by a permanent guardianship agreement may be necessary in some countries when the adopters are not old enough or have not been married long enough to meet the adoption requirements.

This method is used in both agency- and parent-initiated adoptions in Chile and in Argentina. The adoptive parents immigrate the child under a permanent guardianship.

Method 5: Custody transfer, usually with escort service, is used by some international adoption agencies with child-placing agreements in Korea and the Philippines. It transfers custody of the child from the foreign institution to a U.S. international agency until the child is adopted in his/her state of residence. This method can only be used by international agencies.

Method 6: A final formal adoption decree, issued at the end of the adoption process.

PREPARING YOUR FOREIGN DOSSIER

Once you have made a decision, your agency or its foreign counterpart will provide you with a packet of materials and instructions for preparing your dossier for the foreign country. Completing the dossier is a big task, but you will have already done much of the work in preparation for your home study.

Cover Letter

Your completed dossier will need to be accompanied by a cover letter. If you are working with an international agency, you typically won't need to write the letter yourself, unless it is specifically requested by the child-placing country. The letter should be translated, but notarization is not usually required.

The cover letter should describe your motive for adoption. In the length of two or three pages, your cover letter must clearly explain why you plan to adopt.

Formally request the child you wish to adopt with a description: State your preference for a boy or girl. Specify the age of the child. Explain your preference, if any, for the child's ethnic background. Indicate the name(s) you have chosen for the child, or if you will consider keeping all or part of the child's original name. (Research indicates that children whose names are retained have an easier adjustment.) Your wait will usually be shorter if you will accept a boy or a girl and if you will accept a child within the age range of one to three years. If you are considering a child with a chronic illness or handicap, state the medical conditions you are willing to accept.

Through the activity of formulating your ideas and communicating your knowledge of international adoption, you will create a letter that should lay to rest some of the fears we have heard foreign nationals express concerning international adoptions. (Occasional rumors assert that Americans are adopting children to use as servants or for organ transplants. Nothing of the sort has ever happened.)

Required Documents

STEP 11

Obtain documents required for your foreign dossier.

Most likely you will have already assembled many of these documents to support the facts you gave the social worker during the home study process. Now is the time to check to make certain you have all of the necessary documents and to move them into a complete dossier for the foreign country. See Chapter 5 for specific details on requesting this information.

Foreign countries change their documentation requirements occasionally; however, they will inform you or your agency of their current procedures. They will also state which documents need notarization, verification, authentication, and translation. (A section at the end of this chapter describes this process.)

It's best to keep this information in a protective folder or binder, just be sure not to punch holes in the documents.

Required documents for your dossier will include:

1. Application form of the child-placing entity. Government authorities in charge of adoption in many countries have their own application forms. These forms are also used by their adoption committees for preapproval in some countries.

2. Certified birth certificates for each member of the family.

3. Certified marriage license, if applicable.

4. Certified divorce decrees, if applicable.

5. Certified death certificates of former spouses, if applicable.

6. Job letter (one for each applicant) from your employer, stating your length of employment and annual salary. If you are self-employed, a public accountant can provide this.

7. A statement of net worth written by you or your accountant.

8. The first two pages of last year's federal income tax return.

9. Current medical examination forms for all household members. (Good for one year from the date of the exam.)

10. Letters of reference from at least three people who are acquainted with the family unit. These letters should come from professionals or community leaders, if at all possible.

11. Letter(s) from your local police, stating that you have no criminal record.

12. Pictures of you in front of your home and individual close-ups (or passport pictures), three of each. Pose in business attire for all photos.

13. Specific forms particular to the foreign child-placing entity.

14. International processing contract. This document explains the agency's responsibilities and yours in locating a child for you and arranging your legal custody of the child.

15. Copies of the first two pages of your passports.

Changes to Countries or Adoption Programs

If for any reason you change the country you are adopting from, you will need to transfer your INS file from the original country to the one you are now planning to adopt from. Request Form I-824 (Application for Action on an Approved Application or Petition) from the INS, fill it out, and mail it in with a money order for $120.00.

TRANSLATING SERVICES

STEP 12

Obtain translations for documents in your foreign dossier.

Your international agency or foreign liaison will advise which documents need translating and at what point this should take place. Most translations of dossiers are accomplished abroad by official translators. If translations must be accomplished in the United States, most U.S.-based international agencies can recommend a skilled translator who can produce legal documents for review by a foreign court. In addition, skilled translators can be found through international institutes. About forty international institutes are located around the nation in the larger cities. Consult the telephone book to find the institute nearest you. Before submitting your letter to a translator, agree on a price. Twenty dollars or more per typewritten page is typical. Some translators charge by the word.

A cover letter certifying the translator's competency must be attached to the translated document. One letter will suffice for all documents translated by the same person. Notarize and verify this letter. Some countries also require authentication of this letter. (A sample for the translator's statement of competency appears at the end of this chapter.) On the other hand, some countries require that translations be accomplished in their Department of Foreign Ministry. In this case, your U.S.-based international agency will air courier your documents there. Whether you work with an independent translator or a Department of Foreign Ministry, you should supply the translator with a photocopy rather than the original document in order to keep the originals pristine.

NOTARIZATION, VERIFICATION OR APOSTILLE, AND AUTHENTICATION

STEP 13

Obtain notarization, verification (or apostille), and authentication of documents in your dossier.

All documents must go through the process of notarization and verification before they can be authenticated by the consul of the country from which you are adopting. To make sure that the information you provide is reliable, the consulates require that the papers sent to them for authentication be notarized by a notary public and verified by your county clerk or secretary of state.

Check with your international agency or foreign source to find out exactly what documents need to be notarized, verified, and authenticated. Differences occur even among the courts in a foreign country. Any supporting documents that you choose to submit, such as a cover letter or tax return, need not be notarized.

Obtaining Notarization

A notary public verifies that the signatures on your documents are valid by affixing his or her seal.

You can find a notary public in the phone book. Fees may range from free to $5.00 per document. Legally, the persons who provide the documents or letters of reference — your doctor, banker, employer, friends, and so on — must sign their name in the presence of the notary public. If a doctor, police chief, or so on, cannot leave the office to sign before a notary, the alternative is for you to also sign the form as a release of information and have your signature notarized. Ask your notary to use a jurat form similar to the one found at the end of this chapter.

Sending for Verification or Apostilles

Verification or an apostille is the process by which the state or county verifies the validity of the notary's signature. (Mexico and some Eastern European countries request apostilles rather than verifications.) Verification and apostille sheets are available from the county clerk or secretary of state who verifies that the notary's signature and seal are valid. Fees for verification or apostille vary from state to state. Do not verify documents until you have chosen an adoption source. Not every country requires this step. (Samples of verification and apostille forms for the state of Texas can be found at the end of this chapter.)

Send a typewritten sheet with the name, county, and expiration date of your notary's commission, along with the fee for each signature, to obtain apostille or verification sheets with state seals to the secretary of the state in which the document was issued. Check with the appropriate office before sending in your fees and sheets. In some other states, you may be able to send a photocopy rather than the original document, if they need to see the document. Check before sending. Remember that even if one notary signs six documents, you will need six verifications, not just one.

Birth and marriage certificates are certified documents; they should not require additional verification before they are accepted by the consul.

A county clerk can legally verify the seals of only those notary publics who reside in his or her county and register with his or her office. All notaries, however, must register with the Secretary of State.

All documents must be verified in the states where they originated; for this reason, it is advisable that all of your documents be prepared by persons living in your present state of residence. Out-of-state documents will require verification out of state, which just creates one more hassle.

Obtaining Authentication

After notarization and verification, most countries require that certain documents be authenticated by a consul representing the country from which you wish to adopt that has jurisdiction in your locality. Consuls attest to the authenticity of the document or the signer of it by their seal, stamp, and signature. U.S.-based international agencies will provide a list of documents requiring authentication by the country from which you plan to adopt. Check with your international agency or foreign liaison to ensure that you follow the correct steps, especially if you are adopting from a country not mentioned here.

To locate the nearest consul, look in the phone book under U.S. Government Offices, Federal Information Center. These centers have consulate addresses and phone numbers. The INS also has the addresses and phone numbers of various consulate offices.

The process with foreign consulates is as follows: Send your notarized and verified documents, with translations if required, to the foreign consulate for authentication. Enclose a check or money order for the total amount and a stamped, self-addressed envelope when you send your documents. Obviously, you will have to call the consulate first to inquire about the fees per document. Fees for authentication range from as low as $10.00 per document for Guatemala to $85.00 per document for Bolivia. Most consulates will double the charge for rush services. China triples their fee for rush services.

If the consulate is located in your city, you may be able to handle this much more quickly in person. Be certain to dress in business attire since the cooperation of the consul is essential. Treat the consul with the dignity to which he or she is accustomed. However, if the consul is not cooperative, call the embassy of the country from which you are adopting for help. All of the foreign embassies are located in Washington, D.C. Ask your telephone operator for the number.

Some states near the Washington, D.C. area and some foreign countries without consulates outside of Washington, D.C. require that the U.S. Department of State certify the notarized and verified documents before they will authenticate them. This is always required if you deal with a consulate attached to a foreign embassy. For instance, Russia has only two consulates in the United States, one of which is attached to its embassy. Romania has no consulates outside the D.C. area, nor does Vietnam. At present there is a $5.00 charge per document for this service. Call them before sending your money order or certified cashier's check made payable to the U.S. Department of State. The address and telephone number are as follows:

Supervisor, Authentication Office
U.S. Department of State
518 23rd Street N.W.
State Annex 1
Washington, D.C. 20520
Tel: (202) 647-5002

A WORD OF CAUTION: DOCUMENTS AND FEES

Safeguard your documents. After your documents have been notarized, verified, and authenticated, make one photocopy of each before they are sent abroad. This is your proof in case of loss in the mail or elsewhere. Hand-carry these copies with you on your adoption trip abroad.

Do not give your dossier of original documents to anyone in the United States except a licensed adoption agency or licensed social worker. Be suspicious of unlicensed individuals who for any reason keep their sources secret, insist upon handling your dossier, or expect payments, whether these payments are to be made in advance or at a later date to a for-profit corporation or individual.

INTERNATIONAL COMMUNICATION

If you are working with a U.S.-based international agency, your agency will send your dossier to their representative abroad and handle the communications for you. If you are not using an agency, you should send this information to your lawyer or foreign representative. Several methods of international communication are available.

1. E-mail. Your adoption agency, as well as its representatives or agencies abroad, communicates by e-mail on a frequent basis.

2. Telegrams. Many foreign businesses and institutions have short, registered cable addresses, usually acronyms. A return voucher is sent along with the message if a reply is expected.

3. Faxes. Faxes are becoming quite common around the world.

4. Telephone. Long-distance phone calls range from $4.00 to $12.00 per minute, person-to-person. When dialing most countries from the United States, you must dial 011, followed by the country code, the city code, and then the number you are trying to reach. For some countries, especially some Caribbean countries, it is only necessary to dial 1, rather than 011.

5. Courier Service. International air courier services, such as Federal Express and DHL, guarantee service from pickup in a foreign country to personal delivery here and vice versa. The cost varies. U.S. Postal EMS (Express Mail Service) is the least expensive and now goes to most foreign capital cities. Unfortunately, it is not as reliable as Federal Express or DHL.

Power of Attorney

TO WHOM IT MAY CONCERN:

This is to certify that we, the undersigned _____

presently living at _____

are herewith granting full power of attorney to _____

presently living at _____

to carry through and complete on our behalf any and all formalities required for the process of

the adoption of a _____ born child.

This is also to confirm that we herewith grant full power of attorney to _____

to carry through and complete on our behalf any and all formalities required by the American

Consulate in _____ in this matter.

Name _____ Date _____

Name _____ Date _____

Subscribed and sworn to before me on the _____ day of _____ 199_ to which

_____

Notary Public

My commission expires: _____

Statement of Competency

I, _____ , hereby certify that I am competent to translate from the _____

language to the _____ language and that the above translation is accurate.

Date: _____   _____   (name printed or typed)

                       _____   (address)

                       _____

Jurat

Subscribed and sworn to before me on the _____ day of _____ , 199 ____
to which witness my hand and seal of office.

_____

Notary Public in and for the State of _____ , County of _____

My Commission Expires _____ .

Verification

The State of Texas
Secretary of State

I, _____ , Secretary of State of the State of Texas, DO HEREBY CERTIFY that according to the records of this office,

(name of notary)

qualified as a Notary Public for the State of Texas on July 27, 1999. for a term ending on July 27, 2000.

Date Issued: November 13, 1999

_____
Secretary of State   sai

Apostille

STATE OF TEXAS

APOSTILLE
(Convention de La Haye du 5 Octobre 1961)

1. **Country:**   United States of America
   This Public document

2. **has been signed by**   (name of notary)

3. **acting in the capacity of** Notary Public, State of Texas

4. **bears the seal/stamp of**   , Notary Public,
   State of Texas, Commission Expires: 07-27-00

CERTIFIED

5. **at Austin, Texas**   6.   on December 3, 1999

7. **by the Deputy Assistant Secretary of State of Texas**

8. **Certificate No. N-118607**

9. **Seal**   10. **Signature:**

Deputy Assistant Secretary of State
LSW/NO/ sai

CHAPTER 8

The Referral

STEP 14

Prepare for the referral of your child.

Once your completed and authenticated dossier has been sent, you are ready for a referral for your child. Waiting for a child to be assigned is the most difficult part of the process. Make good use of the time by volunteering to babysit for friends, taking child care classes (see the section below), finding a good pediatrician or family doctor (consider looking for a foreign-born pediatrician or one who specializes in health conditions in developing countries), attending adoptive parent support group functions, subscribing to their newsletters (see Bibliography), and researching the culture and customs of your child's native land. Buy a book on child care that explains the signs and symptoms of childhood illnesses. Study the language. Assemble what you will need to pack, using our tips in Chapter 10. Most reputable agencies offer a six-week course on international adoption travel and parenting. The Joint Council on International Children's Services also offers a booklet called *The Adoptive Parent Preparation System*. The pamphlet is $30.00, and the Council's phone number is 301-322-1906.

PREADOPTIVE RESOURCES

The American Red Cross, local hospitals, and some adoption agencies offer courses on infant care. While these courses are essential for every inexperienced new mother, the courses do not cover problems typical of orphans from developing countries and malnourished babies with infectious diarrhea. (See Chapter 13 for more information on health issues of babies and children from developing countries.)

Also contact adoptive parent groups and child development centers for information. Also, see Chapter 15 for more information on parenting adopted children and refer to the Bibliography for additional resources.

THE REFERRAL CALL

When the call comes with the referral of your child, panic may render you nearly witless and speechless. So, make a list of questions you have about the child such as the name, age, and clothing size. Ask if the child has any health problems, and, if a baby, whether the child needs a special formula. Have names ready in case the child does not have a name.

In the event that you are assigned an abandoned child without a name, your foreign lawyer will draw up a birth certificate with the name you have chosen. You can find books of names for children in the public library that list endless derivations of names along with their foreign origins.

Don't hang up without asking for the name and the phone number of the person who is calling you. Write it down. You will need to contact that person again.

Usually, you are given as much time as you need to make a decision. In the meantime, depending upon the policies of the child-sending country, you will be sent a photograph or possibly a video, health, educational, social, and genetic information, possibly a power of attorney form, and a custody contract. After telephoning your acceptance of the child to your adoption agency, follow this up formally by mail or fax. Adoption agencies send along an approval form for you to sign. The child-placing entity will send copies or fax the child's documents to your agency or you if required by INS, the Department of Public Welfare in your state, or ICPC. The originals are retained for their court.

Most people are quite happy with the babies and children they are assigned, unless they object to the skin color, the age, or there is a serious health problem they are worried about. In Russia, for example, infants are often over-diagnosed or misdiagnosed. While the medical record can be alarming, the video may show a normal child who is healthy according to institutional standards in developing countries. Medical information and tests are not always accurate; record keeping is poor. You can take the translated information, photos, and videos to discuss with a pediatrician. In addition, you might contact an international adoption clinic (see Chapter 13 for names and contacts) and send them the information for an opinion. Developmental delays in orphanage children are common. Your child may lag far behind infants and children of the same age level in your neighborhood. Generally, the children overcome developmental delays fairly quickly.

The same is even more true for older children. The social worker at the orphanage will include her observations about the child's personality and behavior. However, the behavior may be different for a while when the child is interacting in a family. The other scenario is that the parents and established siblings may have more trouble adjusting to the child than the child does to the family. The main reason adoptive parents reject children after adoption is not health, but behavior. Sometimes the reactive behavior of the existing children rather than that of the newcomer is more than the parents can tolerate and they decide that the new child has to leave.

However, if the child's medical information indicates problems you cannot or do not wish to handle, or if the child does not fit the guidelines you originally specified, then by all means, turn down the referral. You will eventually be given another. If you are in a foreign country when you make a decision not to adopt a particular child, it is extremely important that you cooperate with the authorities abroad and also with your child-placing agency in the United States if you wish to try again.

The referral of a child is a nerve-wracking time for everyone. The new parents start worrying about who is taking care of the child, his or her state of health, and possible legal hitches. The agency starts worrying about getting the adoptive parent's approval in order to begin coordinating the travel itinerary with the adoption hearing. This can get complicated. Sometimes the adoptive parents or their doctor request an updated medical evaluation, which can take a month or two for the physician, lab, and translator to complete. An aggravating problem at this point can be the rescheduling of the adoption hearing. That means changing travel plans and more days off at the workplace.

Consider the referral of a child tentative until you have left your child's native land while holding him or her in your arms. Refrain from telling everyone about your child right away and don't pass out copies of his or her photo. Wait until you're ready to leave the country — the adoption situation could change.

You can help prepare a child over age two for adoption. Mail the following items to the authorities in charge of your child: pictures of yourselves, your home, your parents, and, if applicable, the child's future siblings. Also include pictures of the local playground, pets, and/or a fabulous toy like a tricycle. And, include translations of short letters from new family members that can be read to him or her.

OBTAINING A VISA OR TOURIST CARD

American citizens do not usually need visas except in formerly or presently communist countries. If you are adopting from Africa, China, Vietnam, Russia, or other former Iron Curtain countries, your international agency or the consulate of that country will advise you regarding the type of visa needed. They will also tell you how to use special expediting services in order to get the visa in a day or two.

STEP 15

Obtain visa or tourist card (if neccessary) for travel to your child's country.

Once the authorities abroad know that you have accepted the referral of a child, they will send you an invitation to travel to their country. When you have this letter and your travel itinerary, you will fill out their visa application forms. If you are adopting from an international agency, they will furnish these forms. Otherwise, they can be obtained at the consulate of that country. The length of stay will depend on the length of the adoption process; about one or two weeks in the above-mentioned countries should be sufficient. The question regarding the object of the journey should be answered. "To conclude business and carry out humanitarian aid." In Russia, you can write in "adoption." Be certain to sign and date the form.

Send copies of the letter and itinerary along with the visa application to the consulate. Obtaining a visa can take a week or two unless you use special expediting services.

Most tourist cards or visas are issued in duplicate. The original is surrendered upon entry. The copy is turned in at the time of departure. The other documents required to enter a country are needed again to leave it.

CHAPTER 9

Filing the Orphan Petition

ELIGIBILITY TO FILE FOR AN ORPHAN PETITION

In order to be able to file a petition, parents must meet INS eligibility requirements.

A Petition to Classify an Orphan as an Immediate Relative (Form I-600) for issuance of a visa may be filed by a married or unmarried United States citizen. (If married, they must adopt jointly; if unmarried, the citizen must be at least twenty-five years of age.) The spouse need not be a United States citizen. It must be established that both the married petitioner and spouse, or the unmarried petitioner, will care for the orphan properly if the orphan is admitted to the United States. If the orphan was adopted abroad, it must be established that both the married petitioner and spouse, or the unmarried petitioner, personally saw and observed the child prior to, or during the adoption proceedings. If both the petitioner and spouse, or unmarried petitioner, did not personally see and observe the child during the adoption proceedings abroad, they must establish that the child will be adopted in the United States and that any preadoption requirements of the state of the orphan's proposed residence have been met. This generally means an approved home study. The petitioner must submit, if requested, a statement by an appropriate official in the state in which the child will reside that the prospective parents are approved to adopt in that state. If the orphan has not been adopted abroad, the petitioner and spouse, or the unmarried petitioner, must establish that the child will be adopted in the United States by the petitioner and spouse jointly, or by the unmarried petitioner, and that the preadoption requirements, if any, of the state of the orphan's proposed residence have been met. Again, this means an approved home study.

DOCUMENTATION OF ORPHANS

In addition, in order for approval of Form I-600, it is crucial that the child you are adopting meets the INS definition of an orphan and that proper supporting documentation of the child's status be available.

In the first paragraph of the application and the petition, the INS definition of an orphan is provided:

> "*The term orphan under the immigration laws means a foreign child who is under the age of 16 years at the time the visa petition in his behalf is filed and who is an orphan because both parents have died or disappeared, or abandoned or deserted the orphan, or the orphan has become separated or lost from both parents.*"

> "*If the orphan has only one parent, that parent must be incapable of providing for the orphan's care and must have in writing irrevocably released the orphan for emigration and adoption. An illegitimate child whose father acknowledges paternity and signs a relinquishment along with the mother is also considered an orphan. In addition, the orphan either must have been adopted abroad or must be coming to the United States for adoption by a United States citizen and spouse jointly or by an unmarried United States citizen at least 25 years of age. [Section 101] (b)(i)(F) of the Immigration and Nationality Act.*"

A child who is abandoned to a government institution by both parents may qualify for classification as an orphan under immigration law, but immigration law does not define the term abandonment, and the subject is only discussed once in INS regulations.

According to the regulations, a child who has been unconditionally abandoned to an orphanage is considered to have no parents. A child is not considered to be abandoned, however, when he or she has been placed temporarily in an orphanage, if the parent or parents are contributing or trying to contribute to the child's support, or the parent or parents otherwise show that they have not ended their parental obligations to the child.

DIFFICULT ISSUES IN ORPHAN CASES

Under U.S. immigration law, the child of a sole or surviving parent may be considered an orphan if that parent is unable to care for the child properly and has forever or irrevocably released him or her for emigration and adoption.

The child of an unwed mother normally may be considered to be an orphan as long as the mother does not marry. The child of a surviving parent may also be considered to be an orphan if it is proven that one of the child's parents died and the surviving parent has not since married. However, marriage results in the child's having a stepfather or stepmother under immigration law.

Legitimate versus Illegitimate Designations

Most countries have legal procedures for the acknowledgment of children by their natural fathers. Therefore, adoptive and prospective adoptive parents of children who were born out of wedlock in any country should find out whether the children have been legitimized. Legitimized children from any country have two legal parents and cannot qualify as orphans (until the passing of the proposed amendments).

Some countries have passed laws that eliminate all legal distinctions between legitimate and illegitimate children. In those countries, all children are considered to be legitimate or legitimized children of their natural fathers as of the effective date of the laws in question. Of course, paternity must be established. A child born out of wedlock and living in a country that has such a law and whose paternity has been legally established has two parents even though the parents never married and may not be living together.

Adoptive and prospective adoptive parents of children who were born out of wedlock should become familiar with the legitimacy laws in the countries where the children are born and reside. If a child born out of wedlock is from a country that has eliminated all legal distinctions between legitimate and illegitimate children, the child could still qualify for classification as an orphan under immigration law.

Refugee Children

Every year the world experiences significant natural disasters. Earthquakes, hurricanes, and epidemics create hundreds of orphans. "Ethnic cleansing," war, and famine create even more. Media coverage of such traumatic events and the children left orphaned by them often motivates individuals to seek information on adopting these children. Unfortunately, adopting children orphaned by these sudden and extreme circumstances is much more difficult than adopting a child already relinquished by a parent to an institution. Documented evidence must prove that the child has no living relatives, and investigating a child's social history and creating identifying documents is a slow process, particularly in an area that has been destroyed by nature or man. American Consulates may be overwhelmed and unable to issue orphan visas, and the INS does not have a special category for refugee orphans. In exceptional cases, the INS might be able to issue a humanitarian visa, but again, such an occurrence is rare.

Many people remember all too well the painful lessons learned during the Vietnam War when American agencies placed refugee children in U.S. homes. Many parents of the "orphans" actually survived the fall of Saigon and eventually made their way to America to find their children. In such cases, the courts returned the children to their biological parents. This is the only instance in which an international adoption has resulted in a custody suit.

FILING THE I-600 ORPHAN PETITION

STEP 16

File Form I-600 (Orphan Petition) if this is to be filed in the United States. (This is usually filed abroad if the adoption is finalized in the child's country and both parents travel to meet the child.)

Where you file the I-600 Orphan Petition depends upon the country and the kind of adoption you are planning, such as an agency-initiated adoption requiring one or both spouses to travel abroad; an agency-initiated adoption with escort for the child to the United States; or a parent-initiated adoption. Your U.S.-based international adoption agency or INS will advise you whether to file the Orphan Petition with your local INS office or the U.S. Consulate in the child's native country. For most foreign adoptions, Form I-600 is filed at the U.S. Consulate abroad. However, if you are advised to file the form in the United States, you will file it at the same INS office where the Application for Advance Processing (Form I-600A) was filed. If the petition is filed in the United States, a cable of approval of Form I-600 will be forwarded at your request to the appropriate U.S. visa-issuing post abroad. Ask your INS office to send abroad to the U.S. Consulate a "Visa Cable 39." This message indicates that your INS office has issued approval of your Form I-600 and supporting documentation.

Filing in Absence of Form I-600A

If no Application for Advance Processing (Form I-600A) has been filed because you located a child who meets INS criteria before you knew and understood their requirements, file Form I-600A and Form I-600, and then register with an adoption agency and follow the remaining steps, beginning in Chapter 3.

Required Documents

1. Form I-600, Orphan Petition. Both spouses must sign the form. (See sample form at the end of this chapter.)

2. Birth certificate of orphan. If the birth certificate cannot be obtained, the prospective adoptive parent should submit an explanation together with the best available evidence of birth.

3. Death certificate(s) of the orphan's parent(s), if applicable.

4. Form of relinquishment, if applicable, which shows evidence that the orphan's sole or surviving parent cannot provide for the orphan's care and has in writing forever or irrevocably released the orphan for emigration and adoption. If the orphan has two unmarried parents, both must sign relinquishments. However, a child with two parents must be relinquished to a government agency prior to the adoption.

5. Certificate of abandonment, if the orphan is institutionalized, which shows evidence that the orphan has been unconditionally abandoned to an orphanage.

6. A final or initial decree of adoption or permanent guardianship.

7. Evidence that the preadoption home study requirements, if any, of the state of the orphan's proposed residence have been met, if the child is to be adopted in the United States. A statement to this effect is often included in the home study. If, under the laws of the state of the child's proposed residence, it is not possible to submit this evidence when the petition is first filed, it may be submitted later. The petition, however, will not be approved without it.

8. The home study and supporting documents previously listed with Form I-600A, Application for Advance Processing, unless this evidence was already

U.S. CITIZENS RESIDING ABROAD

Transferred business employees of international companies, military personnel and U.S. government employees, missionaries, students, Peace Corps volunteers, and other U.S. citizens who are not expatriates (residing abroad voluntarily without a contract or military orders) and who will be residing abroad should follow these procedures for the following situations:

U.S. citizen departing for a foreign post.
    Filing Form I-600A, Application for Advance Processing, will be easier if your move is still in the planning stages. Ask an adoption agency to give you top priority if you are planning to leave the United States in the near future. You must get advance processing before you leave if you wish to avoid future delays.

U.S. citizens residing abroad who have been living with an adopted orphan for less than two years.
    At least three to six months before you plan to return home, you must process Form I-600, Petition to Classify an Orphan as an Immediate Relative. Contact the nearest U.S. Embassy or Consulate

for the names of social workers who conduct home studies and for the appropriate INS service office in order to file Form I-600. Allow enough time before your departure to obtain a home study that meets the legal requirements of your state of residence. If the country only places children through U.S. agencies they have licensed, you will need to contact the U.S. Consulate in that country for a list of approved agencies.

U.S. citizens who have adopted abroad or had legal custody and have been living abroad for two years with the foreign orphan.

You may file Form I-130, Petition to Classify an Alien as an Immediate Relative. Form I-130 is for aliens of any age who can be classified as immediate relatives. The U.S. Embassy located in the country where you reside will provide you with Form I-130 and the list of supporting documents that you will need in order to file for the child's IR-2 visa. If you can prove that the child has lived with you for two years, you do not need a home study or an FBI clearance.

submitted with a pending Form I-600A application or it is within one year of a favorable determination in a completed advance processing case.

Documents 2-6 are obtained by the foreign lawyer or foreign child-placing entity, who also arranges for the translation of these documents. Two sets of certified copies are needed to complete the legal immigration and readoption in your home state. The adoptive parent, or international agency in the case of an escort, is responsible for submitting a complete set of these translated originals to the American Consulate abroad. If you are traveling to meet your child, be sure to take the originals on your adoption trip unless, of course, your agency has already sent them.

Exceptions to the Process

If documentary evidence relating to the child or the home study is not yet available, the I-600 Orphan Petition and fee may be filed without that evidence.

If the necessary evidence relating to the child or the home study is not submitted within one year from the date of submission of the petition, the petition is considered abandoned and the fee is not refunded. If the petitioner later decides that he or she wants to petition for the same child or a different child, it will be necessary to file a new Application for Advance Processing (Form I-600A) or a new Orphan Petition (Form I-600) and pay a new fee.

Updating the I-600 Orphan Petition

As with Form I-600A, Form I-600 is ~~~~ or 18 months. If an orphan has not immigrated ~~~~ tion, updated home study and ~~~~ be filed.

FORM I-600

2 pgs.

OVERSEAS ORPHAN INVESTIGATION

When an I-600 Orphan Petition is ~~~~ a U.S. Consulate or Embassy for ~~~~ When an Orphan Petition is filed ~~~~ orphan investigation as part of ~~~~ ickly, and the adopting parent ~~~~ alize this process. The purpose ~~~~ ild is an orphan as defined in ~~~~ ignificant illness or disability ~~~~ Form I-604, Request for and ~~~~ be found at the end of this chapter.

If a child is not eligible for classification as an orphan under immigration law, INS notifies the petitioner and spouse, if married, and gives them the choice of withdrawing the petition or having the question considered in revocation proceedings. Revocation proceedings give the petitioner a chance to submit evidence to overrule the stated grounds for revoking the approval of the petition.

Form I-600

Orphan Petition, Page 1 of 2

OMB No. 1115-0049

U.S. Department of Justice
Immigration and Naturalization Service

Petition to Classify Orphan as an Immidiate Relative [Section 101 (b)(1)(F) of the Immigration and Nationality Act, as amended.]

Please do not write in this block.

TO THE SECRETARY OF STATE:

The petition was filed by:
☐ Married petitioner   ☐ Unmarried petitioner

The petition is approved for orphan:
☐ Adopted abroad   ☐ Coming to U.S. for adoption. Preadoption requirements have been met.

Remarks:

Fee Stamp

File number

DATE OF ACTION

DD

DISTRICT

Please type or print legibly in ink. Use a separate petition for each child.

Petition is being made to classify the named orphan as an immediate relative.

BLOCK I - Information About Prospective Petitioner

1. My name is: (Last)   (First)   (Middle) (name of notary)

2. Other names used (including maiden name if appropriate):

3. I reside in the U.S. at: (C/O if appropriate)   (Apt. No.)

    (Number and street)   (Town or city)   (State)   (ZIP Code)

4. Address abroad (if any): (Number and street)   (Apt. No.)

    (Town or city)   (Province)   (Country)

5. I was born on: (Month)   (Day)   (Year)

    In: (Town or City)   (State or Province)   (Country)

6. My phone number is: (Include Area Code)

7. My marital status is:
    ☐ Married
    ☐ Widowed
    ☐ Divorced
    ☐ Single
        ☐ I have never been married.
        ☐ I have been previously married _____ time(s).

8. If you are now married, give the following information:
    Date and place of present marriage

    Name of present spouse (include maiden name of wife)

    Date of birth of spouse   Place of birth of spouse

    Number of prior marriages of spouse

    My spouse resides ☐ With me   ☐ Apart from me
        (provide address below)

    (Apt. No.)   (No. and street)   (City)   (State)   (Country)

9. I am a citizen of the United States through:
    ☐ Birth   ☐ Parents   ☐ Naturalization   ☐ Marriage
    If acquired through naturalization, give name under which naturalized, number of naturalization certificate, and date and place of naturalization:

    If not, submit evidence of citizenship. See Instruction 2.a(2).
    If acquired through parentage or marriage, have you obtained a certificate in your own name based on that acquisition?
    ☐ No   ☐ Yes
    Have you or any person through whom you claimed citizenship ever lost United States citizenship?
    ☐ No   ☐ Yes (If yes, attach detailed explanation.)

Continue on reverse.

Received	Trans. In	Ret'd Trans. Out	Completed

Form I-600 (Rev. 8/25/89) Y

Form I-600

Orphan Petition, Page 2 of 2

BLOCK II - Information About Orphan Beneficiary

10. Name at birth (First) (Middle) (Last)	20. To petitioner's knowledge, does the orphan have any physical or mental affliction? ☐ Yes ☐ No If "Yes", name the affliction.
11. Name at present (First) (Middle) (Last)	
12. Any other names by which orphan is or was known.	21. Who has legal custody of the child?
13. Sex ☐ Male ☐ Female 14. Date of birth (Month/Day/Year)	22. Name of child welfare agency, if any, assisting in this case:
15. Place of birth (City) (State or Province) (Country)	23. Name of attorney abroad, if any, representing petitioner in this case. Address of above.
16. The beneficiary is an orphan because (check one): ☐ He/she has no parents ☐ He/she has only one parent who is the sole or surviving parent.	
17. If the orphan has only one parent, answer the following: a. State what has become of the other parent:	24. Address in the United States where orphan will reside.
b. Is the remaining parent capable of providing for the orphan's support? ☐ Yes ☐ No	25. Present address of orphan.
c. Has the remaining parent, in writing, irrevocably released the orphan for emigration and adoption? ☐ Yes ☐ No	25. If orphan is residing in an institution, give full name of institution.
18. Has the orphan been adopted abroad by the petitioner and spouse jointly or the unmarried petitioner? ☐ Yes ☐ No If yes, did the petitioner and spouse or unmarried petitioner personally see and observe the child prior to or during the adoption proceedings? ☐ Yes ☐ No Date of adoption Place of adoption	26. If orphan is not residing in an institution, give full name of person with whom orphan is residing.
19. If either answer in question 18 is "No", answer the following: a. Do petitioner and spouse jointly or does the unmarried petitioner intend to adopt the orphan in the United States? ☐ Yes ☐ No b. Have the preadoption requirements, if any, of the orphan's proposed state of residence been met? ☐ Yes ☐ No c. If b. is answered "No", will they be met later? ☐ Yes ☐ No	27. Give any additional information necessary to locate orphan such as name of district, section, zone or locality in which orphan resides.
	28. Location of American Consulate where application for visa will be made. (City in Foreign Country) (Foreign Country)

Certification of Prospective Petitioner

I certify under penalty of perjury under the laws of the United States of America that the foregoing is true and correct and that I will care for an orphan/orphans properly if admitted to the United States.

(Signature of Prospective Petitioner)

Executed on (Date)

Certification of Married Prospective Petitioner's Spouse

I certify under penalty of perjury under the laws of the United States of America that the foregoing is true and correct and that my spouse and I will care for an orphan/orphans properly if admitted to the United States.

(Signature of Prospective Petitioner)

Executed on (Date)

Signature of Person Preparing Form if Other Than Petitioner

I declare that this document was prepared by me at the request of the prospective petitioner and is based on all information of which I have any knowledge.

(Signature)

Address

Executed on (Date)

Form I-604

Overseas Orphan Investigation, Page 1of 2

U.S. Department of Justice

Immigration and Naturalization Service

Request for and Report on Overseas Orphan Investigation

	File
TO: U.S. CONSUL, _____ (City and country)	
FROM: DISTRICT DIRECTOR, _____	Date

☐ 1. Attached is an approved visa petition in behalf of an orphan. Please complete this form concerning the orphan. If you develop information which indicates that the child is not an orphan as defined in section 101(b)(1)(F) of the Immigration and Nationality Act or that the child has an affliction or disability not set forth in the petition, suspend action on the visa application and return this form with the attached petition to the INS office of origin. If no adverse information is developed, attach this form and the petition to the visa application.

☐ 2. Attached is an application for advance processing of an orphan petition with a favorable determination concerning the prospective petitioner's ability to furnish proper care to a beneficiary orphan. When the prospective petitioner files an orphan petition at your post, please complete this form concerning the child. If you develop information which indicates that the child is not an orphan as defined in section 101(b)(1)(F) of the Immigration and Nationality Act, forward the petition with this form, Form I-600A and all attachments to the Service office having jurisdiction over the beneficiary's place of residence. If you determine that the child has an affliction or disability not set forth in the petition, furnish all details to the petitioner, and spouse, if married. Should the petitioner and spouse, if married, elect to proceed with the petition, the information concerning the affliction or disability should be incorporated at the bottom of page 1 of Form I-600 and initialed by the petitioner and spouse, if married. If the petitioner and spouse, if married, choose not to proceed with the petition, Form I-600A should be returned to the INS office of origin with Form I-600, this form, and all attachments.

Orphan's present name

Date and place of orphan's birth	(name of notary)

Ethnic origin of orphan	Does orphan live in an orphanage?	If not, where does orphan live?

If orphan lives with relatives, what are their relationships to the orphan?

If orphan lives with non-relatives, explain.

How many years of formal education has orphan received?	As a student, orphan is ☐ Average ☐ Above average ☐ Below average

Is child's mental level the same as that of other children the same age?	Does child get along well with other children the same age?

Does child participate in games or athletic activities with other children the same age? If not, explain.

Has the orphan had serious difficulties with any adult authority, including the persons having charge of the orphan? If so, explain.

Form I-604 (Rev. 12-15-82) N

111

Form I-604

Overseas Orphan Investigation, Page 2 of 2

Does child require medical attention frequently. If so, explain.

Does child require any special care, attention, medication or diet?

Indicate by check mark whether orphan has any of the following

☐ physical defects   ☐ speech defects   ☐ nervous disorders   ☐ mental defects

Is child normal in appearance? If not, explain.

Give ages of brothers and sisters, if any.	Does child reside with brothers or sisters?

When and under what circumstances did child become an orphan?

| If orphan has remaining parent and is residing with that parent, give the following: | Ability of that parent to care for orphan |
| | Reason remaining parent has released child for emigration and adoption |

Did either parent of orphan ever have a mental disease? If so, explain.

If either parent of orphan is dead, give cause of death.

(Complete only if orphan has one parent). Set forth circumstances resulting in child having only a sole or surviving parent.

Known travel arrangements of the orphan to the United States

Other pertinent facts

If conflicting information is developed as to any of the above matters, or "Yes" or "No" answer would leave the issue unsettled, attach narrative report and place notation."See narrative" beside the pertinent item on this form.

Investigating officer's signature	Date investigation completed

GPO 896-386

CHAPTER 10

The Adoption Trip

This is the moment you've been waiting for. If you're feeling happy and frightened at the same time, it's to be expected. You're about to become a parent in the midst of a whirlwind of activity.

Your adoption trip will be planned down to the last detail if you are adopting through an international agency. They will make certain that you are in the right place at the right time for all of your appointments. If this is a parent-initiated adoption, you will plan the trip yourself, scheduling your travel around the adoption-related appointments.

Depending upon the country you have chosen, you might leave in just a few weeks to initiate the adoption. If you have chosen a country where power of attorney is used, you may not leave for one to three months.

Your adoption experience in a foreign country is uniquely your own. If you have never spent much time in a foreign country before, the food, customs, and language can give you a first-rate case of culture shock. The average stay for adopters is two weeks, just long enough to reach a peak in exasperation, frustration, anger, and shock. No one has ever died of it, but recovery requires several months. After a year back home, almost everyone has fully recovered and wants to make the trip again — either to adopt more children or to visit.

INTERNATIONAL TRAVEL

Adopters traveling to foreign countries become unofficial ambassadors for the United States, especially for the U.S. adopters who come after them. Adopters who wish to make and leave a favorable impression do their homework first — a study of the host country's language, culture, and etiquette. While orphans are usually from the lower classes, social workers, directors, lawyers, and liaisons are from the privileged classes. Proper social form and behavior are important to them. Most North Americans are in a hurry to return home. This is understandable. What is not understandable is rude and pushy behavior, which, incidentally, does not get the family home any faster. Most delays occur during the court procedure. The court cannot be rushed, no matter what part of the world you are in. Be accessible, responsive, and cooperative to avoid further delays.

Several excellent travel books explain how we should behave in foreign countries as well as 1,001 things every traveler should know. New editions are published each year. The language barrier appears to present the greatest obstacle to bridging the gap between the two cultures. Books, tapes, records, and hand-held computers are available to assist or help you learn most of the major languages. In most cases, a representative associated with your U.S. agency will meet you abroad and stay with your group, but the more you know, the more independent you will be when you arrive at your destination. Consult the Internet for more information.

As you prepare for your adoption trip, learn the travel requirements and procedures in the foreign country, too. After sending your dossier, gather your travel documents together; then you will be ready to travel when your referral comes. While the average adoption stay is two weeks, your stay could last up to eight weeks, depending upon your foreign source and other variables.

Following Entry and Exit Requirements

Foreign immigration authorities only permit travelers with proper documents to enter their countries. Be aware that many foreign governments change their entry and exit requirements frequently. For up-to-date information on entry and exit regulations, contact your airline or the consulate of the foreign country you wish to visit.

If you are working with an international agency, they will advise you about your travel documents. Otherwise, you will need to consult a travel agent.

Generally the following documents are required:

1. A passport. Married couples should obtain separate passports since one spouse may need to return home ahead of the other spouse.

2. A tourist card or visa (if required).

3. A round-trip ticket. Nonpenalty tickets are more expensive, yet they are the best way to purchase airline tickets for an adoption. That way, if the hearings are rescheduled or other problems occur overseas, you won't lose any money. You can exchange the tickets.

4. Identifying photos. A passport photo will be sufficient.

If for some reason you were not able to get your passport earlier, keep in mind that one-day service for passports can be found in most major cities. You may need to present evidence that you must leave the country within forty-eight hours. Call ahead about this as well as their office hours.

Most tourist cards or visas are issued in duplicate. The original is surrendered upon entry. The copy is turned in at the time of departure. The other documents required to enter a country are needed again to leave it.

Making Travel Arrangements

STEP 17

Prepare for your adoption trip.

Arrange your trip by phone or on the Internet. U.S.-based international agencies as well as some travel agencies are aware of adopters' needs and will advise you about fares and nonpenalty tickets. Do not make reservations until the INS sends a cable of clearance and the court hearing is scheduled. Remember to arrive at the airport three to four hours before any international flight and two hours before a domestic flight.

Since different excursion rates are offered from time to time by various airlines and since airfares are subject to sudden changes, you should check the fares of several airlines before your adoption trip is scheduled. You will also need to purchase a one-way ticket back to the United States for your child. Because adoption hearings are sometimes rescheduled or the process takes longer than planned, you should look for nonpenalty tickets that can be exchanged without additional costs.

In most circumstances, your international agency will arrange for your lodgings. If you are traveling individually to adopt, the agency representative abroad will help you find lodgings according to your taste and budget. If you are traveling in a group, your lodgings will be arranged ahead of departure.

Prior to leaving, try to find a doctor knowledgeable about health problems in developing countries. Arrange for a consultation with the doctor before you leave. The most commonly recommended vaccines are for hepatitis A and B with updating of your tetanus and polio series. Other vaccines are not generally indicated. You can reference the Centers for Disease Control and Prevention (CDC) Web site (http://www.cdc.gov/travel/) for the most up-to-date recommendations for travelers. This is also a good time to investigate what kinds of specialists your insurance plan covers as well as where laboratory testing is conducted.

HEALTH PRECAUTIONS FOR TRAVELERS

Your adoption trip will be one of the peak experiences in your life. It's definitely not the time to get sick. Taking some simple precautions listed below should minimize your risk of becoming ill while overseas.

Travelers to developing countries must be extremely careful about what they eat and drink if they want to avoid spending a substantial portion of their trip in search of a bathroom. Rule number one is to eat only in first-class restaurants or to dine in the homes of the upper-class nationals. However, this is not always guaranteed safe or even possible.

Even then, do not eat raw salads. And, don't eat raw vegetables or fruits unless you disinfect them with iodine before peeling them yourself. The tried and true mantra "Boil it, peel it, wash it, or forget it," still holds true.

Do not eat raw meat or raw fish. Don't eat or drink milk products unless you know they are pasteurized. And avoid foods, including condiments, that have been sitting around at room temperature for long periods of time.

So what do you do if you are far from an AAA-rated restaurant and hungry? Find a bakery and buy some just-out-of-the-oven rolls or the equivalent staff of life for that country, such as steaming hot rice or boiled or roasted potatoes. Hot noodle soup or hot tea or coffee should also be safe. Clean your hands before you eat with the packaged pre-moistened towelettes you brought from home. Or, stash some U.S. breakfast bars or other high protein bars in your pockets.

What should you drink? Bottled mineral water, with seal intact, with or without carbonation, or other carbonated beverages, preferably drunk from the bottle through a straw. You should purify water for hygienic use. The easiest method is to purchase a pint-sized water purifier from a camping outfitter to take along. Otherwise, you can purify water by boiling it for twenty minutes. (Take a hot pot and, if necessary, an electrical current adapter, if you plan to boil water.) If boiling is not possible, treat water with Halazone tablets or mix in 10 drops of 2% tincture of iodine to one quart of water and let stand for 30 minutes. (Keep in mind that Halazone only treats bacterial agents, not viruses. Use this method only as a last resort.) If the water is cloudy, filter it through a cotton cloth.

In Latin American countries, U.S. adoptive parents who stay in better hotels will have little to worry about regarding food and water. Luxury hotels post notices in each room explaining the purity of the water supply. However, if you stay in lower rate hotels, bottled water can be ordered. Check to make certain that the seal isn't broken. For all of the former Soviet Union, Eastern Europe, and all of Asia, except Japan, you must use bottled water at all times. This includes water for rinsing your toothbrush as well as for brushing. With the frequency of international travel, most hotels will provide boiled and filtered water.

Should you be unlucky enough to ingest contaminated food or water, the vomiting and/or diarrhea are more of a threat to your health than the particular pathogen, whether it be a virus, bacterium, or parasite. Mild diarrhea in adults can be managed with Imodium (available over-the-counter) or Lomotil (available by prescription). However, diarrhea drains salts and fluids from the body, causing the dehydration that accounts for the deaths of babies worldwide. While an adult's diarrhea is not usually life threatening, grown-ups should replace the salts and fluids they are losing with almost any fluid. If diarrhea is severe (more than one stool every two hours), adults should use an oral rehydration solution (ORS) such as Pedialyte. An ORS powder to be mixed with boiled water is available over the counter at pharmacies around the world.

Should you or your child feel ill the first year after your trip, alert your doctor as to which country you visited. The doctor will then order the appropriate series of stool examination kits. Most diarrhea-producing parasites such as Crypotosporidium or Giardia are transmitted by contaminated water. Even if the diarrhea abates, you may still be harboring the parasite. Get rechecked at home if you are not completely back to normal.

Other parasites, such as tapeworms and flukes, are transmitted by contaminated foods and, occasionally, by water. Some, like hookworms and schistosomes, which cause schistosomiasis, are acquired through the skin by walking barefoot outside or swimming in contaminated water. Most of these parasites require an intermediate animal host and are not contagious from person to person. These parasites typically do not give diarrhea and may be detected only months or years after travel.

Since most parasites are transmitted in a food-fecal chain, consider each diaper a transmitter. Make certain that all members of your family keep up a scrupulous hand-washing ritual. All orphans and their new parents with symptoms should be tested for parasites after their arrival home. Some worms and parasites have dormant periods and will not show up in every stool sample. You or your child should be rechecked if symptoms persist. (Chapter 13 provides a more detailed overview of the potential health problems of children from developing countries.)

Most bacterial pathogens, such as Salmonella and Shigella resolve on their own. There is no need to recheck after arrival unless symptoms persist or new problems develop. A few viral pathogens may be spread by travelers after arrival home, especially hepatitis A and hepatitis B. Of course, strict hand washing should be practiced even after arrival back home. An ill person should not prepare food for the family, nor share food or utensils with anyone.

Vaccinations and Immunizations

Adopters planning international travel may phone the Centers for Disease Control and Prevention (CDC) hotline in Atlanta at (404) 639-3311 or log on to the Centers' Web site at www.cdc.gov for information on epidemics, diseases, and the precautions as well as the inoculations necessary for travel to each country. Bear in mind that you usually will be in urban, not rural areas. A short stay in a foreign city requires fewer inoculations than a stay in a rural area or a long stay abroad. If you will be staying in an orphanage or living in a remote area for several weeks, you may need more extensive health precautions.

At the minimum, individuals traveling abroad should update their tetanus and polio vaccinations and should receive the vaccination series for hepatitis A and B. The vaccination for hepatitis B requires a series of three inoculations given over several months. In addition, you might consider immunizing all household members (even those not traveling) for hepatitis A and B.

Most travelers should consider immunization against influenza between November and April. Adults traveling to Asia, Eastern Europe, or any part of the former Soviet Union should also receive the one-time adult polio booster. If you have never had chicken pox or received the vaccine before, consider an inoculation before you leave. Although generally a mild disease, chicken pox may be severe in adults. Adults are more likely to contract a serious case and have a higher rate of complications from the virus. Some doctors also recommend an MMR vaccine (measles, mumps, and rubella) if the prospective parents were born after 1957, have not had the diseases, or had only one shot.

Malaria

Malaria is carried by certain kinds of mosquitoes in coastal and jungle areas, including parts of Mexico, Central America, some Caribbean Islands, and the northeastern half of South America. The disease is also present in parts of Asia, including China. Since most adoption programs are in large cities where malaria outbreaks are rare, antimalarial drugs are not usually necessary, but check the CDC's Web site before you travel. The site is updated daily as needed and carries the most current recommendations for each country, region, and season of travel. Do not depend on your travel agent or the consulate of the country you are traveling to for accurate advice. Malaria prophylaxis is rarely needed for adoption travel. Finally, if you are bringing your other children with you, read carefully the CDC's advice for child travelers as many of the recommendations differ by age, weight of the child, etc.

PACKING FOR HEALTH AND CONVENIENCE

Practice packing two weeks before you leave. Take any necessary pharmaceuticals along as well as a mix and match wardrobe that doesn't wrinkle or show stains. You should be able to pack everything you need for yourself in one large piece of rolling luggage and a medium-sized piece that fits on top. In addition, pack one medium-sized bag on wheels for your baby or child. Put the baby's diaper bag or the child's carry-on inside the bag for the trip abroad. This pared down set of luggage will make transfers from one mode of transportation to another much easier. By the time you get your child, your hands will be full. Porters and skycaps are not available in many Asian and Eastern European countries. Jetways are not common either. Passengers often board the plane by climbing a metal stairway pushed up against the airplane while it's parked on the tarmac.

The Essentials

Suitcases and Bags: For checked luggage, two pieces per passenger is the limit. One suitcase can be no larger than sixty-two inches; the other, no larger than fifty-five inches. In order to compute the size allowed by airlines, measure the height, length, and width and add them together. Each suitcase can weigh no more than 70 pounds. You will be charged for overweight and oversized luggage. (Luggage restrictions may vary according to country. Check with your travel agent or air carrier for the exact requirements for your particular trip.)

In addition, each passenger is allowed one carry-on bag, forty-five inches wide, plus a purse or camera. If your bag is stowed overhead, it cannot weigh more than fifty pounds; if stowed beneath the seat, it can weigh no more than seventy pounds.

Be certain to get all of the documents for the adoption in your carry-on luggage. You may reach your destination, but your checked luggage may not arrive for another day or two (or ever)! Plan for this emergency by placing nightwear and clothes for the next day in a soft-sided bag or folding garment bag that will fit under the seat ahead of you. Items for the child can be purchased abroad. In most cities, you'll be able to find wonderful handmade toys, national costumes, unique children's clothing, children's books and music tapes, fancy mosquito nets or bedspreads for beds and cribs, weavings, pictures, hats, baskets, and native jewelry. You can also buy an inexpensive bag to bring them all home in.

Clothing for adults: Plan a coordinated wardrobe to cut down on the number of clothes and shoes you will need. Check the Internet or a travel book for climate. Most of the time you will be dressed in casual clothes. However, for business appointments, you should dress like the attorneys and social workers. Suits for men and a suit or modest dress for women are the acceptable clothing for appointments with government officials and lawyers. This will help make a favorable impression and will look good on the pictures you show your child when he or she is older.

Dress conservatively but comfortably for your flight. Low heels for women — you never know how much running you may have to do when you change planes, especially if your flight schedule is changed at the last minute.

Foreign money: Take only American Express, Cook's, or Citibank traveler's checks. Check with your bank to see if ATM machines in the country to which you are traveling will accept your bankcard. When using an ATM overseas, it's important that you know the approximate rate of exchange as the money will be dispensed in local currency. However, some countries do not use ATMs and do not routinely accept traveler's checks. Check with your agency for recommendations on how much cash to bring.

Have some foreign money handy for the first taxi and probable expenses for your first day. You can obtain it at exchange houses in most international airports. It is helpful to inquire about the rate of exchange a day or two before traveling, and to make up your own rate-of-exchange chart in a notebook for $1, $2, $5, $10, etc. Pay attention to when your flight is arriving overseas to be sure that you will have access to a bank the following day. If you are arriving on a weekend or national holiday, you may need to take more foreign currency with you. Be certain to get small change for tips. We take $20 or $30, in $1 bills, for tips. American dollars are prized in most foreign countries. Request newly printed U.S. bills without any marks or tears. Damaged U.S. currency is not accepted in most foreign countries.

What to Take — Packing for You

If your trip will only be for a few days, you won't need to take most of these items. For a trip of two weeks or more, you will need most of these items. However, if you stay with families most of the time, you won't need the hot pot or food items.

Camera: If you have a digital camera, practice with it before you leave and take extra batteries. If you have a new 35mm or other camera, shoot a roll of practice film and use all of the camera's features before you leave. Make certain that you know how to use the camera or you may end up with nothing. If your camera takes 35mm film, extra rolls can be purchased abroad. Other film is difficult to find. Don't forget extra batteries. You may also want to take an x-ray safe film bag; your film may go through 20 or 30 security checks before you get home!

Polaroid, with film: Good for making friends with children.

Video camera: As light in weight as possible. Again, practice with it and be certain the charger and batteries are working.

Electrical current adapter: Ask your travel agent or consult a travel book to see if your hotel has outlets for A/C current. If not, you need the adapter for U.S. electrical appliances. You may also need special plug adapters as well.

Water supply: Ask if the hotel has its own potable water supply. Water for the baby's formula must be boiled twenty minutes, regardless. Bottled water is available in most countries. Buy a supply as soon as you arrive overseas or order it at your hotel. Asian hotels usually give you a thermos of boiled, hot water every day — more if you ask for it.

Remember that you can buy almost anything in most large, international cities. However, depending on the country, your accommodations, and the length of time abroad, you might also need:

A hot pot: Easily packed and handy for boiling water. Take a thermos to store the boiled water in. A water purifier is also a good idea. Pint-sized purifiers are available through camping outfitters.

Travel alarm: To make sure you make it to those early morning appointments.

Flashlight with extra batteries: Most countries have blackouts. Hotels provide candles, but a flashlight is better.

Instant foods: Many couples bring packets of foods — cocoa, instant coffee, cup-of-soup, Tang, crackers and peanut butter, etc., for their own use, making some meals convenient and less expensive than eating out or depending upon room service. Take a supply of drinking straws for carbonated beverages.

Entertainment: In countries where the wait is more than a week, you will have time to read, play board games, and do handiwork. Pack your favorites. Include a travel dictionary, phrase book of the native language, or a hand-held computer translator.

Small notebook: A small, bound notebook will provide a convenient place to write down names and addresses of people you meet, notes about your rolls of film, and brief notes about your trip. You may think you'll never forget the details of this important trip, but you will!

Laundry aids: Try to be as self-sufficient as possible and also be prepared to do the baby's wash in the sink. Hotels in Asia will launder your clothes overnight. Hotels in other countries may also have laundry service, but your child may be using clothes faster than the hotel can wash them. A portable clothesline is helpful. Dryer sheets or other lightweight forms of fabric softeners are great in the rinse water; they make line-dried clothes softer. Also, bring a small bottle of liquid detergent (or use shampoo) and plastic bags with closures of assorted sizes.

Insect repellent: Mosquito and insect body lotion and room spray. You may also want to bring roach spray if you will have a kitchenette.

Sewing kit: Tiny size, with basics: threads, shirt buttons, needles, and several sizes of safety pins.

Wash cloths: Some foreign countries use natural or synthetic sponges. Thus, few hotels furnish wash cloths. Take some with you.

Stationery supplies: Writing pad, Post-it notes, folder, pens, paper clips, and tape.

Roll of nylon tape: To repair suitcases or close bottles, etc. Carry a roll in your pocket or purse.

Tape player (small): Also bring children's music tapes and batteries.

What to Take — Packing for Your Child

You'll need to be as self-sufficient as possible in caring for your baby while at the hotel and on the plane ride home. Items you'll need to care for your new child are listed below.

Baby bottles: We suggest you buy the old-fashioned baby bottles with the large nipples as close as possible to what the orphanage is using abroad. If you are in touch with others who adopted from the same orphanage, ask them what kind to buy. Otherwise, buy an assortment. Babies often refuse to suck from unfamiliar nipples. You may need to try different kinds. Babies over five months of age usually reject the bottles with small nipples and plastic inserts. If your child is very young or of low weight, take "preemie" nipples, which are available at larger drug stores — it makes nursing much easier for the little ones. Special nipples are also manufactured for babies with cleft palates. Also, remember to bring tongs for removing nipples from the boiling water.

Baby carrier: Cloth baby carriers, such as a Snuggly or Bjorn, in which the baby is carried in front of you, can be purchased for babies under a year. Larger, older babies can be carried behind you where the weight is better distributed.

Baby stroller: Find one that folds down for sleeping and folds up for storage in the overhead rack of the plane. Buy stroller netting to keep insects off the child.

Booties, socks, and shoes: In developing countries, people without shoes are the poorest of the poor. Never take your baby outdoors without something on his or her feet.

Caps and bonnets: Summer caps and bonnets should have visors or brims. For winter, hats should cover the ears.

Baby clothing: A few changes, prewashed for softness.

Baby soap and lotions: Bring mild baby soap for the baby's bath. Babies react to changes in temperature. By lining the hotel basin with a towel and filling it with water, the bath should be accomplished fairly peacefully. Test the water with your wrist or elbow first before easing the baby in. For a sponge bath, uncover the baby slowly, one body part at a time. Start with the feet and work up. Wash and dry the first part before uncovering another part of the body. Most children are used to showers, usually cold ones in most countries. Many have learned to hate water and may need to be gently coaxed into a warm bubble bath by floating some toys in it first. This might take several days.

Baby food: Canned baby food and instant baby cereal are readily available overseas. Some restaurants will make it for you. Buy just a small supply to take along. Be sure to bring a can opener for food and formula.

Formula: Continue using the same formula and baby bottle as used by the orphanage while you are abroad. We recommend that you pack one or two cans of powdered formula in case you don't have time to buy it when you receive the baby. Ask your agency or others who have adopted from the same orphanage what kind of formula to purchase. Generally, the switch from one formula to another should be made gradually, since many babies suffer stomach upsets from drastic changes in food. You may wish to take soy-based formula along in case the infant is lactose intolerant. When traveling, put the prescribed amount of dry formula in as many bottles as you will need. Take about six extra preparations. Add sterile water to a bottle when the baby needs it.

Diapers: Be certain to take an adequate supply of disposable diapers — estimate ten per day. Diarrhea warrants an extra supply. If you bring too many, excess diapers are welcome gifts at the foster home as you leave and lifesavers for other American couples you will meet who may have not brought enough. Take a good supply of pre-moistened towelettes. Be sure to bring plastic bags for soiled diapers.

Diaper changing pads: Waterproof pads to put under the child, especially for messy jobs.

Pacifiers: Bring several kinds of pacifiers and clips to attach on a short ribbon to the baby's clothes.

First aid kit: A good first aid kit is essential. See the nearby boxed insert for a list of basic supplies you'll need to carry.

Hand puppets: (For children over one year). Bring enough for the whole family. Actions speak louder than words, and puppets can help you break the language barrier. Also bring picture books of your state, pictures of your home, relatives, and pets, as well as a small, musical, stuffed toy animal to sleep with.

FIRST AID KIT

The items listed below will cover most needs. It is better to keep a few standardized items than have a large mixed collection that can confuse. Anything you use should be replaced with new items as soon as possible. Replace sterile items any time you open their sealed contents.

Instruments:
Infant/child medicine dropper marked in ml or cc
Syringes (3, with a needle attachment) in case you or your child needs an injection due to accident or illness

Thermometer (to take a baby's temperature, put the thermometer under the armpit for three minutes)
Tweezers and scissors (used only for this purpose)
Safety pins
Small scissors

Bandages:

White gauze; absorbent cotton; paper tissues; 2-inch and 3-inch wide plain bandages; ready-to-apply sterile dressings, each packed singly in its protective covering (these are obtainable in various sizes); 2-inch and 3-inch wide adherent dressing strips that can be cut to size for covering simple wounds; 1-inch wide adhesive tape.

Medicines/Salves:

The following pharmaceutical preparations should help you deal with most common infant/childhood ailments. The ones marked with an asterisk are most important and useful. The others are nice, but you can usually buy them if necessary.

Allergies

Benadryl 12.5 mg per 5 ml (dose is 1.25 mg/kg/dose)

*Analgesics

Tylenol (infant 80 mg/0.8 ml or children's Tylenol 160 mg/5ml), Motrin (100mg/5ml)

Antibiotics

Amoxicillin (prescription — do not add bottled water until ready to use/111cc for 150 ml bottle)
Bacitracin Ointment — Skin cuts, burns, rashes
Pink Eye (Conjunctivitis) — Prescription for Tobrex; 2 drops in each eye three times a day for one week

Coughs and Colds

Saline nose drops (Ocean, Nasal, Ayr)
Bulb aspirator

*Diaper Rashes (Apply with each diaper change)

Baby wipes (unscented and without alcohol)
Desitin, A & D Ointment, Balmex (any of these)
Nystatin cream 1% for diaper rash (prescription)

Diarrhea and Vomiting
KAO Lectrolyte packets to mix with 8 oz. of bottled water (plain, bubble gum, and grape)
ORS powder for adults

Skin Problems
Aquaphor or Cetaphil cream for eczema
Hydrocortisone 1% cream or ointment
T-gel shampoo (Neutrogena)
Soap — unscented
Elimite cream 5% for treating scabies (prescription)
Eucerin, also for treating scabies

Lice
Nix cream rinse shampoo
Fine-tooth comb

Water Purification Tablets (if necessary)
Halazone tablets

U.S. EMBASSY AND CONSULATE SERVICES

In addition to issuing visas, embassies and consulates perform many other functions. The responsibility of the Department of State, as well as U.S. Consular offices overseas, is to do everything possible to protect the rights of U.S. citizens abroad while, at the same time, alerting the U.S. traveler to his or her responsibilities and obligations.

Few of us know exactly what services consular offices can provide. For example:

If you lose your passport, you can get an on-the-spot free temporary passport from the nearest U.S. Consulate. Keep a record of your passport number, some extra photos, and a photocopy of your original passport.

If you become seriously ill, destitute, are arrested, or die, a consular official can provide assistance.

If there is political turmoil in the country where you are headed, check for travel advisories and warnings from the State Department or call the U.S. Consulate there for an on-the-spot analysis of the situation before you leave. The U.S. State Department Web site (http://travel.state.gov/) offers an up-to-date list of travel warnings and consular information sheets.

If you register at the U.S. Consulate upon arrival in a country of political unrest, you will be notified of an emergency evacuation. If you get into difficulties, the Consulate will be aware of it.

The Office of Special Consular Services offers these recommendations for worry-free travel:

1. Provide family and friends with complete itinerary.

2. Take twice as many dollars and half as many clothes as you originally planned. Take a combination of cash, personal checks, credit cards, ATM card, and worldwide brands of traveler's checks. Always take traveler's checks that can be cashed, or replaced if stolen, in the country of your destination.

3. Keep your documents and some of your money in the hotel safe. Or, split up money with your spouse. It is better to lose half rather than all of it.

4. In a separate inner pocket, carry each other's passport numbers and the names and phone numbers of people to contact in an emergency. The next piece of advice is extremely important, but is often overlooked by traveling spouses and friends. Write down the name, address, and phone numbers of the places you will be staying and the dates you will be there. Should you and your traveling companion get separated in a crowd, on a bus, or a train, you will know how to get back to your hotel or apartment.

CHAPTER 11

Meeting Your Child

STEP 18
Meet your child.

You've carried a picture around for months. In the meantime, your child-to-be has not been frozen in time like the photo. The real child may look quite different by the time you get there.

Adoptive parents with high expectations are more likely to experience some initial disappointment with their child than new parents who have few expectations. The happiest parents have disengaged the dream child they carried around in their minds for so long. They have considered the fact that this child not only descends from different ancestors, but has survived in conditions that they have never experienced. They have opened their hearts and minds to let this real child enter their lives at a time and in a place they could never have imagined when they first thought of having children.

In most Asian and Latin American countries, you will usually be presented with your child the first or second day after your arrival. In most Eastern European countries, on the other hand, you will not meet your child until the final adoption decree is issued. When you receive your child, you will be expected to provide his or her going-home clothes and shoes, just as you would for a newborn birth-child. You must also be prepared to feed the child according to the directions given you. You may see your child for the first time at the adoption agency abroad, a foster home, or a hotel.

Placements are joyous occasions. After so much longing, work, and struggle, the placement is climactic. But we express emotions differently. We look at the child with awe. Can this really be our child? Your joy is superimposed upon the birth parents' grief. I remember shedding a few tears. "They look just like I thought they would," I said. (We had not been sent pictures.) Heino said in a voice quavering with emotion, "They are lovely girls."

Your first moments together are cinematically recorded in your memory. Even newborns lock eyes with their new parents. A month later, they focus on faces and in response to your voice, will babble and coo. This is where differences in language and ways in which various cultures talk to babies begin to make a difference. For example, the Chinese clap their hands before they pick up a baby. Babies are distressed by extremely loud noises and soothed by quiet sounds. Unfortunately a quiet place is difficult to find in the frenzy and clamor of most cities.

Wear something soft the day you first meet your baby or child. Holding and rocking becomes an even more enjoyable experience when you feel soft and cuddly. Studies confirm that infants are more sensitive to developing attachment behaviors between four months and six months. Hard plastic baby carriers and infant seats should be used as little as possible. The child needs holding to promote bonding.

Between six and nine months, relinquished and abandoned children may not be fearful of strangers. Most likely, they have been cared for by many people and try to keep a mother figure nearby with smiles and coos, since the urge for attachment is extremely strong. Adoptive parents at this stage must interact warmly with the baby, showing approval for this behavior and must not reject clingy and whiny behavior. To reject this negative behavior will only intensify it. Your goal here is to promote attachment, which in turn will help them relax. Then they can play and learn.

Children between eighteen months and three years of age are able to recognize that they are separate individuals. Institutionalized babies spend most of their lives cooped up in a box or crib, simply observing. When they finally climb out, they seek out adults, watching them work, and imitating their motions. They have learned there is no one to go to for comfort if they are hurt or afraid. One of your tasks is to win the child's trust and to prove that you are now there to give aid and comfort. Children are now able to talk and to understand most of what is being said in their native language. Suddenly they must learn a new language and a new routine in a new environment.

School-age children have all of these challenges and, in addition, must submit to the discipline required for a formal education. Formidable!

Fortunately, many excellent books address adjustment issues in children of all ages. Please see the Bibliography at the end of the book for a few recommendations.

CARING FOR YOUR CHILD OVERSEAS

You will be caring for your child in his or her native country for two weeks or several months, depending on the country you are adopting from and the length of wait for the final adoption decree. This is a stressful period for most people. It takes a lot of fortitude to focus on the adoption proceedings, to get to know your child, and to begin to win his or her trust.

For children over one, use a hand puppet. The puppet can act out ideas for both of you as well as provide some comic relief. If your child is too large to be carried and held a lot, giving the child smiles, pats, and light back massages when he or she is sitting or standing near you is an excellent way to give the child a feeling of closeness.

New children are fearful, but they may cover it up. Since they were rejected once, they may be again, or so they may reason. Boys and girls who begged on the streets and lived in orphanages have learned some survival techniques, some of which will probably stay with them forever.

Older children need to believe that you will be there for support when they have problems — when something good happens or something bad happens. Be creative these first few days to start winning their trust. Attachment begins when you acknowledge their feelings and share their experiences. Shared laughter and shared tears are the glue of parent-child relationships.

We tend to treat orphans as First World kids, overwhelming them with toys, furniture, and clothes. However, they have never even had the luxury of making personal choices regarding style and color. And, if they had the leisure to play, they probably made their own toys from stones, sticks, and paper. Your carefully chosen educational or trendy toys will probably be played with for five minutes and then carefully put back in the toy box. That was our experience with Omar, and countless other adoptive parents have reported similar behavior. Most psychologists agree that parents should separate a child's rights from a child's rewards. After you provide the basics, teach your child that rewards and privileges must be earned.

Your child has likely been eating the cheapest food available with little variety and no second helpings. Each child responds to this situation differently. They may eat the crumbs off the floor and hoard food. At home, your refrigerator and pantry will become a source of wonder and pride. The child may eat twice as much as you do, creating worries about obesity. Such concerns are usually unfounded. Let the child overeat for several months. You can control the calories by carefully shopping for meals and snacks. Children are no different than adults when it comes to seeing food as a comforter. Since their emotional needs have not been met, food soothes the soul, as well as the stomach. As children become more secure, food will lose its importance. Other children may eat very little and be suspicious of new foods. Introduce new foods a tablespoon at a time. Don't worry or fuss about it. In a few months, things will change. Concentrate on meal time as a happy family time. Turn off the TV and get to know your child. Struggles over food can hurt your relationship.

Many parents also report incidents of bedwetting. If you discover your child is a bedwetter (nocturnal enuresis), do not despair. Most children from developing countries are beaten for this problem, thus they will probably try to hide the evidence. Help is available as soon as you get home in the form of behavior modification, bed alarms available from Sears, or large size disposable diapers for nighttime for a while. See a doctor; the condition often responds to treatment within a few weeks.

ARE YOUR EXPECTATIONS FULFILLED? WHAT TO DO IF THEY ARE NOT

Many people feel rather let down when they first see the child they were assigned. Orphanage children often look too small for their ages; they may have a runny nose, flu symptoms, and a bad skin rash. On top of that, they are usually dressed in worn out, ill-fitting orphanage clothes, and often have shaved heads to treat insect bites or lice. Babies may have bald spots on heads that are flattened on the back or one side from spending too much time lying down. Disappointing. After all the work and all the waiting, the child does not match the dream child parents have been carrying around in their heads for so long. Some of this is normal. Mothers and fathers report similar let downs with biological children.

What this tells you is that you don't have to fall in love with the child immediately. You put your best efforts into nurturing the child and hope for the best. Suddenly, you feel more needed than you ever have in your life! Bonding, that much overused word, is a two-way feeling. A good adjustment takes place when the parents are able to overcome their initial disappointment and let their feelings and the child's feelings of love gradually develop.

If you can't stop emotionally rejecting the child, or the child seems to be rejecting you, what do you do? This depends on the kind of person or people you are. Mothers usually take the lead at a time like this, and fathers support them. Parents who do not have high expectations fare the best. If they believe they are good for the child and that the child has a lot of potential, they will show their admiration for the child and make him or her feel special. The parents will put a great deal of effort into building a loving relationship with the child. They realize that it may take years for the child to trust them completely and to believe that they won't go away.

Prior to the adoption, most parents worry about the child's health; however, the major reason children are rejected is due to behavior. Orphanage children have learned to survive in what could be best described as a 24-hour big city public school. They have found ways to protect themselves. Children on the extreme ends of coping behavior worry parents the most — whether it be the depressed, withdrawn child or the child who cries a lot and rejects them. If children have become attached to a caretaker or another child, they are confused as to why they have to leave their "home." They may not be able to trust this new relationship enough to show genuine affection or to depend on you for a long time. They have no concept of what you can do to make them happier, more comfortable, and secure.

The greatest difficulty in making a decision about adopting a child is that you have to make it so fast; usually, you are only given a few days before you must make up your mind about going ahead with the adoption. No one can really advise a parent caught in such a quandary. You can talk to doctors and psychologists abroad, or even by long distance here, but in the end, only you know whether you have the patience and tolerance to raise this child. Think about it as long as possible before making a decision that will affect both you and the child for a very long time.

If you are flooded with feelings that adoption is wrong for you or that this is not the right child for you, stop the legal proceedings. But be gracious. You may still want to adopt someday. Cooperate with all the authorities involved, to assure that the child gets another chance for an adoptive home. Depending upon whether or not you have a final decree, you will need to communicate with your foreign agency or attorney, the U.S. Consulate, the INS, and your local adoption agency to cancel the placement.

OTHER CHILD-PLACEMENT ISSUES

Unfortunately, the U.S.-based adoption agency does not have as much control as they would like over the referral information sent by the child-placing entity abroad, especially countries of the former Soviet Union. Attempts are constantly being made to make these entities more accountable and accurate with their records. Cases occur in which an orphan has medical problems that are more severe or different than those described in the referral information. In other cases, the child is diagnosed with a multitude of health or development problems that are not actually present. Prospective adoptive parents go through a lot of unnecessary anguish in trying to make an informed decision.

Once in a while, the child you were assigned is not the one placed with you abroad. This occasionally happens in China and Bolivia. If the authorities make a substitution, you can be assured it was for a good reason. Serious health concerns or a death would be the usual reason for making the switch. Adopters who have had this happen have had to make some quick adjustments. In China, because of time constraints, the child you receive will probably have the documents of the child you were assigned. You can change the child's name during the readoption in the United States.

CHAPTER 12

Preparing for the Trip Home: Emigration and Immigration

GUARDIANSHIP AND FINAL ADOPTION DECREES

In some countries, you will be given a temporary custody agreement when your child is placed with you. Placement usually occurs the first or second day after your arrival. Countries of the former Soviet Union usually do not allow you to have custody until the child is adopted in their country, although you may visit the child in the orphanage. You may also take the child away from the orphanage during the day, but you will be required to return the child to the orphanage at night. Orphanage directors in other countries may also ask that you return older children at night in order to make the transition easier. Once you are granted a final adoption decree, the temporary custody agreement is no longer in effect.

While lawyers handle adoptions in some countries, government welfare officials or private, licensed institutions handle adoption in others. If you are working through an adoption agency, the agency will engage a lawyer in countries where adoptions are handled by the courts. If you are adopting independently, you will need to contact your own foreign attorney or the national authority in charge of adoptions.

Required Documents

The foreign attorney or other designated official obtains the birth documents (items 1-3 in the following list). After the court hearing and definitely before applying for the orphan visa, adoptive parents should make sure they have the originals and two sets of certified copies with translations attached of the following:

STEP 19
Obtain the guardianship or final adoption decree.

1. Child's birth certificate, showing date and place of birth. Some countries record the child's original name and birth parents, if known. Other countries amend the certificate to show the child's new name and the names of the adoptive parents.

2. A release form signed by the birth mother, birth parents, court, or government welfare office (or if applicable, the death certificates of one or both parents). The release must state the reason for relinquishing the child. The name of the biological father should be stated if known. A release by two parents must be made to an institution.

3. Certificate of abandonment issued by the court after publishing for the child's relatives prior to the court hearing. The certificate grants custody to a legal child-placing entity or to the adoptive parents.

4. Decree issued in that particular country, such as initial adoption decree, final adoption decree, guardianship, or custody transfer, previously explained.

5. The child's passport photos and passport. You will either receive these from the representative, or you will be instructed and assisted in obtaining them. No copy of this is required.

6. A "Permission to Leave the Country" form signed by a judge or other appropriate official, if required. In some countries, this is included in the decree or guardianship.

Additional documents are required in Eastern European countries, such as Russia and those countries of the former Soviet Union.

7. Documents confirming that the child has been registered with the Central Data Bank of orphans at the Ministry of Education and that relatives did not attempt to claim the child and that nationals have not applied to adopt the child.

8. A statement from local child welfare authorities that the adoption is in the child's best interest.

9. If the child is older than 10, a statement of his or her consent to the adoption.

10. A statement of consent from the director of the institution where the child lives.

The U.S. Consular Service abroad has the authority to certify copies and to notarize documents.

General Adoption Proceedings for Russia and Eastern Europe

Although the process may vary depending upon the country, this is the general process for the adoption proceedings in Russia and some countries in Eastern Europe. When the file is complete, the judge has up to 20 days to prepare for the court hearing after which he or she must schedule the hearing within 30 days. Our experience has been that most judges schedule hearings promptly. Up until the time of the hearing, only a summary of the child's social and medical history has been available to the adopters. By the time of the hearing, the full history has been reviewed and translated. You may hear about siblings for the first time as well as parental neglect and abuse of the child.

Adoption cases are heard by the judges in special, closed proceedings. The prospective parents, a state prosecutor, and a representative from the local child welfare organization must attend the hearing. At its discretion, the court may also call the biological parent(s), other relatives or other interested persons, including the child, if over 10 years of age. Ordinarily a representative of the parents' adoption agency is allowed to attend. The hearing is held in the language of the country and the court is responsible for providing interpreters and for the accuracy and quality of the translation. You may wish to consider offering to pay for your own certified interpreter, to spare the court this expense and to guarantee the quality of the interpreting.

The court's decision is issued on the day of the hearing, and, in Russia, it takes effect ten calendar days later unless the judge waives the waiting period. During the ten-day interval, the decision can be appealed. Once it takes effect, the new parents are granted parental rights and full responsibility for the child.

After the decision takes effect, a copy of the court decree must be sent within three days to the local registry office. When the adoption has been officially registered, the new parents can apply for the adoption certificate, a new birth certificate (issued in the child's new name and showing the adoptive parents as the child's parents), and a passport. In some Eastern European passports, the name appears in Cyrillic and in Latin letters. The Latin version of the name is spelled phonetically, not the way you spell it (for example, Murphy will be "Merfi"). The spelling of the child's name in the passport does not have to agree with the way it is spelled on the visa or other documents. After you're back in the United States, you can change the spelling of the name through readoption or reaffirmation in your country of residence.

General Adoption Proceedings for Asia

Adoptions are granted by government departments or ministries in Cambodia, China, and Vietnam rather than by judges in a court of law. For example, the China Center of Adoption Affairs in Beijing supervises adoptions throughout the country. Approximately five days after the child's placement, the international process is complete. The final adoption is granted in a notary office in the provincial capital where the child is sheltered. A few days after the new family appears, a notarial Adoption Certificate is issued along with a Certificate of Abandonment. With these documents, the child's passport and exit visa are obtained at the Public Security Bureau.

In Cambodia, the National Ministry of Foreign Affairs in Phnom Penh arranges adoptions with a method similar to that of China. In Vietnam, provinces are autonomous in regard to adoption. Provincial representatives of the People's Committee, the orphanage, the Department of Justice, and the Police Department hold a "Giving and Receiving Ceremony" for children and their new parents and issue the final adoption decree.

General Adoption Proceedings for Latin America

Although the process may vary slightly depending on the country, in most cases, the foreign attorney will prepare a presentation letter to the family welfare department or the family court of the child's country, if one exists. The presentation letter states the adoptive parents' identity according to the documents you have prepared; the parents' motives for adoption (that the only intention is to make the orphan a legal child and heir); that the adoptive parents will honor the adoption laws of the child's native country; that the adopted child will emigrate to your home address; and that you will notify the family welfare department of any change of address that might occur before you receive the final adoption decree. Adopters who travel abroad may be required to sign this document in the presence of a family welfare official.

Next, the attorney presents the case for preliminary review to the Civil Court for Minors, or a similarly named court. The attorney delivers your dossier of translated, notarized, verified, and authenticated documents to the court for legal consideration and secures a date on the court calendar. When the attorney presents the case, the court verifies that the documentation is legal and complete. Then, it either issues an initial adoption decree and a permanent custody agreement (which is effective until a final adoption decree is issued), or a final decree, or a permanent guardianship agreement (which is effective until the child is adopted in the country of the adoptive parents). Possibly, a family welfare department official may hold the adoption decree for one day to several weeks while he or she reviews the case. This person represents the orphan in court.

After this review, the attorney may direct the adopters to the judge's chambers. The judge may ask for a personal interview with the adoptive parents to study their dossier with them. Depending upon local procedures, the court may issue the final adoption decree anywhere from one week to one month after the case has been presented in court by your attorney. The law office will obtain notary seals for the final decree and present the decree to you in person. The attorney also obtains the child's documents and organizes and helps present them for the child's U.S. visa.

The time needed to complete the foreign adoption process varies from country to country. When all of the required documents are provided, foreign attorneys can complete the adoption process. It may take anywhere from a few days to several months, although two weeks is typical.

No matter where you adopt your child from, remember that your child is still a foreign citizen, traveling on a foreign passport. If you plan to transit a third country (e.g. England, Germany, Holland) on your way back to the United States, check with that country's embassy in Washington, D.C. before your adoption trip to find out whether your child will need a visa. Most embassies abroad do not offer same-day visa service.

MEETING AND COMMUNICATING WITH BIRTH MOTHERS

In Guatemala, it is possible that you may meet the birth mother around the time of the court appearance in order to transfer custody. Naturally, this is an emotionally stressful time for everyone concerned. However, you must remember that the decision was made in the best interest of the child by the birth mother. Such meetings are unlikely in most adoptions. They are illegal in most countries, as well as prohibited by the Hague Convention.

It is important that you keep your last name and address confidential. Some families have received letters from their child's birth mother or relatives requesting money. These are impoverished people who have real needs; however, experience tells us that these requests for money will continue for the rest of your life. Your obligation to the child does not extend to the child's birth mother and her other children and relatives. We strongly recommend that you do not send gifts or money to the birth mother, during or after your trip. Your generosity could be interpreted as buying the baby. If you wish to correspond with the birth mother or family, let the orphanage or your international agency act as your post office.

OBTAINING THE ORPHAN VISA

STEP 20

Apply for the orphan visa and file Form I-600 (Orphan Petition) if this was not filed earlier.

After the child's adoption or guardianship has been granted, the adoptive parents must obtain an orphan visa before the child can enter the United States. An orphan's U.S. visa is obtained at the U.S. Embassy or Consular Section that has jurisdiction over the country in which the child resides. U.S. Embassies are usually located in the capital city of foreign countries. Your adoption agency will take the lead in coordinating most of this. If not, make an appointment at the visa section of the U.S. Embassy or, in some cases, the U.S. Consulate abroad. Since some consuls require additional documents, ask what is required before you appear. Usually, visas are issued the same day as the interview or the day after.

INS requires that the orphan's documents are originals or certified copies. INS also requires English translations of documents in foreign languages. For most adoptions, either the foreign child-placing entity or the U.S.-based adoption agency will arrange for translations. If not, contact the American Consulate for names of translators. The translation must be attached to the original or certified copy. To certify the competency of the translation, a brief statement signed by the translator must accompany the orphan's documents. Typically, this letter must be notarized and/or authenticated for INS. (A sample of a statement of competency letter can be found at the end of Chapter 7.)

Present the original set of documents to the U.S. Consulate abroad and keep the certified copies and copies of the translations. You will need your certified copies when you reaffirm the foreign adoption or readopt, as well as when you apply for the child's social security number and for U.S. citizenship.

Required Documents

You'll need documents 1-10 listed in the discussion of the Guardianship and Final Adoption Decree at the beginning of this chapter. In addition, you'll need the following required documents, which are available at the visa section of the U.S. Consulate.

11. Form I-600, Petition to Classify an Orphan as an Immediate Relative. Depending on the country from which you are adopting, you will file Form I-600 either in the United States or while you are abroad. If you are supposed to file while in the United States, you will be sent a full set of the child's documents prior to your adoption trip. (See Chapter 9). If you are supposed to file while abroad, the orphan's original documents will be given to you or your agency's representative. The completion of Form I-600 and Form OF-230 (the orphan's visa application) is usually done at the same time, at the end of the adoption process. (A sample of Form I-600 can be found at the end of Chapter 9.)

12. Form OF-230, Application for Immigrant Visa and Alien Registration, and a $325.00 filing fee. These forms are available at the U.S. Embassy or Consulate. You will need two copies. (A sample of Form OF-230 can be found at the end of this chapter.)

13. Affidavit by Adoptive Parent or Prospective Adoptive Parent. This form certifies that the new parents will take responsibility to obtain medically appropriate vaccinations for the child in 30 days. (A sample of this form can be found at the end of this chapter.)

14. Medical examination report form for the child issued by a U.S. Embassy-approved doctor. This form is available at the U.S. Consulate. Your agency representative may be able to help you get the form, exam, and vaccination record from the orphanage or the doctor. (A sample of the medical examination report can be found at the end of this chapter.)

15. Three color photographs of the child for the U.S. visa application. Your agency representative may be able to help you obtain the correct visa photos. (Photo specifications for a U.S. visa are included at the end of this chapter.)

You'll also need the following documents, which are generated in the United States. Note: If you file Form I-600 at your local INS office in the United States, INS cables your clearance to the U.S. Consular Office abroad. You will need to take a set of documents 16-20 with you on your trip. You will obtain documents 1-10 from your representative or agency abroad.

16. Copy of your home study. The original is filed in court.

17. Copies of your last three years (most recent) federal income tax forms complete with W-2s and schedules — signed and notarized as "true copies of the original."

18. A recent letter from your employer with an original signature.

19. INS Form I-864, Affidavit of Support, and Form I-864A, Contract Between Sponsor and Household Member. The Affidavit of Support is available at INS offices. Even though the instructions on Form I-864 indicate otherwise, if you are a married couple you must prepare both Form I-864 and Form I-864A. File the originals. One set of forms is required for each child adopted. (A sample of Form I-864 and I-864A can be found at the end of Chapter 6.)

20. INS Form I-171H, Notice of Favorable Determination Concerning Application For Advance Processing. The U.S. Consular office must receive this form. In most states, this clearance is either sent by diplomatic pouch or cable, via Washington, D.C. Bring a copy of your I-171H in case the copy at the U.S. Consular office is missing.

Early Return of One Spouse

If one of the parents plans to return to the United States before the end of the adoption process, the following documents must be provided for the spouse attending the interview. Items 1-3 must be signed by the returning spouse and notarized at the consulate.

1. Power of Attorney form.

2. Form I-600, Petition to Classify an Orphan as an Immediate Relative.

3. Form I-864, Affidavit of Support, and Form I-864A, Contract Between Sponsor and Household Member.

4. A statement from the parent who is returning to the United States confirming that he or she saw the child and reviewed the medical report.

5. Picture of both parents with the child.

6. Copy of the passport of the returning spouse.

Photography for the Orphan Visa

Three photographs of the child in color with a white background must be presented for the orphan visa.

The U.S. Consulate will advise you regarding their approved photographers. INS forms M-370 and M-378, Color Photograph Specifications, show and explain the requirements (see sample at the end of this chapter).

Size of photograph: 4cm x 4cm (1 1/2 inch square).
Head size: 2.54 cm (about 1 inch) from chin to top of hair.
Subject should be shown in 3/4 frontal view showing right side of face with right ear visible.

Lightly print name on the back of each photograph and sign your name on the front left side of two photographs using pencil or felt pen.

Arranging a Medical Evaluation for the Orphan Visa

Every foreign child must have a physical exam conducted by a U.S. Embassy-approved doctor before departing for the United States. In some countries, adoptive parents can also request that the child be taken to a pediatrician for a more thorough evaluation before they obtain custody.

Waivers must be signed by U.S. citizens who adopt foreign orphans with certain disabilities, and this is the reason a medical report from the U.S. Embassy-approved doctor or clinic is required. Before approving the visa, the U.S. Consular service needs to know that the parents are aware of a child's disability and will take full responsibility for the child's care. Waivers must be applied for, but are not necessarily granted for, children diagnosed as Class A and Class B. No waiver is needed for those diagnosed as Class C.

The U.S. Embassy will direct you to an approved physician or clinic that will fill out a medical form. (See sample form at the end of this chapter.)

According to an article in the *American Journal of Diseases of Children*, March 1989, "International Adoption," by Margaret Hostetter, M.D. and Dana E. Johnson, M.D.:

"The quality of this visa medical evaluation is so extraordinarily variable that an assurance of health should be viewed by parents and their physician as confirming only that the child is alive rather than free of unsuspected medical problems. Parents may ask their physician to interpret the classification system (A, B, or C) used by the federal government in the examination. Class A includes psychiatric disorders, mental retardation, and dangerous contagious diseases, including chancroid (venereal ulcer), gonorrhea, granuloma inguinale (inflamed lesion of the groin), infectious leprosy, lymphogranuloma venereum (inflamed lymph nodes of the groin), infectious syphilis, active (untreated) tuberculosis, and as of December 1, 1987, human immunodeficiency virus (HIV) infection."

"Parenthetically, testing for HIV-seropositivity is not required in children younger than 15 years unless they have a history (hemophilia or an HIV-positive parent) or signs and symptoms suggestive of the disease. Therefore, few children will actually be screened for acquired immunodeficiency syndrome (AIDS) before their arrival in the United States. Class B is defined as physical defect, disease, or disability serious in degree or permanent in nature amounting to a substantial departure from normal physical well-being. Although this category sounds ominous, minor cosmetic defects, such as occipital hemangiomas or dark red birthmarks (stork bites), are often placed in Class B. Class C is defined as minor conditions. If the overseas investigation is successfully concluded, the child is issued a permanent resident's visa and can then be admitted to the United States."

When an orphan is so ill that he or she must travel to the United States immediately, adopters who have fulfilled their state and federal requirements may apply for a visitor's visa for their child that is specifically issued for medical emergencies. Before attempting to have the child emigrate for emergency medical reasons, adoptive parents should discuss the procedures with the appropriate U.S. Consular Service Office. They must present a statement from a doctor that describes the medical emergency and explains the need for that child to undergo medical treatment at once in the United States. Once in the United States, adopters must apply for permanent resident status for the child.

When an orphan is not only critically ill but resides in a war-torn country, the potential adopters may apply for a humanitarian parole, with as much documented evidence as possible. The help of a member of Congress is essential, but does not guarantee success.

Orphan Visas IR-2, IR-3, and IR-4

Upon completion and submission of all of the required paperwork, your child will be issued one of the three types of U.S. visas listed below. The visa number is stamped in your child's passport. Check the visa number stamped in the passport; immigration officials can make mistakes and record the wrong type of visa.

- ***Visa IR-4.*** Orphan to be adopted in the United States by a citizen and spouse (or single parent). IR-4 is used in countries where the adoption process is not completed before the visa is filed. The court issues a guardianship agreement or an initial adoption decree. This visa is also issued if both adoptive parents have not observed the child prior to final adoption, since the child must be readopted in the United States.

- ***Visa IR-3.*** Orphan adopted abroad by a U.S. citizen and spouse (or single parent). IR-3 is used for orphan visas in countries where the adoption decree can be presented to the U.S. Consulate before the visa is issued. Both adoptive parents must observe the orphan prior to adoption in the foreign country to receive this visa.

- ***Visa IR-2.*** Applies to orphans who have lived abroad with their adoptive parents for at least two years. Documented proof that the orphan has lived with the parents for two years must be provided.

It should be noted here that you do not need a U.S. lawyer until three to six months after the child has immigrated with an IR-4 visa under a guardianship or initial adoption decree. Then you will need to consummate the adoption in your state of residence. If the child immigrates with an IR-3 visa, under a final adoption decree, your state may recognize this final decree and you will only need to reaffirm or certify the adoption in court. If you were unable to change the child's name abroad, you will need to change it at the readoption or reaffirmation, unless a simpler means of a name change is available in your county. The name change is important for the child's social security number and U.S. citizenship.

U.S. State Requirements and Importation Laws

Since each of our fifty states has its own set of laws concerning adoptions, every adopter must take the responsibility for knowing and understanding his or her state's requirements concerning the importation of a foreign child into that state.

In some countries, a permanent guardianship decree is issued rather than a final adoption decree. This document permits a child to leave the country based on the adopter's promise of a future adoption at home. In all cases, adopters must have completed their home study, their state's preadoption requirements, and INS requirements. To discover which countries issue permanent guardianships or final decrees, see the adoption law summaries in the Compendium.

THE TRIP HOME

Once you have your child's visa, you are ready for the trip home.

Book your return trip before leaving the United States. Request bulkhead seats where there is more room. Also request a baby bed on your return flight. It cannot be reserved for you, as they are given on a first-come, first-serve basis.

Confirm your international return flight seventy-two hours before departure so as not to get bumped. Be at the airport at least two hours early. If you have a baby, prepare six bottles of the formula for the flight. Pour the amount of powdered formula needed into each bottle. Ask the cabin attendants to add water for one bottle at feeding time. Include pre-moistened towelettes to clean the child, since washing on board is difficult.

On the airplane during takeoff and landing, be certain the baby is sucking on a bottle or pacifier. This will prevent painful pressure on the delicate eardrum. Older children can be given candy to suck or gum to chew. You may consider taking children's Dramamine along, in case the child has motion sickness. Some kids fight being buckled in. Bring toys and activities for the flight.

The flight home is symbolic, recalled almost as a rebirth to children age two and up. Make it as pleasant as possible — the memory will be with them forever.

The Airport Tax

Have foreign cash ready at the airport to pay a departure tax for yourself and your child. People leaving foreign countries, regardless of whether they are citizens, adopted children, or travelers, usually have to pay the foreign governments this kind of tax. In Asia and European countries, the tax is included in your ticket. If it is not included, find out how much it is when you buy your airline tickets. The tax must be paid in foreign currency or U.S. dollars. Traveler's checks are not accepted. You will need to have this amount with you when checking in for your trip home.

U.S. Immigration upon Arrival

At the same time that the child's temporary U.S. visa is presented to you, the visa-issuing office will also give you a sealed envelope containing the original supporting documents you filed for the child's visa. A list of the contained documents appears on the outside of the envelopes. (Officials in some countries must see this when you exit.)

When your flight arrives in the United States, the child's foreign passport will be stamped by INS with a temporary visa, valid for several months. Present the sealed envelope to U.S immigration. INS will forward the papers to the office where you filed Form I-600A, Application for Advance Processing of Orphan Petition. If you were unable to retain a set of originals or certified copies, you can get them once they arrive at your district INS office. To receive a set of the documents you presented in the sealed envelope at the U.S. port of entry, request from the INS Form G-884, Request for Return of Original Documents. The alien card will be mailed to you. If the alien card does not appear within three months, request INS Form G-731, Inquiry About Status of I-551 Alien Registration Card.

Form OF-230

U.S. Visa Application, Page 1 of 4

OMB APPROVAL NO. 1405-0015   EXPIRES 8-31-92   *ESTIMATED BURDEN: 1 HOUR

APPLICATION FOR IMMIGRANT VISA AND ALIEN REGISTRATION

PART 1 - BIOGRAPHIC DATA

INSTRUCTIONS: Complete one copy of this form for yourself and each member of your family, regardless of age, who will immigrate with you. Please print or type your answer to all questions. Questions that are not applicable should be so marked. If there is insufficient room on the form, answer on a separate sheet using the same numbers as appear on the form. Attach the sheet to this form.

WARNING: Any false statement or concealment of a material fact may result in your permanent expulsion from the United States.

This form is Part I of two parts which, together with Optional Form OF-230 PART II, constitute the complete Application for Immigrant Visa and Alien Registration.

1. FAMILY NAME   FIRST NAME   MIDDLE NAME

2. OTHER NAMES USED OR BY WHICH KNOWN (If married woman, give maiden name)

3. FULL NAME IN NATIVE ALPHABET (If Roman letters not used)

4. DATE OF BIRTH
   (Day)   (Month)   (Year)

5. AGE

6. PLACE OF BIRTH
   (City or town)   (Province)   (Country)

7. NATIONALITY (If dual national, give both)

8. SEX
   ☐ Male
   ☐ Female

9. MARITAL STATUS
   ☐ Single (Never married)   ☐ Married   ☐ Widowed   ☐ Divorced   ☐ Separated

   Including my present marriage, I have been married _____ times.

10. PERSONAL DESCRIPTION
    a. Color of hair _____   c. Height _____
    b. Color of eyes _____   d. Complexion _____

11. OCCUPATION

12. MARKS OF IDENTIFICATION

13. PRESENT ADDRESS

    Telephone number: Home   Office

14. NAME OF SPOUSE (Maiden or family name)   (First name)   (Middle name)

    Date and place of birth of spouse:

    Address of spouse (if different from your own):

15. LIST NAME, DATE AND PLACE OF BIRTH, AND ADDRESSES OF ALL CHILDREN

NAME	DATE AND PLACE OF BIRTH	ADDRESS (If different from your own)

THIS FORM MAY BE OBTAINED GRATIS AT CONSULAR OFFICES OF THE UNITED STATES OF AMERICA

NSN 7540-00-149-0919
50230-106

OPTIONAL FORM 230 I (English)
REVISED 4-91
DEPT. OF STATE

Form OF-230

U.S. Visa Application, Page 2 of 4

16. PERSONS NAMED IN 14 AND 15 WHO WILL ACCOMPANY OR FOLLOW ME TO THE UNITED STATES.

17. NAME OF FATHER, DATE AND PLACE OF BIRTH, AND ADDRESS (If deceased, so state, giving year of death)

18. MAIDEN NAME OF MOTHER, DATE AND PLACE OF BIRTH, AND ADDRESS (If deceased, so state, giving year of death)

19. IF NEITHER PARENT IS LIVING PROVIDE NAME AND ADDRESS OF NEXT OF KIN (nearest relative) IN YOUR HOME COUNTRY.

20. LIST ALL LANGUAGES YOU CAN SPEAK, READ, AND WRITE

NAME	SPEAK	READ	WRITE

21. LIST BELOW ALL PLACES YOU HAVE LIVED FOR SIX MONTHS OR LONGER SINCE REACHING THE AGE OF 16.

CITY OR TOWN	PROVINCE	COUNTRY	OCCUPATION	DATES (FROM - TO)

22. LIST ANY POLITICAL, PROFESSIONAL, OR SOCIAL ORGANIZATIONS AFFILIATED WITH COMMUNIST, TOTALITARIAN, TERRORIST OR NAZI ORGANIZATIONS WHICH YOU ARE NOW OR HAVE BEEN A MEMBER OF OR AFFILIATED WITH SINCE YOUR 16TH BIRTHDAY.

NAME AND ADDRESS	FROM/TO	TYPE OF MEMBERSHIP

23. LIST DATES OF ALL PREVIOUS RESIDENCE IN OR VISITS TO THE UNITED STATES. (If never, so state) GIVE TYPE OF VISA STATUS IF ANY. GIVE I.N.S. "A" NUMBER IF ANY.

LOCATION	FROM/TO	VISA	I.N.S. FILE NO. (If known)

SIGNATURE OF APPLICANT

DATE

NOTE: Return this completed form immediately to the consular office address on the covering letter. This form will become part of your immigrant visa and your visa application cannot be processed until this form is complete.

*Public reporting burden for this collection of information is estimated to average 24 hrs per response, including time required for searching existing data sources, gathering necessary data, providing the information required, and reviewing final collection. Send comments on the accuracy of this estimate of the burden and recommendations for reducing it to: Department of State (OIS/RA/DR) Washington, D.C. 20520-0264, and to the Office of information and Regulatory Affairs. Office of Management and Budget, Paperwork Reduction Project (1405-0015), Washington, D.C. 20503

Form OF-230

U.S. Visa Application, Page 3 of 4

EXPIRES 00-00-00
*ESTIMATED BURDEN: 24 HOURS

APPLICATION FOR IMMIGRANT VISA AND ALIEN REGISTRATION

PART II - SWORN STATEMENT

INSTRUCTIONS: Complete one copy of this form for yourself and each member of your family, regardless of age, who will immigrate with you. Please print or type your answer to all questions. Questions that are not applicable should be so marked. If there is insufficient room on the form, answer on a separate sheet using the same numbers as appear on the form. Attach the sheet to this form. DO NOT sign this form until instructed to do so by the consular officer. The fee for filing this application is listed under tariff item No. 20. The fee should be paid in United States dollars or local currency equivalent, or by bank draft, when you appear before the consular officer.

WARNING: Any false statement or concealment of a material fact may result in your permanent expulsion from the United States. Even though you should be admitted to the United States, a fraudulent entry could be grounds for your prosecution and/or deportation.

This form is a continuation of Form OF-230 Part I, which together, constitute the complete Application for Immigrant Visa and Alien Registration.

24. FAMILY NAME   FIRST NAME   MIDDLE NAME

25. ADDRESS (Local)

Telephone No.

26. FINAL ADDRESS TO WHICH YOU WILL TRAVEL IN THE UNITED STATES (Street Address including ZIP code)

Telephone No.

27. PERSON YOU INTEND TO JOIN (Name, address, and relationship)

28. NAME AND ADDRESS OF SPONSORING PERSON AND EMPLOYER

29. PURPOSE IN GOING TO THE UNITED STATES

30. LENGTH OF INTENDED STAY (If permanently, so state)

31. INTENDED PORT OF ENTRY

32. DO YOU HAVE A TICKET TO FINAL DESTINATION?
☐ No   ☐ Yes

33. United States laws governing the issuance of visas require each applicant to state whether or not he or she is member of an class individuals excluded from admission into the United States. The excludable classes are described below in general terms. You should read carefully the following list and answer YES or NO to each category. The answers you give will assist the consular officer to reach a decision on your eligibility to receive a visa.

EXCEPT AS OTHERWISE PROVIDED BY LAW, ALIENS WITHIN THE FOLLOWING
CLASSIFICATIONS ARE INELIGIBLE TO RECIEVE A VISA.
DO ANY OF THE FOLLOWING CLASSES APPLY TO YOU?

a. An alien who has a communicable disease of public health significance, or has or has had a physical or mental disorder that poses, or is likely to pose a threat to the safety or welfare of the alien or others; an alien who is a drug abuser or addict. [212(a)(1)]   YES ☐   NO ☐

b. An alien convicted of, or who admits committing a crime involving moral turpitude, or violation of any law relating to a controlled substance; an alien convicted of 2 or more offenses of which the aggregate sentences were 5 years or more; an alien coming to the United States to engage in prostitution or commercialized vice, or has engaged in prostitution or procuring within the past 10 years; an alien who is or has been an illicit trafficker in any controlled substance; an alien who has committed a serious criminal offense in the United States and who has asserted immunity from prosecution. [212(a)(2)]   YES ☐   NO ☐

c. An alien who seeks to enter the United States in espionage, sabotage, export control violations, overthrow of the Government of the United States, or other unlawful activity; an alien who seeks to enter the United States to engage in terrorist activities; an alien who has been a member or affiliated with the Communist or any other totalitarian party; an alien who under the direction of the Nazi government of Germany, or any are occupied by, or allied with the Nazi government of Germany, ordered, incited, assisted, or otherwise participated in the persecution of any person because of race, religion, national origin, or political opinion; an alien who has engaged in genocide. [212(a)(3)]   YES ☐   NO ☐

d. An alien who has become a public charge. [212 (a)(4)]   YES ☐   NO ☐

e. An alien who seeks to enter for the purpose of performing skilled or unskilled labor who has not been certified by the Secretary of Labor; an alien graduate of a foreign medical school seeking to perform medical services who has not passed the NMBE exam or its equivalent. [212(a)(5)]   YES ☐   NO ☐   Not Applicable ☐

f. An alien previously deported within one year, or arrested and deported within 5 years; an alien who seeks or has sought a visa, entry into the United States, or any U.S. Immigration benefit by fraud or misrepresentation; an alien who knowingly assisted any other alien to enter or try to enter into the United States in violation of the law; an alien who is in violation of Section 274C of the Immigration Act. [212(a)(6)]   YES ☐   NO ☐

THIS FORM MAY BE OBTAINED GRATIS AT CONSULAR OFFICES OF THE UNITED STATES OF AMERICA

Previous editions obsolete

OPTIONAL FORM 230 II (English)
REVISED 4-91
DEPT. OF STATE

g. An alien who is permanently ineligible to U.S. citizenship; a person who has departed the United States to evade military service in time of war. [212(a)(8)] Yes ☐ No ☐

h. An alien who is coming to the United States to practice polygamy; an alien is to a guardian required to accompany an excluded alien; an alien who withholds custody of a child outside the United States from a United States citizen granted legal custody. [212(a)(9)] Yes ☐ No ☐

An alien who is a former exchange visitor who has not fulfilled the 2-year foreign residence requirement. [212(e)] Yes ☐ No ☐

If the answer to any of the foregoing questions is YES or if unsure, explain in the following space on a separate piece of paper.

34. Have you ever been arrested, convicted, or ever been in a prison or jailhouse; have you ever been the beneficiary of a pardon or an amnesty; have you ever been treated in an institution or hospital or other place for insanity or other mental disease? [222(a)] Yes ☐ No ☐

35. I am unlikely to become a public charge because of the following:
☐ Personal financial resources (describe)　　☐ Employment (attach)　　☐ Affidavit of Support (attach)

36. Have you ever applied for a visa to enter the United States? Yes ☐ No ☐
(If answer is yes, state where and when, whether you applied for a nonimmigrant or an immigrant visa, and whether the visa was issued or refused)

37. Have you ever been refused admission to the United States? Yes ☐ No ☐
(If answer is yes, explain)

38. Were you assisted in completing this application? Yes ☐ No ☐
(If the answer is yes, give name and address of person assisting you, indicating whether relative, friend, travel agent, attorney, or other)
Name　　　　　　　　　Address　　　　　　　　　Relationship

39. The following documents are submitted in support of this application:

☐ Passport	☐ Military record	☐ Evidence of own assets
☐ Birth certificate	☐ Police record	☐ Affidavit of support
☐ Marriage certificate	☐ Medical records	☐ Offer of employment
☐ Death certificate	☐ Photographs	☐ Other (describe)
☐ Divorce decree	☐ Birth certificate of all children who will not be immigrating at this time. (List those for whom birth certificate is not available.)	

DO NOT WRITE BELOW THIS LINE
The consular officer will assist you in answering items 40 and 41.

40. I claim to be exempt from ineligibility to receive a visa an exclusion under item _____ in part 33 for the following reasons:

212(a)(5)　　　　　　　　Beneficiary of a waiver under:

☐ Not applicable	☐ 212(a)(3)(D)(ii)	☐ 212(e)	☐ 212(h)
☐ Not required	☐ 212(a)(3)(D)(iii)	☐ 212(g)(1)	☐ 212(j)
☐ Attached	☐ 212(a)(3)(D)(iv)	☐ 212(g)(2)	

41. I claim to be:
☐ A Family-Sponsored Immigrant
☐ An employment based Immigrant
☐ A diversity Immigrant
☐ A special category (Specify) _____
(Return resident, Hong Kong, Tibetan, Private Legislation, etc.)

☐ I derive foreign state chargeability under Sec. 202(b) through my _____

I am subject to the following:
☐ Preference: _____
☐ Numerical limitation: _____
(foreign state)

I understand that I am required to surrender my visa to the United States Immigration Officer at the place where I apply to enter the United States, and that the possession of a visa does not entitle me to enter the United States if at that time I am found to be inadmissible under the Immigration laws.
I understand that any willfully false or misleading statement or willful concealment of a material fact made by me herein may subject me to permanent exclusion from the United States and, if I am admitted to the United States, may subject me to criminal prosecution and/or deportation.
I, the undersigned applicant for a United States Immigrant visa, do solemnly swear (or affirm) that all statements which appear in this application, consisting of Optional Forms 230 PART I and 230 PART II combined, have been made by me, including the answers to items 1 through 41 inclusive, and that they are true and complete to the best of my knowledge and belief. I do further swear (or affirm) that, if admitted to the United States, I will not engage in activities which would be prejudicial to the public interest, or endanger the welfare, safety, or security of the United States; in activities which would be prohibited by the laws of the United States relating to espionage, sabotage, public disorder, or in other activities subversive to the national security; in any activity a purpose of which is the opposition to or the control, or overthrow of, the Government of the United States, by force, violence, or other unconstitutional means.
I understand all the foregoing statements, having asked for and obtained an explanation on every point which was not clear to me.

The relationship claimed in Items 14 and 15 verified by documentation submitted to consular officer except as noted:

_____
(Signature of applicant)

Subscribed and sworn to before me this _____ day of _____, 19_____ at:_____

_____
(Consular Officer)

TARIFF ITEM NO. 20

Affidavit of Adoptive Parent

AFFIDAVIT BY ADOPTIVE PARENT OR PROSPECTIVE ADOPTIVE PARENT

I, _____, certify that I am the
        (Name)
adoptive parent or prospective adoptive parent of a child,

_____, on whose behalf I have
        (Name if known)
filed or will file an I-600 Petition (Petition to Classify
Orphan as Immediate Relative) according said child status as an
orphan as defined by Section 101(b)(1)(F).

I have read the statement on the reverse of this form and I am
aware of the vaccination requirement set forth in Section
212(a)(1)(A)(ii) of the Immigration and Nationality Act. In
accordance with Section 212(a)(1)(A)(ii), I will ensure that my
foreign adopted child receives the required and medically
appropriate vaccinations within 30 days after his or her
admission into the United States, or at the earliest time that
is medically appropriate.

Signed this _____ day of _____, ____, at _____.
            (date)   (month) (year)   (location)

_____
(Signature of parent)

Subscribed and sworn to (or affirmed) before me this _____ day
                                                        (date)
of _____,____, at _____.
   (month) (year)   (location)
My Commission expires on _____.
                                (date)

_____
(Signature of Notary Public or Officer Administering Oath)

Form M-370

Color Photo Specifications

U. S. IMMIGRATION & NATURALIZATION SERVICE

COLOR PHOTOGRAPH
SPECIFICATIONS

IDEAL PHOTOGRAPH ◄

IMAGE MUST FIT INSIDE THIS
BOX ►

THE PICTURE AT LEFT IS IDEAL SIZE, COLOR, BACKGROUND, AND POSE. THE IMAGE SHOULD BE 30MM (1 3/16IN) FROM THE HAIR TO JUST BELOW THE CHIN, AND 26MM (1 IN) FROM LEFT CHEEK TO RIGHT EAR. THE IMAGE MUST FIT IN THE BOX AT RIGHT.

THE PHOTOGRAPH
* THE OVERALL SIZE OF THE PICTURE, INCLUDING THE BACKGROUND, MUST BE AT LEAST 40MM (1 9/16 INCHES) IN HEIGHT BY 35MM (1 3/8IN) IN WIDTH.

* PHOTOS MUST BE FREE OF SHADOWS AND CONTAIN NO MARKS, SPLOTCHES, OR DISCOLORATIONS.

* PHOTOS SHOULD BE HIGH QUALITY, WITH GOOD BACK LIGHTING OR WRAP AROUND LIGHTING, AND MUST HAVE A WHITE OR OFF-WHITE BACKGROUND.

* PHOTOS MUST BE A GLOSSY OR MATTE FINISH AND UN-RETOUCHED.

* POLAROID FILM HYBRID #5 IS ACCEPTABLE; HOWEVER SX-70 TYPE FILM OR ANY OTHER INSTANT PROCESSING TYPE FILM IS UNACCEPTABLE. NON-PEEL APART FILMS ARE EASILY RECOGNIZED BECAUSE THE BACK OF THE FILM IS BLACK. ACCEPTABLE INSTANT COLOR FILM HAS A GRAY-TONED BACKING.

THE IMAGE OF THE PERSON
* THE DIMENSIONS OF THE IMAGE SHOULD BE 30MM (1 3/16 INCHES) FROM THE HAIR TO THE NECK JUST BELOW THE CHIN, AND 26MM (1 INCH) FROM THE RIGHT EAR TO THE LEFT CHEEK. IMAGE CANNOT EXCEED 32MM BY 28MM (1 1/4IN X 1 1/16IN).

* IF THE IMAGE AREA ON THE PHOTOGRAPH IS TOO LARGE OR TOO SMALL, THE PHOTO CANNOT BE USED.

* PHOTOGRAPHS MUST SHOW THE ENTIRE FACE OF THE PERSON IN A 3/4 VIEW SHOWING THE RIGHT EAR AND LEFT EYE.

* FACIAL FEATURES **MUST BE IDENTIFIABLE.**

* CONTRAST BETWEEN THE IMAGE AND BACKGROUND IS ESSENTIAL. PHOTOS FOR VERY LIGHT SKINNED PEOPLE SHOULD BE SLIGHTLY UNDER-EXPOSED. PHOTOS FOR VERY DARK SKINNED PEOPLE SHOULD BE SLIGHTLY OVER-EXPOSED.

SAMPLES OF UNACCEPTABLE PHOTOGRAPHS

INCORRECT POSE

IMAGE TOO LARGE

IMAGE TOO SMALL

IMAGE TOO DARK
UNDER-EXPOSED

IMAGE TOO LIGHT

DARK BACKGROUND

OVER-EXPOSED

SHADOWS ON PIC

Immigration & Naturalization Service
Form M-378 (6-92)

Medical Examination for U.S. Visa

MEDICAL EXAMINATION OF APPLICANTS FOR UNITED STATES VISAS	PLACE
	DATE OF EXAMINATION (Mo., Day, Yr.)

At the request of the Amercian Consul at | CITY | COUNTRY

| I certify that on the above date I examined | NAME (Last in CAPS) (First) (Middle) | DATE OF BIRTH (Mo., Day, Yr.) | SEX ☐ F ☐ M |
| | WHO BEARS PASSPORT NO. | ISSUED BY | ON |

GENERAL PHYSICAL EXAMINATION
I examined specifically for evidence of the conditions listed below. My examination revealed:
☐ No apparant defect, disease, or disability
☐ The conditions listed below were found *(Check boxes that apply)*

CLASS A CONDITIONS *(Give pertinent details under remarks)*   **CLASS B CONDITIONS**

☐ Chanorold
☐ Gonorrhea
☐ Granuloma Inguinale

☐ Hansen's Disease, Infectious
☐ Lymphogranuloma Venereum
☐ Syphilis, Infectious

☐ Tuberculosis, Active
☐ Human Immunodeficiency Virus (HIV) Infection

☐ Tuberculosis, Not Active
☐ Hansen's Disease, Not Infectious
☐ Other Physical Defect, Disease or Disability: _____

☐ Mental Retardation
☐ Insanity
☐ Sexual Deviation

☐ Previous Occurance of One or More attacks of Insanity
☐ Psychopathic Personality

☐ Mental Defect
☐ Narcotic Drug Addiction
☐ Chronic Alcoholism

EXAMINATION FOR TUBERCULOSIS

CHEST X-RAY REPORT

☐ Normal   ☐ Abnormal   ☐ Not Done

Describe findings:

DOCTOR'S NAME *(Please print)* | DATE READ

TUBERCULIN SKIN TEST *(See USPHS Instructions)*

☐ No Reaction

☐ Reaction _____ mm

☐ Not Done

DOCTOR'S NAME *(Please print)*

DATE READ

SEROLOGIC TEST FOR SYPHILIS

☐ Reactive Titer (Confirmatory test performed - Indicate treatment under Remarks)
☐ Nonreactive
☐ Not Done

TEST TYPE:

SEROLOGIC TEST FOR HIV ANTIBODY

☐ Positive (Confirmed by Western Biot or equally reliable test)
☐ Negative
☐ Not Done

TEST TYPE:

DOCTOR'S NAME *(Please print)* | DATE READ | DOCTOR'S NAME *(Please print)* | DATE READ

OTHER SPECIAL REPORT(S) *(When needed)*

DOCTOR'S NAME *(Please print)*

REMARKS

APPLICANT CERTIFICATION

I certify that I understand the purpose of the medical examination and I authorize the required tests to be completed. The information on this form refers to me.

Signature | Date

DOCTOR'S NAME *(Please type or print clearly)* | DOCTOR'S SIGNATURE | DATE

OPTIONAL FORM 157
Revised 2-88
DEPT. OF STATE

CHAPTER 13

Health Problems of Orphans from Developing Countries

Acute medical conditions that adoptive parents might need to cope with during their first weeks with their child are covered in this chapter. Long-term medical and developmental problems are not within the scope of this book. The Bibliography cites organizations that provide information on chronic medical conditions, such as maternal lifestyles and their effect on the fetus, as well as fetal alcohol syndrome, fetal alcohol effect, prematurity, and low birth weight. Other issues prospective adoptive parents need to educate themselves about are the effects of parental abuse and neglect, institutional-ization, and developmental disabilities, especially speech.

The general health of children adopted internationally depends a great deal upon the condition of the child at the time of relinquishment and the quality of the orphanage or foster care. We have seen children in excellent health, but more often, they have a degree of malnutrition, some intestinal parasites, and acute illnesses, such as colds. These are quickly remedied with a loving home and medical attention. Babies and children come from impoverished environments and often arrive at orphanages and foster homes with malnutrition, lice, scabies, skin problems, worms or parasites, diarrhea, and infectious diseases. Sometimes the orphanage or hospital where the child lives may expose him to all these health conditions and even more.

U.S. health insurance coverage is now regulated by a federal health insur-ance act, Public Law 104-91, which, among other things, limits the ability of some group insurance providers to exclude coverage of pre-existing conditions in adopted children. Most group insurance plans will cover adopted children — sometimes even while the children are still abroad.

Contact your insurance provider for complete details of your plan's coverage. Adoptive parents must notify their insurance carriers within 30 days of the child's placement or adoption.

Children of developing nations get all of the diseases U.S. children do with an important difference. Many foreign children have never had the series of vaccinations commonly administered to U.S. children. Consequently, complications and disabilities are sometimes caused by entirely preventable childhood diseases, such as measles or poliomyelitis. Their effects, as well as birth defects, injuries, and common illnesses often go untreated since the poor cannot afford medical care. In addition, simple conditions are often complicated by the effects of poor nutrition. Most disabled orphans face a bleak future in these countries. As adopted children, they have made some spectacular recoveries.

In the United States, all children are eligible for free orthopedic correction or surgery for burns from the Shriners Hospital network. Middle-income families whose quality of life will change if they must pay for a child's expenses themselves may apply to the nearest Shriners Hospital for Crippled Children. Donations from the Shriners make it possible for these hospitals to serve newborns and children up to sixteen years of age. The Shriners maintain twenty-one hospitals on the U.S. mainland, one in Hawaii, one in Mexico City, and one in Manitoba. Families apply to the Shriners Medical Board and Board of Governors, who review and accept applications within two to three weeks.

Many states also have federally funded programs for children with disabilities (usually called Children's Special Health Care Services). Some states have free eligibility for adopted children while others have a sliding scale for fees.

The immigration evaluation for visa approval is not a stamp of approval of the child's health. Most of the health conditions affecting internationally adopted children are not "excludable conditions" and may not be noted at the visa physical.

The American Academy of Pediatrics recommends the following for all newly arrived, adopted, immigrant children, regardless of age, country of origin, or apparent health.

Blood tests for
   HIV 1 and 2
   Syphilis
   Hepatitis B
   Hepatitis C
   Complete blood count
Stool samples for ova and parasites
Skin test (Mantoux) for tuberculosis
Update of all immunizations

The following sections include introductory information about common and more severe illnesses.

IMMUNIZATIONS

Most countries begin immunizations at birth with the BCG or tuberculosis vaccine. Other immunizations are typically given by the World Health Organization (WHO) schedule, which is different than the U.S. schedule (fewer diseases covered, doses at younger ages, and closer intervals). If your child has not been immunized, wait until you are home to begin the series of inoculations. Regardless of whether your child has an existing record of immunizations, you should consult your pediatrician about reimmunizing upon your return home. Many pediatricians do not accept vaccination records from developing countries because the vaccines may not have been kept refrigerated or they may have expired before being used. Both circumstances diminish their effectiveness. Infants and toddlers may be revaccinated without harm. Blood serum tests may be conducted on older children to determine their immunity to diphtheria, tetanus, measles, mumps, rubella, and chicken pox. The tests may indicate a need for booster vaccines.

DETERMINING THE AGE OF CHILDREN

In the case of abandoned children, or those without records, a doctor must make an educated guess as to the child's age. Neglected and malnourished children are usually quite short for their age and, generally, look and act much younger than they actually are. This is to the child's benefit since he or she has a lot of catching up to do, both physically and socially. U.S. doctors and dentists can make educated guesses about a child's age by looking at the teeth and bone x-rays, although the variation in these tests is great — typically plus or minus six to twelve months. However, because of catch-up growth, it is usually best to delay deciding on an age for as long as possible, preferably a year.

MALNUTRITION

Most children arriving in the United States from institutional care have mild caloric deprivation or mild to serious psychosocial dwarfism. Given love, nourishment, and medical care, they rapidly develop into normal little kids. Although the relationship of severe malnutrition in infancy and childhood to brain damage is a well established fact, seriously affected children are not typically selected for adoptions. Studies of severe malnutrition in infancy and childhood do show that children may experience persistent and permanent cognitive, behavioral, and social defects — the severity of the effects are impacted by the age of onset of malnutrition, the length of time of caloric deprivation, and other existing health conditions, such as premature birth and fetal alcohol syndrome (FAS). However, the damage of even severe malnutrition may be ameliorated by the age of rehabilitation (the younger the better), better social environments, and adequate educational support. Long-term studies of malnourished children show generally good outcomes, especially if the child is adopted before the age of three years. Prospective adoptive parents with concerns about the effects of malnutrition should visit with parents who have adopted foreign children who were once in this condition.

Many adopted children have phenomenal appetites and will eat whatever is presented to them. Some children will not know when to stop eating. They may gain weight initially, although their weight will level off as catch-up growth ensues and they begin growing taller. Serve them well balanced meals and snacks. A daily multi-vitamin tablet is also helpful. If the child shows no acceleration in growth, an underlying illness such as tuberculosis may be suspected.

U.S. pediatricians use the National Center for Health Statistics growth chart, which is also used by the World Health Organization. This chart indicates population standards divided into the fifth, tenth, twenty-fifth, fiftieth, seventy-fifth, ninetieth, and ninety-fifth percentiles. Ninety percent of the population should be covered by these charts. By plotting the child's growth, the doctor knows what percentile is normal for this child and can also see if the child's growth has slowed. In normal growth, the child's measurements follow along one of the percentile lines on the chart. If growth slows, the measurements cross percentile lines. The doctor can see if the child has recovered by plotting his or her return to normal. This system depends on taking repeated measurements in order to establish the normal patterns of growth.

Malnourished or neglected children, of course, do not have a normal growth pattern. Adoptive parents are usually very disappointed at their first appointment with a pediatrician because their child does not measure up to ideal U.S. standards. Upon placement in a nurturing adoptive home, however, the children's sizes change dramatically, due to the advent of "catch-up" growth. Catch-up growth may continue for years after placement. Your child's recovery from malnutrition is complete when height and weight are in proportion to each other, and the child is growing at a steady pace in a typical growth diagram.

DEVELOPMENTAL DELAYS

The majority of internationally adopted children are mildly to severely delayed due to malnutrition, neglect, or illness. Upon your return, make contacts with Early Childhood Intervention (ECI) specialists through your county or public school system. Ask them to send their literature for review. ECI specialists meet with parents and children in their homes and in the community to demonstrate techniques to assist children with the development of speech and fine and gross motor skills, etc. ECI is funded by the federal government and provides a range of services to developmentally delayed children under the age of three. Free ECI programs have been established throughout the United States.

General information about developmental delays and ECI programs can be found at http://www.nectas.unc.edu/. In addition, the main contact number for each state can be found by following links on the same Web site or by going directly to http://www.nectas.unc.edu/makecx/cendir.html. Also, see the section on screening tests at the end of this chapter.

COMMON WORMS AND PARASITES

Adopted orphans have had as many as five varieties of parasites at once, some active, some in a cyst-like stage, and some in an ova (egg) stage. Most chronic parasitic infections produce no symptoms at all. The child's stool should be tested two or three times, two to three weeks apart after arrival.

For diaper changes, be certain to lay the baby on a washable or disposable surface and wash your hands thoroughly afterwards. If needed, antiparastic drugs can be special ordered by your pharmacy or from the Parastic Drug Division of the Centers for Disease Control and Prevention in Atlanta at (404) 639-3311. Adoptive parents and siblings also should be tested if they exhibit any symptoms after the arrival of the adopted child.

Within the first month, if an infant or child has profuse diarrhea (more than one stool every two hours) or there is obvious blood or pus in the stool, seek help immediately. Begin an oral rehydration solution (ORS) such as Pedialyte, while taking the child to the nearest medical care.

The most common worms and parasites found among adopted children are amoebas, roundworm, tapeworm, pinworm, giardia, hookworm, lice, and scabies.

Amoebas (one-celled organisms): The symptoms of amoebas are dysentery, dizziness, nausea, weight loss, or failure to gain weight. Left untreated, amoebas can cause colitis, bleeding ulcers, and in rare cases a liver abscess. The treatment is Metronidazole. Amoebas are transmitted through contaminated food or water.

Roundworm (ascaris): There are usually no symptoms. Infection is often discovered when the child passes a large, white, pencil-sized worm. The worms may be passed months or years after immigration, much to the consternation of parents. Treatment is Mebendazole. Roundworms are not typically contagious with normal hygiene.

Pinworm (enterobiasis): Pinworms are tiny thread-like worms in the stool. They may cause the child to scratch around the anus. Treatment is Mebendazole. Pinworms are highly contagious, especially to other children.

Giardia lamblia (one-celled protozoa): Symptoms include stomach cramps, nausea, vomiting, weight loss, bloating, fatigue, and foul-smelling gas. Children often have no symptoms at all. Nonsymptomatic giardia can multiply and cause the above problems. The treatment is

Metronidazole Furazolidone. Giardia is contagious (typically to the mother!) and is often transmitted by poor attention to hand washing.

Hookworm (ancyclostomatidae): Symptoms are iron deficiency anemia, abdominal, and pulmonary symptoms. Treatment is Mebendazole. Hookworm is not contagious.

Tropical tapeworm (hymenolepsis nana): This worm is usually asymptomatic and is not contagious with normal hygiene. Treatment is Niclosamide or Praziquantel.

Lice: Detected by looking for white eggs or nits at the base of the hair in a good light. It is a good idea to take along Nix cream rinse and a fine-tooth comb just in case. Some toddlers and older children have had them and have infested their new families and schools.

Scabies: Adoptive parents who did not read this section have infected their friends and family with scabies by not treating the baby and by passing him or her around for everyone to hold. Scabies is caused by tiny mites that lay eggs under the skin. Symptoms include blistering of the skin and intense itching. Partially treated scabies and scabies complicated by impetigo may be very difficult to diagnose. Any persistent, itchy rash should be suspect. The treatment is a bath and applications of Elimite (permethrin lotion). A steroid cream will help with the itching as it may take up to two or three weeks to eliminate all of the eggs and mites from the skin.

Schistosomiasis (Bilharziasis): Schistosomiasis is caused by microscopic blood flukes (worms) present in fresh water lakes and streams of Asia, Africa, the Antilles, and the northeastern and eastern parts of South America. Snails are the intermediate hosts for these worms, which penetrate human skin and later develop into larger worms in the abdominal blood vessels. Schistosomiasis is usually only seen in older children who have worked in the fields — not in institutionalized children. Symptoms are not usually present. Treatment is Praziquantel.

Whipworm (trichuris): These are contagious. Symptoms include nausea, stomach pain, diarrhea, anemia, and, infrequently, rectal prolapse. Whipworm is treated with Mebendazole.

INFECTIOUS DISEASES

Shigellosis (bacillary dysentery): This acute bacterial disease occurs worldwide. It is highly contagious under poor sanitary conditions. Most infections and deaths are in children under ten years of age. Symptoms include diarrhea, fever, vomiting, cramps, and tenesmus (straining). In severe cases, stools contain blood, mucus, and pus. The treatment includes fluid and electrolyte replacement. Antibiotics are not usually necessary.

Helicobacter pylori: The symptoms are abdominal pain, gastritis, or gastrointestinal bleeding; children show no symptoms when infected with this bacterium. The treatment is a course of triple antibiotics. Left untreated, the disease is mildly contagious and is the cause of most gastric ulcers.

Salmonella: The symptoms are severe abdominal pain, nausea, vomiting, and diarrhea, often with blood in the stool. Treatment is supportive. Antibiotics may actually prolong the disease.

Acquired Immune Deficiency Syndrome (AIDS): All children should be evaluated for the presence of HIV infection after arrival in the adoptive home. Tests in other countries are not reliable and should always be repeated. A positive ELISA or screening test in a baby under eighteen months of age may indicate the mother's infection, rather than the baby's. The incidence of true infection is very low. Less than 2 dozen cases have been documented over the past decade.

Hepatitis: Hepatitis is an inflammation of the liver. Some types of hepatitis can cause permanent liver damage. Tests for hepatitis conducted in another country should be considered unreliable.

Hepatitis A — Prevalent in all countries, including American day care centers, hepatitis A is transmitted by contaminated food and water. The majority of infected children are asymptomatic. Hepatitis A does not cause chronic liver disease and is only contagious for a few days or weeks at the time of infection. Routine testing is not recommended.

Hepatitis B — Hepatitis B is prevalent in many developing countries and is transmitted through contact with blood or body fluids. Hepatitis B may also be transmitted by mother to fetus. Five to ten percent of Asian and Eastern European children have chronic infection. Many more children have been exposed to the disease. Children who test positive for hepatitis B should be tested for hepatitis D, a disease found only in the presence of chronic hepatitis B.

Medical problems are highly unusual for most children with hepatitis B. Most of the intervention in the first twenty years of life is merely monitoring for possible clearing of infection or the rare early complication. Because hepatitis B is also found in the American population, newborns here are inoculated.

Hepatitis C — Hepatitis C is spread by direct blood contact. It's possible for an infected mother to transmit the disease to her child during birth, although the incidence is low (about 5%). Hepatitis C causes chronic infection in up to 80 percent of people, but it takes 30-40 years for complications to develop. Interferon and other drugs are used to treat and manage hepatitis C.

Malaria: Malaria is carried by certain kinds of mosquitoes in coastal and jungle areas in most tropical and subtropical regions. Malaria may not be apparent for weeks to months after infection. Symptoms are often nonspecific (fever, malaise, diarrhea, etc.). Malaria should always be considered in any febrile illness that is not responding to treatment as expected. Malaria is not common among internationally adopted children.

Infantile paralysis (poliomyelitis): This disease no longer exists in North or South America, but is still prevalent in the former Soviet Union, Eastern Europe, and all parts of Asia except Japan. Paralysis in a Latin American child is more likely to be cerebral palsy or other neurological conditions. Sudden paralysis in Asia is most likely due to polio. However, the diagnosis should always be confirmed after arrival in the United States.

Syphilis: If your child's medical history states that the child had syphilis — which is usually acquired from the birth mother — make sure that the child is tested again in the United States. Treatment abroad may have been inadequate.

Tuberculosis (TB): Tuberculosis cases turn up often, especially in Chinese and Eastern European orphanages. The staff is the main source of infection. Unlike adults, children with tuberculosis do not spread the disease. Active tuberculosis must be treated for at least two weeks before an orphan immigrant visa will be issued. Because of the high rate of drug resistant tuberculosis worldwide, a doctor or clinic specializing in infectious disease should manage cases of active tuberculosis.

In all countries except in North America, a BCG (tuberculosis vaccine) is given at birth or soon after. The BCG scar looks like an old smallpox scar on the shoulder, back, or upper thigh. All children, regardless of BCG scar history, need an evaluation for tuberculosis after arrival, usually a PPD or Mantoux test. Occasionally, a chest x-ray is also needed. The 4-prong "tine" test is not appropriate for immigrant children.

U.S. bacteria and viruses: Newly arrived orphanage babies should be protected from well meaning U.S. visitors who have colds and flu. These illnesses can become critical in babies already weakened from malnutrition and/or parasites.

OTHER HEALTH CONCERNS

Anemia (low hemoglobin): Anemia in most children is due to iron deficiency; it should be treated and followed. Some children, especially African or Asian children, will have other blood disorders, such as thalassemia, hemoglobin disorders, and G-G-PD deficiency.

Circumcision: Most of the world does not routinely circumcise. Ask your doctor if this operation is really necessary for your particular boy. The risks include possible mutilation of the penis, hemorrhage, and local infection.

Lactose intolerance: Lactose intolerance is the inability to digest the milk sugars found in most formula and cow's milk. It is fairly common in all dark-skinned populations and in Asia. Mother's milk, soybean formulas, or yogurt are substituted. Tolerance to cow's milk may eventually be attained, especially if the lactose intolerance was due to infection or malnutrition rather than inherited.

Mongolian spots: Adoptive parents who do not read this section are aghast when they change their baby's first diaper and see what looks like bruises. Babies of Asian, Indian, or African ancestry may have blue/black spots on their bottoms and along their spines called Mongolian spots. The spots may also occur on their shoulders, as well as the backs of their hands and the tops of their feet. These spots gradually disappear as the baby grows older.

Rickets: Rickets is a disease of infancy and childhood, which prevents the proper development of bone. The disease, which is prevalent in Chinese, Romanian, and Russian orphanages, is caused by inadequate exposure to sunlight and insufficient intake of Vitamin D. Signs of rickets include bow legs, raised bony bumps on the ribs, exaggerated roundness of the forehead, and a poorly shaped, sweaty head.

Rickets can be diagnosed by blood tests, physical exam, or x-ray. The disease is treated with milk and food fortified with calcium and Vitamin D and exposure to natural light.

Sickle-cell disease: Sickle-cell disease is a serious anemia due to a recessive gene and is found in African, Latin American, Mediterranean, as well as other non-Caucasoid groups. Other hemoglobin or red blood cell diseases, such as alpha or beta thalassemia syndromes, are common in Asians. Anemia not responding to iron is often the first clue to the condition.

Skin pigmentation: Cuts and scrapes on dark skin heal at the same rate as on light skin, but may require many more weeks for the pigmentation to return or may become hyperpigmented as they scar. Even brown, black, or olive children may have delicate complexions that sunburn and windburn easily. Severe malnutrition can cause a genetically olive-skinned, black-haired child to be pale and blond or red-haired. With a balanced diet, the pigment gradually becomes normal.

Teeth: Some orphans need a lot of expensive dental work. Others have perfect teeth. Most dentists believe the birth mother's diet has a great influence over her child's first set of teeth. The practice in lower classes of weaning babies with bottles of sugar water contributes to tooth decay. Orphans with yellowed teeth may have been treated with tetracycline, a drug that can cause this kind of side effect. Upon returning home, a dental exam should be scheduled for any child over 18 months of age.

PREADOPTION CONSULTATIONS

Over the past few years, a new pediatric specialty has evolved that assists adoptive singles and couples with their decision regarding the acceptance of the child they were referred. Adoptive parents receive a lot of information in a referral, especially from former Iron Curtain countries. Adoptive parents can then forward this information to an international pediatric specialist who will review the existing information.

After the doctor receives a video, photos, and a medical and social history on the child, a consultation takes place by phone or in person for a summary of medical problems, congenital anomalies, possibilities of other problems, and a discussion of services and treatment that might be required.

Since the pediatricians do not have the child before them, they explain the uncertainties in such consultations. For example, most medical evaluations from Russia contain archaic terms and diagnoses not easily understood in the United States.

If the information is inadequate or worrisome, the pediatrician will request updated information, typically new growth and developmental parameters or family or social history. A wait of several weeks for updated, translated information is not unusual.

Pediatricians will not make adoption decisions for potential parents. Parents, not pediatricians, must take the responsibility for the adoption decision. They need to trust their ability to use their hearts as well as their heads to make an informed decision. Ultimately the decision must be based on the best interest of the child and the adoptive family (i.e. What are the child's needs, the family's expectations and resources, and do these two areas match?)

PREADOPTIVE MEDICAL CONSULTATIONS

Several international adoption clinics will review the medical information and videos of the child you have been assigned. Contact information for a few of these follows. They will let you know the fee or donation required for each record and/or video. Send a self-addressed, prepaid envelope if you want the information returned. Please call them first for the specific instructions before mailing any items. (See nearby box for more information on preadoption consultations.) You can also contact the Joint Council for International Children's Services for additional contacts. There are more than two dozen clinics in the United States and Canada and many more experienced practitioners in this field.

Dr. Jane Ellen Aronson
Director, International Adoption Medical Consultation Services
Winthrop Specialty Center
200 Old Country Road, Ste. 440
Mineola, NY 11501
Tel: (516) 663-9400
Fax: (516) 739-6535

Dr. Jerri Jenista
551 2nd St.
Ann Arbor, MI 48103
Tel: (734) 668-0419
Fax: (734) 668-9492

Dr. Dana Johnson
International Adoption Clinic
University of Minnesota
Box 211 420 Delaware St. NE
Minneapolis, MN 55455
Tel: (612) 626-2928

Courier delivery address:
Mayo Building, Room C432
420 Delaware St. NE
Minneapolis, MN 55455

Dr. Laurie Miller
The International Adoption Clinic
The Floating Hospital for Children
750 Washington Street, Box 286
Boston, MA 02111
Tel: (617) 636-8121

Dr. Todd Ochs
841 W. Bradley Place
Chicago, IL 60613-3902
Tel: (773) 975-8560
Fax: (773) 975-5989
Email: t-ochs@nwu.edu

Dr. Sarah H. Springer
The Mercy Center for International Adoption Medicine
Mercy Hospital of Pittsburgh
Department of Pediatrics
1515 Locust Street, Room 315
Pittsburgh, PA 15219
Tel: (412) 575-5805
Fax: (412) 232-7389

The Rainbow Center for International Child Health
11100 Euclid Ave., MS 6038
Cleveland, OH 44106-6038
Tel: (216) 844-3224
Email: RCIC@po.cwru.edu
Dr. Karen Olness, Pediatric Behavior and Development
Dr. Anna Mandalakas, International Child Health
Dr. Barbara Baetz-Greenwalt, Pediatric Infectious Disease
Dr. Mariasa Herran, General Pediatrics
M. Adele DiMarco, MA Medical Anthropologist

SCREENING TESTS

About two weeks after children arrive home, the following tests should be administered, even if the child appears healthy and normal. In addition, a dental exam should be scheduled for any child over 18 months of age.

Complete Physical Examination
Documentation of bruises, old scars, scars from surgeries, deformities, rickets, or abuse.

Recommended Screening Tests For All International Adoptees
* *Assessment for vision, hearing (parents need to be aware that recurrent ear infections may interfere with hearing) and dental health for children over 18 months old.*

* *Blood count, complete with erythrocyte indices.*

* *Evaluation for anemia, iron deficiency, iodine deficient hypothyroidism, lead poisoning, malnutrition, rickets, thalassemia*

* *Examination of child with suspected prenatal exposure to alcohol for fetal alcohol syndrome or alcohol-related disorders*

* *Examination/testing of child with signs or symptoms of sexual abuse.*

* *Growth assessment*

* *Hepatitis B profile*

* *Hepatitis C serology for children from Eastern Europe, the former Soviet Union, and China*

* *HIV 1 and 2 screen in all children; PCR or viral culture in a child under two years*

* *Immunizations review and update*

• *Fecal examination for ova and parasites, three times at least one week apart*

• *PPD (Mantoux) skin test for tuberculosis for all children, regardless of whether they had the BCG (Bacille Calmette-Guerin) vaccine*

• *Urinalysis*

• *VDRL screen for syphilis*

Recommended Assessments for Development and Mental Health

• *Development to be followed at one to three-month intervals for the first year after arrival.*

The majority of internationally adopted children from institutional care are mildly to severely delayed. Formal developmental testing should be performed on any and all children with suspected developmental delays through Early Childhood Intervention (ECI) or other programs. ECI childhood specialists meet with parents and children in their homes and in the community to demonstrate techniques to assist the children with speech, fine and gross motor skills, etc. Call your county or local public school system for contact information or visit their Web site (http://www.nectas.unc.edu). Federal law mandates that any child over age 3 must be offered testing in his or her native language.

• *Assessment of mental health for older children, those with known prior abuse or loss, and any child with behavior that is developmentally inappropriate.*

Testing and Referrals

Planning for testing for new or previously diagnosed conditions and referrals to specialists.

CHAPTER 14

After You Return Home: Postplacement, Readoption, and Citizenship

Under the Family Medical Leave Act, new parents are entitled to twelve weeks of unpaid leave from their jobs, providing that the company they work for has more than 50 employees. Medical insurance and other benefits are maintained during your leave. You'll need this time to relax and bond with your child, to schedule appointments with the pediatrician, and to fill out and file the appropriate forms with the Social Security Administration, IRS, and INS.

In some foreign countries, the child's name is not changed on the adoption decree or on the new birth certificate. Since it can take six months or more to readopt or reaffirm in order to legally change the name, it's best to file for a social security number and U.S. citizenship for your child as soon as possible. Table 14-1 includes a list of government forms that may be useful during the postplacement stage of international adoption. More information on readoption and filing for citizenship can be found later in this chapter.

To apply for a social security number for your child, order Form SS-5, Application for a Social Security Card, from the Social Security Administration (toll-free, 1-800-772-1213) or download the form from the administration's Web site at http://www.ssa.gov. A sample of this form is found at the end of this chapter. In order to complete the filing, you will need photocopies of the translations of the adoption or guardianship decree, the birth certificate, the child's passport including the page showing the INS stamp, and your own identification, such as a passport, driver's license, or military I.D. (But not a birth certificate.) If they want to see originals, take them in person. Don't leave the originals at the Social Security Administration or mail them in with the

TABLE 14-1 GOVERNMENT FORMS – POSTPLACEMENT

Form Number	Name of Form	Purpose
IRS Form W-7	Individual Taxpayer Identification Number	Tax Filing
INS Form 8839	Qualified Adoption Expenses	Tax Filing
INS Form N-643	Application for Certificate of Citizenship on Behalf of an Adopted Child	Naturalization
INS Form N-600	Application for Certificate of Citizenship when only one parent is a citizen	Naturalization
INS Form N-565	Application for Replacement of Naturalization or Citizenship document	Name change after Citizenship Certificate is issued. Or to replace lost citizenship document
INS Form G-844	Request for the Return of Original Documents	Return of documents given to INS on entry into United States
SSA Form SS-5	Application for a Social Security Card	Social Security Number
INS Form G-731	Inquiry about status of I-551 Alien Registration Card	Green card Status
INS Form G-639	Freedom of Information/Privacy Act Request	Access to your INS records
INS Form I-90	Application to replace Alien Registration Card	Replace lost card or one that was never received

Helpful Contacts

Toll-Free number for INS forms: 800-870-3676
To download INS forms: http://www.ins.usdoj.gov

Toll-free number for Social Security Administration: 800-772-1213
To download Social Security forms: http://www.ssa.gov

Toll-free number for IRS tax forms: 800-TAXFORM
Toll-free number for IRS assistance: 800-829-1040
To download IRS forms: http://www.irs.ustreas.gov

form. You'll need them again later. Later, if you need to change the child's name, you will need to notify the Social Security Administration. Your child will retain the same social security number.

If you don't have your child's social security number by the time you file your tax return, you will need IRS Form W-7, Individual Taxpayer Identification Number, to complete your tax return. You'll also need IRS Form 8839, Qualified Adoption Expenses, along with your agency receipt for the legal expenses incurred in order to qualify for a tax credit, which can be as much as $5,000. To request forms from the IRS, call 1-800-TAXFORM, or you can download IRS forms from their Web site at http://www.irs.ustreas.gov/.

You may also want to consider opening an Educational Individual Retirement Account for your child, which allows you to set aside up to $500 a year after federal income taxes. Your child will not have to pay taxes on the money or its future earnings if it is used for college expenses. Or, you can open a custodial account with your child's name and social security number.

This is also the time to make out a will or revise your current one. Choose a guardian for your child who will also be the executor of your estate. Read your life insurance policy. Take a look at the beneficiaries of your life insurance, 401(k) and other investment or retirement funds. This is the time to make changes.

ICCC POSTPLACEMENT REQUIREMENTS

International Concerns Committee for Children (ICCC), Report on Foreign Adoption, 1999, has more to say on postplacement supervision.

"Many countries require that follow-up documentation be returned to the foreign courts to monitor the child's progress for a designated length of time. This is not pure whimsy or curiosity. If these children were left in their birth-countries it is likely that they would be "sold" as servants, or "encouraged" to augment their family's income, or simply to survive by themselves, becoming shoeshine boys or criminals. The documents and reports required allow the placing organizations to prove to the courts that this is not the case in the child's adoptive country, and that the child is, in truth, being loved and cherished for the unique person he is, and not being exploited."

"Failure to comply with these various postplacement requirements means it is entirely possible for foreign governments to shut down further foreign adoptions because no assurance is forthcoming that the children are in any better circumstances or their future is any more favorable than if they were left in their birth countries."

"In short, it is essential these requirements be followed to the letter if future adoptions are going to be allowed at all! Even when postplacement documentation is not required it is strongly encouraged. Not only would pictures, letters, etc., be greatly appreciated by the placing organization who — let's face it — are themselves not only the cause of your dear child being yours, but are very possibly the reason he is alive at all. Former caretakers exult in seeing the rosy face and sturdy

limbs of a child who may have arrived to them on literally the edge of death. All of these caretakers live with children's deaths every day and it is never easy and never without anguish."

"If you have adopted a child from another country, please write to the source from which you adopted and tell them, with photographs if possible, how your child is doing. Apparently some really wild rumors surface from time to time about the reasons U.S. citizens want children. Medical experimentation is not the most far-out example. Write every six months if you can, especially if you adopted from an independent source rather than from one of the well established orphanages or government agencies. Even if you adopt from the latter, it is an extremely good idea to correspond. You will do a real favor to all hopeful adoptive parents who come after you, and to your child, who may wish to visit them some day."

POSTPLACEMENT SUPERVISION

Your adoption agency will also send you forms to fill out and return. These will likely include a postplacement supervision contract, five or more monthly progress reports to fill out on your child after the first month, a publicity release form, a form confirming your child's date of U.S. citizenship, and possibly other forms as well.

STEP 21

Participate in postplacement supervision.

Each state has its own requirements regarding the frequency and length of postplacement supervision. Some states require supervisory contacts over a period of six months to one year. Three to six contacts may be required during this time period.

In addition, the national child-placing authorities in each foreign country have specific requirements as to the kind of information they wish to see, as well as how often and for how long. Your social worker will coordinate your state requirements with those of the foreign country. The nearby table shows a sample of postplacement requirements for some of the child-sending countries.

Depending upon your state requirements and those of the foreign country, your social worker will make one to six postplacement contacts. If you are having any problems, tell the social worker. One of the tasks that this person has been schooled for is helping families make satisfactory adjustments. The social worker will summarize the information she gathers at the interviews as well as referral information in postplacement reports. These are needed for the adoption or readoption in the U.S. courts and may also be translated and sent to your child's foreign agency. A sample of a typical postplacement supervision report guide is included at the end of this chapter.

Adoption agencies are licensed in their states under the child-placement standards in that state. The agencies must follow regulations governing the standards for the placement of a child in an adoptive home. The intent of state licensing departments is to cover the pre- and postplacement studies written by a social worker. The legal adoption in court is governed by the legal code on adoption procedures in the child's country of origin.

The requirements for pre- and postplacement studies by the state licensing department and the requirements set down in the state legal code for local adoptions do not necessarily match. This causes a lot of confusion for the adoptive parents. Judges and lawyers inexperienced in international adoption usually request a new home study and handle the adoption or readoption of a foreign-born child as they would a private adoption.

In such a case, once the situation has been discussed, the judge may write a waiver for the additional home study. Your adoption agency will be requested to send the existing home study and postplacement reports to your lawyer or to the court for the adoption or readoption of your child.

TABLE 14-2 NUMBER OF POSTPLACEMENT REPORTS REQUIRED BY SELECTED COUNTRIES

Country	Social Worker Report	Monthly Parent Report	Translation
Bolivia	Yes – 5	Yes – Every three months for the first year, plus one annually for the next five years	Yes
Bulgaria	Yes – 5	Yes – 5, and also at 12, 18, 24, 30, and 36 months after placement	No
China, Mainland	Yes – 5	Yes – 5	Yes
Colombia, Medellin	Yes – 5	Yes – 5	No
ICBF	Yes – 5	Yes – 5	
Ecuador	Yes – 5	Yes – 5, plus one per year for the next four years	Yes
Guatemala	Yes – 5	Yes – 5	Yes
Peru	Yes – 5, plus one social work report every 6 months for 4 years – legalized by Peruvian Consulate	Yes – 5	Yes
Romania	Yes – 5	Yes—5, and also at 6, 12, 18, and 24 months	Yes
Russia	Yes – 5	Yes – 5, and also at 12, 24 and 36 months	No
Vietnam	Yes – 5	Yes – 5, plus 1 per year until child reaches 18 years of age	No

If your health insurance company needs a letter to confirm the date of your child's placement, ask your agency to send it on your behalf. Insurance carriers must be notified within 30 days of the child's placement or adoption. Be aware that group health insurance coverage is regulated by Public Law 104-191, which mandates that group insurance carriers cannot exclude pre-existing conditions or undiagnosed conditions in adopted children.

ADOPTING OR READOPTING IN YOUR COUNTY OF RESIDENCE

STEP 22

Readopt your child in your county of residence.

Not only is there no national adoption law in the United States, adoption procedures are not even consistent among the counties in each state. The Clerk of Court in your county of residence and a civil lawyer with experience in foreign adoption can advise you on the best way to proceed. If you have a final foreign adoption decree, it may be possible for the court to recognize, reconfirm, or validate it. This saves you time and money.

At this point, you may engage a lawyer to handle the adoption or readoption, or, if local laws allow it, you may handle your own case. The latter is called a *pro se* adoption. If you do hire a lawyer, try to find a family practice attorney with international adoption experience.

Readoption in the child's state of residence can be important for a number of reasons, including future custody disputes, distribution of property, survivor's benefits, and child support. And, a state court decree would also be entitled to full faith and credit in other states, an advantage not available to decrees of foreign nations. However, the ratification by the United States of the Hague Convention and its implementation legislation will provide a U.S. norm for international adoptions in the future.

Pro Se Adoption

Pro se adoption procedures vary from state to state and probably from county to county. *Pro se* adoption may be applied by parents who received a permanent guardianship or custody transfer. Children with final foreign adoption decrees may also be readopted *pro se*, as may children brought into the United States under guardianships or custody arrangements held by international adoption agencies.

The best source of information on how to adopt your child without a lawyer is the Clerk of Court. Your social worker may also have this information, or he or she may know a postadoptive parent who will advise you.

State Adoption Procedures

Ask your social worker to send the necessary adoption papers to you or your lawyer after your last postplacement meeting. From an office form supply company, purchase the forms required by your court. You can contact the

Clerk of Court to determine what forms are necessary.

Send the completed and notarized court-required form to the Clerk of Court. (If you are conducting a *pro se* adoption, enter *pro se* in the blank for the name of the lawyer.) With the form, enclose the filing fee (usually about $200.00). If you are conducting a *pro se* adoption, you will also need to enclose a letter to the judge of the District Court, Juvenile Division, explaining why you wish to represent yourself. (For example, you wish to exercise your constitutional right, and you need to save the lawyer's fee.) You may wish to add that you are adequately prepared because you have read your state adoption laws and you have discussed them with your social worker.

The adoption hearing takes about ten minutes. If possible, ask the Clerk of Court for a photocopy of the questions to be asked at the hearing. Be prepared to pay about $150.00 in court costs in addition to the filing fee and $25.00 for a new birth certificate (in some states). At the hearing, you or your lawyer will attest to the legality of the foreign adoption, guardianship, or other legal arrangement made for your child abroad. Under oath, you will verify all of the facts listed on the adoption forms. You will state that your child has been examined by your family physician and that you are satisfied with the child's mental and physical health. You may also be asked if you are responsible for any other minors living in your home, as well as other questions the judge may decide to ask. In most states, a new birth certificate is issued. If you have second thoughts about the child's name, now is the time to change it.

FILING FOR U.S. CITIZENSHIP

STEP 23

File for U.S. citizenship for your child.

Note: This procedure will change when Congress passes the "Adopted Orphans Citizenship Act."

A month or two after your return home, you will receive an Alien Registration Card in the mail. You triggered the issue of the card when you turned in the envelope with your original adoption documents from the U.S. Consulate to an INS official at the airport. You will need this card at the child's citizenship hearing. The card is mailed to the address listed on Form I-600, Petition to Classify an Orphan as an Immediate Relative, at the time of filing. If you didn't receive the form, order INS Form G-731, Inquiry about the Status of I-551 Alien Registration Card. If you lost the card, order INS Form I-90, Application to Replace Alien Registration Card.

Many adoptive parents believe that adopting in their state of residence automatically confers U.S. citizenship on the child. This is not true. As soon as your child has either a final foreign adoption decree or a U.S. adoption decree, you should apply for citizenship.

If both parents are U.S. citizens, order Form N-643, Application for Certificate of Citizenship on Behalf of an Adopted Child, ($125.00 filing fee) from your INS office. (See sample at the end of this chapter.) If only one parent is a citizen, order Form N-600 ($160.00 filing fee). Send in photocopies of the documents listed on the form and include the following statement: "Copies of the documents being submitted are exact photocopies of original documents. I understand that I may be required to submit original documents to an immigration official at a later date." Sign and date this statement.

Once your documents are in order, you will be notified of the citizenship hearing. Take the originals requested on Form N-643 or N-600 to present to the official. The child's alien card is surrendered in lieu of the Certificate of Citizenship. Keep the Certificate of Citizenship in a safe place. Although it states that this document cannot be photocopied, it is now permissible to do so for legal purposes. The entire process of applying for and receiving citizenship can take anywhere from three to twelve months, depending on the INS office workload. U.S. citizenship bestows rights and privileges and protection. Your child now qualifies for federal programs, grants, college loans, and can travel internationally and return to the United States without restrictions.

Finally, apply for your child's U.S. passport. This will be the preferred form of identification.

Forward information regarding your child's date of citizenship to your U.S.-based international agency. Both the U.S. agency and the foreign child-placing entity need this information to close their files.

Required Documents

Certified copies or originals of the following documents will be required:

1. Adoptive parents' birth certificate(s)

2. Adoptive parents' marriage license, if applicable

3. Child's birth certificate

4. Child's adoption decree

5. Child's passport

6. Child's alien registration card

Take your identification and passports along, as well as all documents (both foreign and U.S.) pertaining to the child's adoption or guardianship, in case the court wishes to examine them.

Once citizenship is awarded, be certain to store the child's documents in a safe place. A safe-deposit box would probably be best. Type the citizenship number and the name and location of the bank where the safe-deposit box is located on a sheet of paper and file it elsewhere for easy reference.

If you would like a flag flown over the U.S. Capital in your child's honor, contact your local U.S. representative regarding the proposed date. They will send you an order form with a selection of sizes and fabrics. After your child's special day, the flag will be sent to her or him as a momento.

Celebration

Once you have obtained citizenship for your child, you have completed the adoption requirements from A to Z. Now is the time to unfurl the Stars and Stripes! Decorate cakes in red, white, and blue for this day and on every anniversary of this memorable occasion. Take pictures of these activities for your child's Life Book.

Changes to or Replacement of the Naturalization/Citizenship Document

If, at any time after receiving the child's citizenship documents, you need to either replace the Certificate of Citizenship because it has been lost or damaged or you need to change the child's name on the document, you'll need to file Form N-565, Application for Replacement of Naturalization/ Citizenship Document, from the INS. The instructions on the form will explain the number, size, and poses of the photographs required. You will also need to send them a copy of the damaged document if one exists. If you need to make a name change, you will also need to submit copies of the original service document and a copy of the court order, or your marriage or divorce certificate, showing the name change.

After you submit the completed form, required photocopies, and the $135.00 filing fee, you may be called in for a hearing prior to being issued a new Certificate of Citizenship.

Form SS-5

Application for a Social Security Card

SOCIAL SECURITY ADMINISTRATION Application for a Social Security Card

Form Approved
OMB No. 0960-0066

1	**NAME** TO BE SHOWN ON CARD ➝	First	Full Middle Name	Last
	FULL NAME AT BIRTH IF OTHER THAN ABOVE ➝	First	Full Middle Name	Last
	OTHER NAMES USED ➝			

2	**MAILING ADDRESS** ➝ Do Not Abbreviate	Street Address, Apt. No., PO Box, Rural Route No.
		City State Zip Code

3 CITIZENSHIP (Check One) ➝
- ☐ U.S. Citizen
- ☐ Legal Alien Allowed To Work
- ☐ Legal Alien **Not Allowed** To Work
- ☐ Other (See Instructions On Page 1)

4 SEX ➝ ☐ Male   ☐ Female

5 RACE/ETHNIC DESCRIPTION (Check One Only—Voluntary) ➝
- ☐ Asian, Asian-American or Pacific Islander
- ☐ Hispanic
- ☐ Black (Not Hispanic)
- ☐ North American Indian or Alaskan Native
- ☐ White (Not Hispanic)

6 DATE OF BIRTH _____ Month, Day, Year

7 PLACE OF BIRTH (Do Not Abbreviate) _____ City   State or Foreign Country   **FCI**   Office Use Only

8
A. **MOTHER'S MAIDEN NAME** ➝ First   Full Middle Name   Last Name At Her Birth

B. **MOTHER'S SOCIAL SECURITY NUMBER** (Complete only if applying for a number for a child under age 18.) ➝ ☐☐☐–☐☐–☐☐☐☐

9
A. **FATHER'S NAME** ➝ First   Full Middle Name   Last

B. **FATHER'S SOCIAL SECURITY NUMBER** (Complete only if applying for a number for a child under age 18.) ➝ ☐☐☐–☐☐–☐☐☐☐

10 Has the applicant or anyone acting on his/her behalf ever filed for or received a Social Security number card before?
- ☐ Yes (If "yes", answer questions 11-13.)
- ☐ No (If "no", go on to question 14.)
- ☐ Don't Know (If "don't know", go on to question 14.)

11 Enter the Social Security number previously assigned to the person listed in item 1. ➝ ☐☐☐–☐☐–☐☐☐☐

12 Enter the name shown on the most recent Social Security card issued for the person listed in item 1. ➝ First   Middle   Last

13 Enter any different date of birth if used on an earlier application for a card. ➝ _____ Month, Day, Year

14 TODAY'S DATE _____ Month, Day, Year

15 DAYTIME PHONE NUMBER ( ) _____ Area Code   Number

DELIBERATELY FURNISHING (OR CAUSING TO BE FURNISHED) FALSE INFORMATION ON THIS APPLICATION IS A CRIME PUNISHABLE BY FINE OR IMPRISONMENT, OR BOTH.

16 YOUR SIGNATURE ▶

17 YOUR RELATIONSHIP TO THE PERSON IN ITEM 1 IS:
- ☐ Self
- ☐ Natural or Adoptive Parent
- ☐ Legal Guardian
- ☐ Other (Specify)

DO NOT WRITE BELOW THIS LINE (FOR SSA USE ONLY)

NPN			DOC	NTI	CAN		ITV
PBC	EVI	EVA	EVC	PRA	NWR	DNR	UNIT

EVIDENCE SUBMITTED	SIGNATURE AND TITLE OF EMPLOYEE(S) REVIEWING EVIDENCE AND/OR CONDUCTING INTERVIEW
	DATE
	DCL DATE

Form **SS-5** Internet (2-98) Destroy Prior Editions   Page 5

Postplacement Supervision Guidelines

GUIDELINES FOR POSTPLACEMENT SUPERVISION

One report per month, written by a social worker, will be required for five months. These reports should be based on two face-to-face interviews with the entire family, one of which must take place in the family's home, and three telephone interviews. If the child is over the age of one year, all of the interviews must be face to face.

After the initial visit, subsequent contacts will cover the same topics — a progress report on the child's development, the family's adjustment, and language acquisition and age appropriate education. Include the integration of the child into the community, as well as the utilization of ECI (Early Childhood Intervention) programs, resources of the public or private school system, and other community resources.

Attach copies of the results of the recommended physical for internationally adopted children, including information on height, weight, and immunizations, as well as periodic check-ups, treatments, or therapies.

Contact No.:_____   (State whether the contact is made in the home
with all members present, face-to-face, or by telephone.)

Date: _____   (Date contact was made.)

Family Name: _____

Address:_____

_____

Phone Number: _____

Child's Original Name: _____

Child's Present Name:_____

Date of Birth: _____

Date of Placement: _____

Name of Child-Placing Entity Abroad: _____

Postplacement Supervision Guidelines

INFANTS UNDER ONE YEAR

- *General appearance.*
- *Habits, behavior, and personality characteristics.*
- *Favorite games and toys.*
- *New developmental milestones or skills.*
- *Sleeping and eating patterns.*
- *Unusual or problematic behavior and your suggestions to modify the behavior.*

Parental Adjustment

- *Adjustments for the parent(s) and any siblings in sharing time and new responsibilities.*
- *Quality of time that parent(s), child, and any siblings enjoy together. Is the family bonding? What is the attachment of the parents to the child like and vice versa?*

See final paragraphs in "Older Children" category for advising parents on the legal and citizenship processes as well as your evaluation and recommendations.

OLDER CHILDREN & FUTURE ISSUES

- *General appearance.*
- *Personality, behavior, favorite activities, sports, and toys.*
- *Attainment of developmental milestones and skills.*
- *Positive and/or negative habits and behaviors.*

Child's Adjustment

- *Language, racial, and cultural differences in the family and neighborhood.*
- *Emotional, social, and physical changes since placement.*
- *Child's personality and integration of past experience with the present living situation.*
- *Evidence of the child's attachment to the family.*

Parental Adjustment

- *Emotional and social adjustments.*
- *Methods of coping with increased responsibility and changing roles.*
- *Feelings of attachment toward the child.*
- *Discussion with parents regarding the differences in the development of institutionalized children.*

Postplacement Supervision Guidelines

- *Discussion with parents of how children learn.*
- *Ability to individualize the special needs of birth child or children and adoptive child.*
- *Interpretation of any community prejudices against the child.*
- *Child-rearing practices regarding discipline, setting limits, and household rules.*
- *Parents' response to the manifestations of the loss and separation trauma in the child. For example, parents' reaction to the child's sleep disturbances, withdrawal, aggression, not eating, inconsolable crying, screaming, bed-wetting, and regression in toilet training.*
- *Child's readiness for and enrollment and adjustment to a nursery, day care, or school.*

EVALUATION OF THE PLACEMENT

- *Family's feelings about their preparation for this experience. Is the child as they visualized? How have their ideas changed?*
- *Child's preparation for placement in the United States. Does the family believe it was adequate?*
- *Changes in residence, number of adult household members, health, or income since the placement.*
- *General appraisal of the placement.*

Recommendations

- *Prognosis for the future. How has placement changed and benefited the child, the new parent(s), and the rest of the family?*
- *Discussion with parents to help the child understand the meaning of adoption at age and language appropriate levels.*
- *Your recommendation for adoption, readoption, or re-affirmation. (Request a Waiver and Citation of Consent to Adoption if required in your county.)*
- *Explanation of the steps required to obtain the child's U.S. citizenship.*

Final Observations: Comment upon the manner in which the child or children are being raised. If this is a sibling group, a child over two years of age, or a handicapped child, state whether you recommend that postplacement supervision continue until the adoption is consummated.

Final Report: Indicate that this is the final report and that "The family understands and agrees with termination of postplacement services." Mention any specific recommendations or referrals that you have made to the family. Are these in place, or do they have a plan to follow through?

_____
Social Worker's Name and Credentials

Form N-643

U.S. Citizenship, Page 1 of 2

U.S. Department of Justice
Immigration and Naturalization Service

OMB No. 1115-0152
Certificate of Citizenship on Behalf of Adopted Child

START HERE - Please Type or Print

FOR INS USE ONLY

Part A.   Information about adopted child.

Last Name | First | Middle

Address:

Street Number and Name | Apt. #

City | State or Province

Country | ZIP/Postal Code

Date of Birth (Mo/Day/Yr) | Place of Birth (City, Country)

Social Security # | A#

Personal Description:

Sex   ☐ M   ☐ F   Height   Ft. _____   In. _____

Marital Status | Visible Marks or Scars

Information about Entry:

Name of Entry (If different from Item A)

Date of Entry | Place of Entry

Date of Adoption (Mo/Day/Yr) | Place of Adoption (City, Country)

Part B.   Information about the Adoptive Parents (If there is only one parent write "None" in place of the name of the parent which does not apply.)

Last Name of Adoptive Father | First | Middle

U.S. Citizen by:
☐ Birth in the U.S.
☐ Birth abroad to USC parents (List certificate of citizenship number or passport number)
☐ Naturalized or derived after birth (List naturalization certificate number)

Last Name of Adoptive Mother | First | Middle or Maiden

U.S. Citizen by:
☐ Birth in the U.S.
☐ Birth abroad to USC parents (List certificate of citizenship number or passport number)
☐ Naturalized or derived after birth (List naturalization certificate number)

Form N-643 (rev. 5/10/93) N   *Continued on back.*

FOR INS USE ONLY column:

Returned | Receipt

Resubmitted

Reloc Sent

Reloc Rec'd

☐ Applicant Interviewed

Action Block

Recommendation of Officer:

Approval ☐   Denial ☐

Concurrence of District Director or Officer in Charge:

I Do ☐   do not ☐   concur

Signature

Certificate # _____

To Be Completed by *Attorney* or *Representative*, if any
☐ Fill in box if G-28 is attached to represent the applicant

VOLOG#

ATTY State License #

Form N-643

U.S. Citizenship, Page 2 of 2

Part B. Continued.

Date and Place of Marriage of the Adoptive Parents

Number of Prior Marriages of Adoptive Father	Number of Prior Marriages of Adoptive Mother

Is residence of parents' the same as the child's? ☐ YES ☐ NO (If no, explain on a separate sheet of paper.)

If the residence address is different from Item A, list actual residence address.	Daytime Telephone # ( ) -

Part C. Signature. *(Read the information on penalties in the instructions before completing this section.)*

I certify that this application, and the evidence submitted with it, is true and correct. I authorize the release of any information from my records, or that of my child, which the Immigration and Naturalization Service needs to determine eligibility for the benefit I am seeking.

_____ _____ _____
Signature   Print Name   Date

Part D. Signature of person preparing form if other than above. *(Sign below.)*

I declare that I prepared this application at the request of the above person and it is based on all information of which I have knowledge.

_____ _____ _____
Signature   Print Name   Date

Firm Name
and Address

DO NOT COMPLETE THE FOLLOWING UNTIL INSTRUCTED TO DO SO AT THE INTERVIEW.

AFFIDAVIT. I, the (parent, guardian) _____ do swear or affirm, under penalty of the perjury laws of the United States, that I know and understand the contents of this application signed by me, and the attached supplementary pages number (   ) to (   ) inclusive; that the same are true and correct to the best of my knowledge, and that corrections numbered (   ) to (   ) were made by me or at my request.

Signature of parent or guardian _____ Date _____

_____ _____ _____
Person Examined   Address   Relationship to Applicant

Sworn or affirmed before me on _____ at _____

Signature of interviewing officer _____ Title _____

CHAPTER 15

Parenting the Adopted Child

This chapter includes an overview of what you might expect as you and your child begin to adjust to one another. Many social workers and child psychologists have much experience and expertise to offer on the issues of bonding and attachment in families. These professionals are able to help adoptive parents through the critical first months of an adoptive adjustment and can be called upon later if further help is needed. Prospective parents can help prepare themselves for the first few months of the adoptive adjustment by reading and talking to postadoptive parents of children of the age group and culture in which they are interested. Recommended books on adoption and adoptive parent magazines are listed in the Bibliography. Concise guidelines and tools are available as well. A postplacement progress questionnaire, a checklist for medical tests, a Life Book outline, and a Forever Family Certificate are available to adoptive families through the Joint Council on International Services for Families and Children.

Abandoned children, who have usually been malnourished over an extended period, are usually small for their ages and physically weak. Unfortunately, their early (birth to three months) emotional and developmental needs were probably never met. Typical orphanage infants and children are normal in their mental development, yet lag behind in fine and gross motor skills. Children like these overcome their physical problems quite rapidly in adoptive homes. At the same time, however, the adoptive parents must temporarily forget their child's chronological age and tend to their child's emotional needs, just as they would to a baby's physical and emotional needs. Thus, parents nurture their children and establish mutual trust, love, and cooperation.

Bonding, the process of attachment to a family, gives children the chance to grow and to change within a family over an extended period of time. In bonding, adoptive children decide to trust their parents to not disappear. Bonding is a process that can take up to five years. Working adoptive couples and singles must plan on one parent spending at least six months at home to carry on this bonding process with the child before returning to a career. Yet, keep in mind, it is quality of attention given to the child rather than the quantity of time that leads to a strong bond.

Parenting institutionalized children who are culturally and ethnically different from ourselves is a unique challenge, especially when the child is past the baby stage and already has a personality, memories, habits, and a different language. Quite often they have developed survival behaviors that are far beyond what is expected of a child of that age in a family. Five-month-olds may hold their own bottles; two-year-olds may never indulge in a temper tantrum; three-year-olds may share without a fuss; and four-year-olds may never ask for help, even when they get hurt. You may have to teach your child how to be a child — more specifically how to be your child.

HOUSEHOLD RULES FOR OLDER CHILDREN

Before you emigrate your child, think about age-appropriate household rules. List what the child will and will not be allowed to do. This is particularly important for school-age children who are accustomed to institutional rules and schedules and feel insecure without them. All children feel more relaxed when they know what their new parents expect of them.

Explain these rules the first day your child moves in. A weekly family meeting to highlight each member's progress, to plan family activities, and to maintain or revise the rules is beneficial to everyone, even if it has to be conducted in hand and body signals because of language barriers.

Help from someone who speaks the child's native language is usually seen as threatening to a child under five or six. They have found security and loving attention with you. They don't know what the native speaker's motives are and may interpret it to mean that they are about to be moved again. A native speaker usually makes the child feel insecure.

Siblings

Brothers and sisters are either happy or neutral when they hear about a new sibling. Many adoptive parents take their children along on the adoption trip. This helps some children feel important, especially if they take responsibility for entertaining the new sibling, in order to give their parents a break. Other children have immediately become jealous and difficult, which has added to the stress of the adoption experience. A family meeting should be held before the new child comes home to establish everyone's responsibilities with the new sibling. Household rules should be developed with everyone's ideas making a contribution. Most orphans are used to a structured environment in an institution. The new child will feel more comfortable with a household routine. Siblings will be able to feel important by cooperating with the care of their new brother or sister.

Toys should be sorted out by siblings and decisions made regarding what the newcomer can play with. Perhaps some favorites should be put out of sight for a while, as well as other items precious to the siblings. Most problems with new children have to do with the destruction of possessions that are important to the established children. Their inability to share toys may be a symptom of the inability to share parental attention. The happiest children are those who are taken out individually for an ice-cream cone or a walk. They feel that they are a valued member of the family. And you can enjoy each other's company away from the demands of the house and the rest of the family.

A family picnic is another great way to share time together. I've never met a child who didn't like picnics. Let everyone help pack the basket and have as many picnics as you can.

The oldest child of a large, adoptive sibling group needs special attention in this respect, since this child has carried the responsibility of the family on his or her small shoulders. The child needs to let go of this responsibility as soon as he or she can trust you. Then the child can relax and be a child.

STAGES IN AN ADOPTIVE ADJUSTMENT

Once your child is in your custody, you may notice some puzzling behavior. Various stages occur in the adoptive adjustment of a child, in varying degrees, depending upon the age, sex, and history of the child.

Compliant: Children's initial presence in an adoptive setting is one of quiet submission. The parent has little to complain about, as the child is good.

Rejecting: Crying and searching for lost caregivers. Children may tell their new mother or father by words or actions, "You're not my parent. You can't tell me what to do."

Disoriented: The child's new environment is in conflict with their old environment concerning what is expected of them. The child is frightened and defensive and may act aggressively.

Nondiscriminatory: These children are always happy and friendly to everyone. They imitate the fads and behaviors of peers and charm their new family, neighbors, and teachers.

All-American boy or girl: Eventually, children reject their old culture more vehemently. They don't want to talk about their past. They say that they are a regular American kid. Adoptive parents must create a climate of acceptance of all kinds of people since the children need a connection with their past.

Adjustment: Children achieve balance by knowing who they were and who they are in order to function in the United States, in their new family structure, and with their new language.

Adoptive Adjustments: Things that Parents Go Through

Like children, parents also go through an adjustment process. The parents' initial behavior is one of anticipating the child's needs and providing consistent care and nurturing. Although "rejecting" children are the most difficult to deal with, they are also the ones most in touch with their feelings. In all cases, your kindness, unconditional love and one-on-one personal attention will bring the child out of numbness and into a close relationship with you. Consistently maintain eye contact and verbal and physical expressions of love and caring to win their confidence.

The number one factor in the adoptive adjustment of parents is their expectation of what the child will be like and the degree to which the child is like or different from that dream. Often the adoptive parent feels somewhat disillusioned. The ability of the parent to resolve feelings of disappointment is the key in bonding with the child.

Adoptive parents must realize that their child will always be different from his or her North American friends and classmates because their child:

> *has already lost several mother figures.*
> *was raised under a different set of child-raising beliefs.*
> *was born in a foreign country.*
> *spoke another language.*
> *does not match the adoptive parents racially or culturally.*
> *has had more than one set of parents.*
> *experienced a disrupted family.*
> *has learned a different way to act with adults.*
> *has experienced serious emotional and/or physical trauma.*
> *has national loyalties to another country.*

All of these problems are potential concerns to the adoptive parents and to a child, depending somewhat on his or her age and history. To achieve a good adjustment within the adoptive family, the children must handle these concerns and ultimately resolve them. Your attitude toward the child's history is key. Nothing is more important to a child's self-esteem than their adoptive parent's high esteem of their birth mother. The adoptive parents' first job is to explain that their child was placed for adoption with the authorities because the birth mother trusted them to provide the care that she could not. There was nothing wrong with the child, and he or she was not rejected.

According to Ronald S. Federici, a child psychologist specializing in international adoption, 20-25 percent of orphans make routine adjustments within six to eighteen months and have no need for ongoing medical or psychological intervention. Forty-50 percent have mild attachment disorders, mild to moderate learning disabilities, speech and language disorders, and need a longer recovery period.

Most social workers agree that the possibility that the family can never adjust is higher when the child is handicapped, more than three years old, or part of a sibling group. Parents should not blame themselves too harshly if they have to ask to have the child removed from their home when they believe another family can do a better job. (Further information on disrupted adoptions can be found at the end of this chapter.) Fortunately, most international families can get all the help and information they need. A growing number of pediatricians, psychologists and other specialists have seen enough institutionalized children to create a body of knowledge for other practitioners. Adoptions can be on the brink of disrupting and be salvaged by skilled intervention.

HELPFUL ACTIVITIES FOR ADOPTED CHILDREN

1. If possible, work through your U.S. international adoption agency to have your child draw a picture to send to his or her foster mother or orphanage.

2. Help the child save money to send to an orphanage or church in the child's native land.

3. Find a pen pal for your child in the native land.

4. Read some relevant books together, such as *Why Am I Different* by Norma Simon or *Filling in the Blanks: A Guided Look at Growing Up Adopted* by Susan Gabel. (See Bibliography for other books.)

5. Discuss minority or foreign-born Americans you admire. You can talk about the qualities of color and nations and all of the good things associated with them. You can discuss children you know, along with their good and bad traits and point out that the traits have nothing to do with color or national origin.

6. Go to the children's department of your public library and check out some books on the child's country with pictures. Plan an imaginary trip to that country and talk about what you would see and do there together.

7. Help your children design a Life Book (described below).

The Life Book

One of the best ways to help a child maintain a sense of identity is to create and maintain a Life Book for your child. Design the book to reflect both families and cultures. A large scrapbook is a good background for placing a copy of your child's birth documents, pictures of the people and places where the child stayed, and pictures and memorabilia connected with the child's first moments with you.

While you are abroad, buy picture postcards for the book, small maps, a small flag, and save some coins to tape into the Life Book. Tickets, menus, and any other paper tourist-type items will fascinate the child later on as you look through the book together.

Add pictures of the child's journey home, the first meeting with other new family members, the readoption, and the ceremony of citizenship. This Life Book is the most meaningful baby book an adopted child can possess since the book gives a child a sense of continuity regardless of the changes in his or her life.

Above all, start a journal once you have made the decision to adopt. Keep this as an open letter for the child to read later on. This record will help the child understand that your waiting time was a very important and meaningful period in your lives.

Your cover letter and the response from your foreign child-placing source should also be saved for the child, as well as the foreign stamps.

YOU AND YOUR CHILD

The challenge ahead is one of adjustment for both parent and child. Foreign-born orphans, regardless of which country they are from, have similar adjustment patterns. There is information available on building close parent-child relationships. You may also find studies on adopted foreign orphans at your public library or perhaps at some adoption agencies.

One important, but often overlooked, part of the adoption adjustment involves vocabulary. "The Language of Adoption," a research paper by Marietta E. Spencer, ACSW, Children's Home Society of Minnesota, begins by saying one important aspect in developing close parent-child relationships is the use of correct terminology.

> *"A vital part of education for adoption must include an inspection of the words we use. Vocabulary helps give meaning to the sensitive human process. One should choose words with care. Alternatives to 'put up for adoption' might be the following:"*

> *"To arrange for an adoption.*
> *To make a placement plan for the child.*
> *To find a family who will adopt the child, and so on."*

"Adoption holds out the promise of the fullest realization of the child's (and family's) potential. Such full potential can only be reached if society provides a benign and supportive climate for both the adopted person and for his family."

Unfortunately, our society is not yet benign or supportive. From kindergarten through adulthood, adopted foreign children, as well as adoptive parents, need a lot of answers to a lot of questions that the children ask, those that strangers ask, and those that we ourselves ask.

Consider joining a support group of adoptive families or starting one. Together, you can discuss the problems institutionalized children have and support each other in order to support them. You can also help your children learn about their cultures with other adopted children and adults of their ethnic origin. As a group, you can also discover resources to aid you in planning transracial, cross-cultural workshops for adoption agency staff and prospective adoptive parents.

RACIAL PREJUDICE

In retrospect, Heino and I realized that our personal experience with minorities in this country had been very limited before we adopted our foreign children. We entered into a transracial, cross-cultural adoption believing that by the time our children grew up there would be less racism. Now we know that they will not see the end of prejudice and discrimination in their lifetime. Nevertheless, our lives were enriched by transracial adoption. Our family befriended people we would not have otherwise met. As our children grew, they chose friends because of their personalities and good character. Race was never their criteria for friendship. When they were old enough to date, they followed the same process of selection. Two are married now to people of different ethnicities and religion. Our family is living out our vision of social change. Our twin daughters have risen to important positions in our adoption agency. They are also as thoughtful and considerate as any parent could wish. Interestingly, girls are still more sought after than boys; about 80 percent of prospective parents prefer to adopt girls. Is it because mothers want to re-experience the joys of their childhood with a little girl? Or, should we believe the reason advanced by cynics — that boys carry on the family name, sire future generations, and, therefore, should look like a member of the family?

Prospective adoptive parents who inquired about adoption almost always mentioned their relatives as either being supportive or dead set against a transracial, cross-cultural adoption. After months of hearing some of these callers complain that they could not consider adopting a foreign child because of their relatives, I began asking them how they personally felt about Asian, Hispanic, black, or other minority groups in the United States. Now that we are placing Asian children and white children from Eastern Europe, we must look at political and religious hatreds, as well.

Not until several years after we adopted our foreign children did we realize that we had been thinking of adoption as a single event, done once and for all. We began talking about the additional responsibility of adoptive parents of foreign children as we helped organize their paperwork. We needed to help parents help their children to develop feelings of self-esteem and a sense of identity with both their old family and their new family.

One way to accomplish this is to find friends within the minority groups in our communities to provide adult role models for our middle-school-age children. The prospective adoptive parents who are unwilling to mingle with minorities or foreigners are not likely to feel comfortable in future social situations with their adopted children. Postadoptive parents tend to neglect this aspect of their children's lives.

Most of our inquirers usually mentioned whether they already had, or planned to have, biological children. Had the couple already decided how to handle the problem if a grandparent showed a preference for their genetic grandchildren? Or, had they given some thought to the opposite problem: the foreign adopted child might be given too much attention by everyone and the biological child would feel left out?

Some of the parents considering adoption wondered if the schoolteachers in their communities might believe that children from certain minority groups were intellectually gifted, while children from other groups were intellectually inferior. Other prospective parents confided that minority children were such a rarity in their communities that teachers might overindulge a foreign adopted child.

Most of the time, adoptive parents gave a great deal of thought to their transracial, cross-cultural adoptions. And, usually, once they understood the prospective adoptive parent's feelings, the relatives were emotionally supportive. If their relatives were truly against the idea, the prospective adopters had to ask themselves if they were strong enough to function well without the emotional support and the child care that their extended family would have provided. Fortunately, very few parents considering adoption had to make such a difficult decision. The children were welcomed into loving, extended families. And, some of the grandparents even flew overseas with their children to help with the care and the adoption of their new grandchild.

Whether your extended family supports your adoption plan or not, you do need to make some arrangements concerning your will as well as who shall care for the child should you and your spouse die before the child reaches adulthood. If you have a relative or friend who agrees to accept this responsibility, a letter to this effect can be attached to your will. If you do not have anyone to assume your parental duties, consider writing a letter to your adoption agency, which may agree to re-place your child in a permanent home. Without these provisions, your child could, upon your death, become a ward of the state and be placed in long-term foster care.

CROSS-CULTURAL AND INTERRACIAL WORKSHOPS

To help widen their own awareness and to continue to help other parents and children learn more about the child's country of origin, some parents have volunteered to organize cross-cultural and interracial workshops on an annual basis. Some ideas for similar workshops are listed below.

Purpose: To grow in awareness and understanding of cultural differences. Adoptive parents need to discover some links to the people and culture of their child's native country.

Organization: Gather educational materials from most of the categories in the Bibliography for a display. Include a map, posters of children, and other book and non-book materials. Those from UNICEF are colorful, informative, and inexpensive.

Preworkshop reading: Have the workshop participants read some of the anthropological studies of families in Asia, Europe, or Latin America and discuss the book they chose with the group (see Bibliography).

Music: Play folk music indigenous to these countries. You can probably find tapes and records at the public library.

Featured guest: Present a pro-adoption foreigner from a developing country who is willing to answer questions concerning the conditions that lead to child abandonment and adoption. Prepare a list of questions about the conditions in the guest's country to discuss before his or her presentation concerning child raising.

Films: Present a slide show or rent a film. Slide presentations complete with scripts showing children struggling for survival in extreme poverty are available through UNICEF at very low cost.

Group leaders: Ask the foreign featured guest, a social worker, and a postadoptive couple who have at least three years experience as adoptive parents to answer questions during the group discussion sessions.

Group discussion: Discuss the following questions:
How can we be one another's teachers:
in researching foreign cultures?
in finding immigrants who are willing to teach us culture and customs?
in seeking awareness and understanding of racial and cultural differences?
in learning child-raising methods of other cultures as a comparison?
in discovering how children are taught in other cultures?

Adopted children's interest in these groups may drop off when children are in elementary school. At this point, the family is involved in church and athletic activities and the child just wants to fit in and be an American kid.

In the meantime, parents should continue to collect information on the subject. As children approach adolescence and relate to changing social groups, they will need this for thought and discussion in order to eventually define themselves.

DISRUPTIONS OF ADOPTIVE FAMILIES

Not every adoptive placement succeeds. In our agency's history of more than 2,000 placements, only nine have disrupted. Other agencies cite similar statistics. The reasons have been varied. One child had a serious hearing loss, which was not noticed by the U.S. Embassy-approved doctor. The adoptive parents did not wish to deal with the handicap. Another was an eight-year-old beggar girl who was not easy to transform into a Girl Scout. Another neglected and abused eight-year-old Panamanian boy was uncivilized at home and unruly at school. Another child turned up with hepatitis B and was rejected. A sibling set of three pubescent boys proved impossible for their mother to control. And we were forced to remove an infant when the adoptive parents split up and neither was capable of raising the child alone. On three separate occasions, Romanian and Russian boys of three years old were returned by their first set of adoptive parents for hyperactive, destructive behavior. In all of these cases, the children adjusted well in their new families, probably because the new families were more tolerant, and their expectations were not as high.

Keep your social worker informed of any concerns. Get counseling. Most problems can eventually be resolved. However, if your family agrees that the placement can never succeed, you will need to make plans. If you do not have a final foreign decree, your agency must be contacted. If they hold managing conservatorship, they will take the child into foster care until they can arrange a new placement. The agency must be given all the child's original documents, passport, and alien registration card in order to re-place the child and notify the authorities of the child's change of address.

If you have a foreign decree or U.S. adoption decree, you will need to enlist the assistance of your agency, or another private or public agency, depending upon the needs of the child. If you are able to secure the help of an adoption agency in order to re-place the child in a new home, you must give them the child's previously listed documents. In addition, you will need to sign relinquishments of parental rights in order to terminate your parental rights in court. Only then can the child be placed in an adoptive home.

In our experience, second placements have been successful. The new adoptive parents are already aware of the child's problems and are ready, willing, and able to help the child overcome them. A family meeting held before the child moves in is mandatory in order to establish household rules. The children, unfortunately, blame themselves for having been rejected. They are generally eager to comply with a new living arrangement in the hope of permanence. If at all possible, the first adoptive family should make a preplacement visit with the new adoptive family prior to the placement. They should be there when the transfer is made. If the first family has other children, they should be part of the process so that they don't worry after the transfer is made. If possible, the children should also be allowed to make a postplacement visit to be certain that the child is OK. If a family cannot be found for the child, you or your agency will need to call your state agency to obtain a list of public and private church-run residential homes.

However, the majority of adoptive parents know their limitations and have the right motives: love for children. To them, children are worth all the paperwork, the expense, and the waiting. They're worth the worry and the endless tending. They feel enriched by their racial and/or national diversity and pleased that succeeding generations will probably be of mixed ethnicity.

Figures from the U.S. State Department show that more than 15,000 foreign children are being adopted annually by U.S. citizens. According to sociologists researching this type of adoption, the odds are in favor of happy, cross-cultural, transracial families.

Internationally adopted children will always be "extraordinary Americans." They're resilient survivors of relinquishment, abandonment, and institutionalization. They're brave children raised and trained by some of the most exemplary women and men in the United States. These "extraordinary Americans" grow up with respect for their homelands as well as loyalty toward the United States. As they grow to voting age and rise to responsible positions in the private sector and government, they offer hope for a broader and gentler perspective toward global problems.

Compendium

Adoption Information for
Participating Countries

Information in this Compendium is based on research from international sources and information from the U.S. Department of State. Much of this information is available on the state department Web site (http://travel.state.gov). This Web site offers direct links to detailed international adoption information for many different countries as well as direct links to the Web sites of U.S. Embassies around the world. You can also receive additional information by calling the Office of Children's Issues in the U.S. Department of State at 202-736-7000.

Foreign sources selected for inclusion in the Compendium were based on the political and legal situations for individual countries relating to international adoption at the time of writing. Keep in mind, however, that political and legal situations for individual countries are subject to rapid change. Countries not listed in the Compendium typically do not place children outside of their countries, either because few children are available for adoption, or because legal requirements make it difficult for non-nationals to adopt unless they reside in the country, or because of other restrictions. For example, Islamic religious law restricts adoption in many African and Middle Eastern countries.

For each country listed in the Compendium, we have tried to list available information on the adoption process and the Adoption Authority (in the case of countries who have ratified the Hague Convention, the Central Authority) or the Competent Authority and the Accredited Organizations. Contact information for the U.S. Embassy and Visa Issuing Post for each country is also listed. In addition, we've provided available information on the number of orphan visas recently issued for each country and summary information on each country's geography, capital, demography, language, currency, and major religions.

If information is not available or is not relevant to that particular country, the section may be omitted. For example, not every country has an adoption agency or a government authority in charge of adoption. In such cases, write to the U.S. Consulate in that country for a list of attorneys who practice family law and speak English.

When evaluating the following information, keep in mind that the personal philosophy and policies of foreign judges, attorneys, and child-placing entities are as important as the national adoption laws concerning international adoptions. Whether an adoption proceeds quickly or slowly depends upon the judge, the lawyer, and the child-placing entity, in that order.

Instructions for the dossier of documents generally required by foreign child-placing entities and courts can be found in Chapter 7. Additional requirements for some countries might include a psychological evaluation; a letter from your adoption agency stating the agency's commitment to supervise the child for a specific period of time; a copy of the agency's license; a letter of authorization from your state; and possibly a copy of your state's adoption laws.

When contacting countries overseas, keep in mind that the time zones may be 12-24 hours ahead of U.S. time zones. When phoning or faxing from the United States, it will usually be necessary to dial 011, followed by the country code, which appears in brackets [ ], the city code, which appears in parentheses ( ), and then the phone or fax number. Some countries may have only a city code or a country code, rather than both. When dialing some countries, especially many Caribbean countries, it is only necessary to dial a 1 followed by the country or city code, rather than 011.

DIVISIONS OF THE COMPENDIUM

The organization of the Compendium is based on the geographic designations used in the *Report of the Visa Office*.

Africa – We list only those countries that place significant numbers of adopted children.

Asia – The geographic designation of Asia includes the countries of Asia as well as the Middle East. Those countries not listed have no history of orphan visas because of Islamic religious laws or other restrictions. Israel does not permit adoption of children by anyone living outside of Israel.

Europe - Most of the sources listed are in Eastern Europe. Western European countries are not listed due to a shortage of babies available for adoption. For the most part, the countries of Europe are presented in alphabetical order. However, Russia and other members of the Commonwealth of Independent States (CIS) are grouped together, as are republics of the former Yugoslavia. We did not list countries of the CIS that have never allowed international adoption.

Latin America – This section of the Compendium includes Mexico and the countries of Central America, South America, and the Caribbean. Those countries not listed have never allowed international adoption or have laws or residence requirements that greatly restrict the possibility of international adoption.

Oceania – This section of the Compendium includes only the Marshall Islands, a country shown considerable interest by prospective adopters.

INDEX TO COUNTRIES IN THE COMPENDIUM

Africa

According to Cheryl Shotts, Director of Americans for African Adoptions, Islamic laws have an impact on the adoption laws and procedures in each country. In countries such as Sudan, where the religious law and the law of the nation are the same, adoption by persons who are non-Muslims and non-residents is impossible. In countries where adoption is possible, such as Ethiopia, adoptive parents can be of any religion.

In 1998, only 172 orphans from the entire African continent were adopted by U.S. citizens

ETHIOPIA

Geography: East African country of 1,221,918 square kilometers bordered by Sudan, Somalia, and Kenya

Capital: Addis Ababa

Demography: 4,200,000

Language: Amharic

Currency: Birr

Major Religions: Christianity, Islam, Judaism

Orphans Admitted into the United States
Fiscal year 1995: 63   Fiscal year 1997: 82
Fiscal year 1996: 44   Fiscal year 1998: 96

Adoption Information: Most adoptions are handled by proxy through international adoption agencies. When the final decree is issued, the international adoption agency arranges for the child to be escorted to the adoptive parents, usually by airline personnel.

Ethiopian authorities require the usual documents, as well as two passport-size photos of each spouse and a statement explaining why you prefer to adopt an Ethiopian child. Another form, called "Obligation of Adoption or Social Welfare Agency," must be signed by your local adoption agency. With this form, the adoptive parents promise to submit progress reports to the Ethiopian Children and Youth Affairs Organization (CYAO).

These documents are authenticated at the Ministry of Foreign Affairs in Ethiopia. Then they are submitted to the Adoption Committee of the CYAO for approval. Upon approval, a child may be located for the adoptive parents. A Contract of Adoption is signed between the CYAO and the adopting parents or their legal representative, after which they file for a court date. The adoption may be initiated by power of attorney and consummated by the prospective parents or their representative. The CYAO issues a final decree.

Adoption Authority
Children's Youth Affair Office (CYAO)
Addis Ababa, Ethiopia
Tel: [251] (1) 55-22-00 ext. 28

U.S. Embassy/Visa Issuing Post
Entoto Street
P.O. Box 1014
Addis Ababa, Ethiopia
Tel: [251] (1) 550-666
Fax: [251] (1) 551-328

Mailing Address:
U.S. Embassy, Addis Ababa
Department of State
Washington DC 20521-2210

SIERRA LEONE

Geography: A small African country of 27,925 square miles on the Atlantic coast. Sierra Leone is bordered by Guinea, Liberia, and the Ivory Coast.

Capital: Freetown

Demography: 3,100,000

Languages: Mende, Temne, Vai, English, Krio (pidgin)

Currency: Leone

Major Religions: Tribal religions, Islam, Christianity

Orphans Admitted into the United States
Fiscal year 1995: 5   Fiscal year 1997: 2
Fiscal year 1996: 10   Fiscal year 1998: 17

Adoption Information: Most adoptions are handled by proxy through an adoption agency. When the final decree is issued, the child is escorted to the adoptive parents by approved airline personnel. Current adoption information may be obtained from the U.S. Consulate.

U.S. Consulate

Corner of Walpole and Siaka Stevens Streets
Freetown, Sierra Leone
Tel: [232] (22) 226-481
Fax: [232] (22) 225-471

Mailing Address:
U.S. Consulate, Sierra Leone
Department of State
Washington DC 20521-2210

Asia

The geographic designation of Asia is used by the U.S. Visa Office to describe the countries of Asia and the Middle East. Countries not listed, particularly in the Middle East, either do not permit or do not encourage intercountry adoptions. Islamic countries usually do not allow adoptions by foreigners except in the case of adoption by relatives.

CAMBODIA

Geography: A Southeast Asian country of 181,035 square kilometers, bordered by Thailand, Vietnam, and Laos

Capital: Phnom Penh

Demography: Population of 8,500,000 is made up of people of Cambodian and Thai descent

Languages: Cambodian (Khmer), French

Currency: Riel

Major Religion: Buddhism

Orphans Admitted into the United States
Fiscal year 1995: 10   Fiscal year 1997: 66
Fiscal year 1996: 32   Fiscal year 1998: 249

Adoption Information: Applicants must be 25 years old and 21 years older than the child. If the adopting parent is married, a doctor's letter stating that the wife is no longer able to have children is also required. The adopting parent(s) must also provide information about the adopted child until it reaches majority age, as requested by the Ministry of Foreign Affairs.

U.S. Embassy
16, Street 228 (between Streets 51 and 63)
Phnom Penh, Cambodia
Tel: [855] (23) 216-436 ext. 38
     [855] (23) 218-931
Fax: [855] (23) 216-437
*U.S. visas are issued at the U.S. Embassy in Bangkok, Thailand.

Visa Issuing Post
   U.S. Embassy, Consulate Section
   120-122 Wireless Road
   Bangkok, Thailand 10330
   Tel: [66] (2) 250-4000
       [66] (2) 254-2990

Mailing Address:
Consulate Section
U.S. Embassy, Bangkok
APO AP 96546

CHINA

Geography: Land mass of 9,561,000 square kilometers bordering Mongolia, Russia, Korea, India, Nepal, Burma, Laos, and Vietnam

Capital: Beijing

Demography: Population of 1,300,000,000, of which 93 percent are Han (ethnic Chinese). The remaining 68 million are distributed among 55 minority groups ranging in size from the 12 million Zhuang to some groups numbering fewer than 1,000.

Languages: Mandarin Chinese, Cantonese, Chuang, Uigar, Yi, Tibetan, Miao, Mongol, Kazakh

Currency: Yuan (Renmin)

Major Religions: Confucianism, Buddhism, Taoism, Islam

Orphans Admitted into the United States
Fiscal year 1995: 2,130   Fiscal year 1997: 3,597
Fiscal year 1996: 3,333   Fiscal year 1998: 4,206

Adoption Information: In a change of the law effective April 1999, the age limit for adoption of Chinese children has been lowered from 35 to 30 years of age. Single individuals may adopt as well as married couples. Another provision of the new law is that families with children can now adopt another, healthy young child. With few exceptions, all children are females. Interested parties have to work through an approved adoption agency via the China Centre for Adoption Affairs (CCAA). Persons over 45 years of age may adopt older children or special needs children.

Adoption Authority
   China Centre for Adoption Affairs (CCAA)
   No. 1 Baiguaang Road
   Zhongmin Building
   Xuanwu District
   Beijing, China 100053
   Tel: [86] (10) 6357-5768   (Administrative Department)
   Fax: [86] (10) 6357-5769
   Tel: [86] (10) 6357-5785   (Liaison and Service Department)
   Fax: [86] (10) 6357-5786

U.S. Embassy/Visa Issuing Post

U.S. Consulate General	*Mailing Address:*
Adoption Unit	U.S. Consulate, Guangzhou
No. 1 South Shamian Street, South	PSC 461, Box 100
Shamian Island 20031	or FPO AP 96521-0002
Guangzhou, China 510133	
Tel: [86] (20) 8188-8911	
Fax: [86] (20) 8186-2341	

HONG KONG

Geography: Hong Kong became a part of China again on July 1, 1997. According to the Sino-British joint declaration of 1984, the transfer of control should allow for the current social and economic policies of Hong Kong to continue for 50 years.

Capital: Victoria (694,500), an island of only five square miles

Demography: Population of 4,400,000, the majority of which are of Chinese descent, with East Indian and European minorities.

Languages: Chinese and English

Currency: Hong Kong Dollar

Major Religions: Confucianism, Buddhism, Christianity

Orphans Admitted into the United States

Fiscal year 1995: 40	Fiscal year 1997: 21
Fiscal year 1996: 36	Fiscal year 1998: 27

Adoption Information: The Adoption Unit of the Social Welfare Department is the government authority in Hong Kong responsible for arranging the adoption of children by local residents and coordinating with non-governmental organizations (including the International Social Service, Hong Kong Branch, and Mother's Choice) for the adoption of children by foreigners. Children to be adopted by foreigners must first be relinquished by the parents to the Director of Social Welfare.

Married couples or single individuals who are at least 25 years of age, in good health, and financially capable of raising a child to independence are eligible to adopt. However, the Social Welfare Department does mention that candidates are more likely to be successful if they are able to stay in Hong Kong for a continual period of 12 months or more to complete the adoption process.

Adoption Authority
Adoption Unit
Social Welfare Department
38, Pier Road

4/F., Harbour Building
Central, Hong Kong
Tel: [852] 5852-3170

U.S. Consulate General/Visa Issuing Post

U.S. Consulate General
26 Garden Road
Hong Kong
Tel: [852] 2841-2412
Fax: [852] 2845-1598

Mailing Address:
U.S. Consulate General,
Hong Kong
PSC 464, Box 30
or FPO, AP 96522-0002

INDIA

Geography: A republic of southern Asia that was once a British colony. With 1,261,482 square miles, India covers most of the Indian subcontinent.

Capital: New Delhi (324,283)

Demography: The population of 853,100,000 includes six major ethnic groups and millions of tribal people.

Languages: Hindi is the official language and English is widely spoken by educated people; however, a total of 141 different languages and dialects are spoken in India.

Currency: Rupee

Major Religions: Hinduism, Islam, Sikhism, Buddhism, Jainism, Zoroastrianism, Animism, Christianity

Orphans Admitted into the United States

Fiscal year 1995: 371   Fiscal year 1997: 349
Fiscal year 1996: 380   Fiscal year 1998: 478

Adoption Information: International agencies have to be accredited by the Central Adoption Resource Agency (CARA). After that they have to link up with an Indian licensed adoption agency that places children domestically. An Indian agency can only place as many children internationally as they have already placed domestically. Children leave India with a guardianship unless the adopters are Hindu, since Indian law allows only Hindus to adopt. Children placed under guardianship with non-Hindus can then be adopted in their new country of residence.

Adoption Authority

Central Adoption Resource Agency (CARA)
Ministry of Social Justice and Empowerment
West Block 8, Wing 11
R.K. Puram

New Delhi, India 110066
Tel: [91] (11) 605-346
Fax: [91] (11) 384-918

U.S. Embassy/Visa Issuing Posts
American Embassy
Shantipath
Chanakyapuri 110021
New Delhi, India
Tel: [91] (11) 688-9033
Fax [91] (11) 419-0017

American Consulate General
Lincoln House
78 Bhulabhai Desai Road
Bombay, India 400026
Tel: [91] (22) 363-3611
Fax: [91] (22) 363-0350

American Consulate General
5/1 Ho Chi Minh Sarani
Calcutta, India 700071
Tel: [91] (33) 282-3611
Fax: [91] (33) 282-2335

American Consulate General
220 Anna Salei Rd.
Madras, India 600006
Tel: [91] (44) 827-3040
Fax: [91] (44) 825-0240

JAPAN

Geography: An island empire consisting of four large islands, eight small islands, and two island groups, covering 142,798 square miles

Capital: Tokyo (11,350,000)

Demography: 123,500,000

Language: Japanese

Currency: Yen

Major Religions: Shintoism, Buddhism, Christianity

Orphans Admitted into the United States
Fiscal year 1995: 63   Fiscal year: 1997: 45
Fiscal year 1996: 34   Fiscal year: 1998: 39

Adoption Information: The law does not prohibit foreigners from adopting, and no specific government requirements exist. Either a final decree or guardianship may be obtained. One or both parents may travel to Japan to immigrate the child, or the child may be escorted.

Adoption Authority
According to the Tokyo Metropolitan Government, there is no national child-placing authority in Japan. Rather, each prefecture is authorized to handle adoption cases independently.

U.S. Embassy/Visa Issuing Post

10-5 Akasaka 1-Chome	*Mailing Address:*
Minato-ku, Unit 45004	U.S. Embassy, Tokyo
Tokyo, Japan 107-8420	APO AP 96337-5004
Tel: [81] (3) 3224-5000	
Fax: [81] (3) 3505-1862	

KOREA

Geography: The Republic of Korea, commonly referred to as South Korea, occupies the southern half of the Korean peninsula, covering 38,452 square miles.

Capital: Seoul (4,100,000)

Demography: 31,683,000

Language: Korean

Currency: Won

Major Religions: Confucianism, Buddhism, Chondogyo, Christianity

Orphans Admitted into the United States

Fiscal year 1995: 1,666 Fiscal year 1997: 1,654
Fiscal year 1996: 1,516 Fiscal year 1998: 1,829

Adoption Information: All international adoptions in Korea must be arranged through one of the Korean adoption agencies listed below, which are authorized by the Korean government. These Korean agencies have child-placing agreements with many adoption agencies in North America and Western European countries.

Adoptive couples must be married for at least three years and be between the ages of 25 and 44. In addition, the adoptive couple should have no more than five children, including the child or children to be adopted and the couple should not have an age difference of more than 15 years. Korean authorities may make exceptions in some cases. The following factors may be considered when making exceptions to the age limit: (1) at least one parent is under 45, (2) the adoptive parents have previously adopted a Korean orphan, and (3) the parents are willing to adopt an orphan with serious medical problems.

Adoption Authority

Family Welfare Bureau
Ministry of Health and Social Affairs
Republic of Korea
#77 Sejongro, Jongro-gu
Seoul, Korea

Adoption Agencies

Eastern Child Welfare Society, Inc.
(Korean Christian Crusade)
#493, Changchun-Dong,
   Sudaemun-Ku
Seoul, Korea
Tel: [82] (2) 332-3941
   (through 3945)

Social Welfare Society, Inc.
#718-35, Yuksam-Dong
Kangnam-Ku
Seoul, Korea
Tel: [82] (2) 552-1015
   (through 1018),
or [82] (2) 555-0810

Holt Children's Services
#382-14, Hapjong, Dong
Mapo-Ku
Seoul, Korea
Tel: [82] (2) 322-7501 (through 7504),
or [82] 322-8102 (through 8103)

Korea Social Service
533-3 Sscenjmum- Day
Dobany-Ku
Seoul, Korea
Tel. [82] (2) 908-9191
   (through 9193)

U.S. Embassy/Visa Issuing Post

U.S. Embassy, Consular Section
82, Sejong-ro
Chongro-ku
Seoul, Korea 110-050
Tel: [82] (2) 397-4114
Fax: [82] (2) 738-8845

Mailing Address:
Consular Section
U.S. Embassy, Seoul
Unit 15550
APO 96205-0001

LAOS

Geography: A country in Southeast Asia, formerly a part of French Indochina, with 236,789 square kilometers

Capital: Vientiane

Demography: Population of about 4,000,000

Languages: Lao, French, English

Currency: New Kip (LAK)

Major Religions: Buddhism, tribal religions

Orphans Admitted into the United States

Fiscal year 1995: 0   Fiscal year 1997: 1
Fiscal year 1996: 1   Fiscal year 1998: 0

Adoption Information: The Ministry of Justice of the Lao People's Democratic Republic notified the U.S. Embassy of the Lao government's suspension of adoption of Lao children by foreigners, pending review of the Lao adoption law. The suspension will not be lifted until the Laos National Assembly completes its review. As of the fall of 1999, the U.S. Embassy had received no indication that such a review had begun or was scheduled to begin.

U.S. Embassy

Box 114, Rue Bartholonie
Vientiane, Laos PDR
Tel: [856] (21) 212-581
Fax: [856] (21) 212-584

Mailing Address:
U.S. Embassy, Laos
Box V, APO AP 96546

*Visas are issued in Bangkok, Thailand.

LEBANON

Geography: A republic on the Arabian Peninsula that borders Turkey and covers 4,015 square miles

Capital: Beirut

Demography: 2,800,000, the majority of whom are of Arab descent. Most of the rest are Turk and Armenian minorities.

Languages: Arabic and French

Currency: Lebanese Pound

Major Religions: Christianity and Islam

Orphans Admitted into the United States
Fiscal year 1995: 20   Fiscal year 1997: 14
Fiscal year 1996: 15   Fiscal year 1998: 17

Adoption Information: Laws concerning adoptions are handled by religious authorities. Islamic law does not provide for adoption; however, adoption is allowed by the various Christian denominations. Christian orphanages may have children available for adoption. The Lebanese Surete General requires that all adoptive parents must travel to Lebanon to complete the adoption procedure and to accompany the child out of Lebanon.

U.S. Embassy/Visa Issuing Post

U.S. Embassy
Awkar
P.O. Box 70-840
Beirut, Lebanon
Tel: [961] (4) 542-600, or
    [961] (4) 543-600
Fax: [961] (4) 544-136

Mailing Address:
U.S. Embassy, Beirut
FPO AE 09836-0002

NEPAL

Geography: Mountain kingdom in the Himalayas between China and India

Capital: Kathmandu

Demography: More than 13 million of Nepalese and Tamang descent

Languages: Nepali, Maithali, Tamang, Newari, Than

Currency: Nepalese Rupee (NPR)

Major Religions: Hinduism, Buddhism

Orphans Admitted into United States

Fiscal year 1995: 8   Fiscal year 1997: 17
Fiscal year 1996: 16   Fiscal year 1998: 19

Adoption Information: On January 14, 1999, the government of Nepal suspended approval of all adoptions of Nepali orphans by foreigners. On March 2, 1999, the government informed the U.S. Embassy in Kathmandu that foreign adoptions would resume, but imposed new requirements that effectively precluded U.S. citizens from adopting in Nepal. At the time of writing, the U.S. Department of State was continuing work with the government of Nepal to try to find a solution that would allow adoptions by U.S. citizens to resume.

Adoption Authority:

Nepal Children's Organization (NCO)
P.O. Box 6967
Bal Mandir, Naxal
Kathmandu, Nepal
Tel: [977] (1) 411-202
Fax: [977] (1) 414-485

U.S.Embassy/Visa Issuing Post

U.S.Embassy
Pani Pokhari
Kathmandu, Nepal
Tel: [977] (1) 413-836
Fax: [977] (1) 419-963

PHILIPPINES

Geography: An island republic covering 115,707 square miles in the Malay Archipelago island group. The Philippines became independent from the United States in 1946.

Capital: Manila, on the island of Luzon (2,000,000)

Demography: 62,400,000 people of Indonesian and Malayan ethnic backgrounds

Languages: Filipino (Tagalog), English, Spanish, Bisayan, Ilocano, Bikol, and many other dialects

Currency: Piso

Major Religions: Roman Catholic, Islam, Protestant, and tribal religions

Orphans Admitted into the United States

Fiscal year 1995: 298   Fiscal year 1997: 163
Fiscal year 1996: 229   Fiscal year 1998: 200

Adoption Information: The Philippine Family Code, which took effect in 1988, made several significant changes in the laws governing adoption of children by foreigners in the Philippine courts. The new law provides that aliens may not adopt children in the Philippines except in the following circumstances: Former Filipinos who seek to adopt a relative by consanguinity, or who seek to adopt the legitimate child of their Filipino spouse, or who are married to Filipino citizens and seek to adopt a relative jointly with their spouse. Aliens not included in the foregoing exceptions may adopt Filipino children in accordance with the rules on intercountry adoptions as may be provided by law. In general, to process an intercountry adoption, a U.S. citizen must be physically outside the Philippines and process the adoption through a licensed agency in conjunction with the Philippine Department of Social Welfare and Development. It will no longer be possible for American citizens living in the Philippines to identify a child and adopt through the Philippine courts, except as noted above. Either a guardianship or final adoption decree is issued. Adoptions are initiated through accredited agencies.

Central Adoption Authority
Bureau of Child and Youth Welfare
Department of Social Welfare
and Development
Batasang Pambansa Complex
Constitution Hills
Quezon City, Philippines

U.S. Embassy/Visa Issuing Post
U.S. Embassy
1201 Roxas Blvd.
Ermita 1000
Manila, Philippines
Tel: [63] (2) 523-1001
Fax: [63] (2) 522-4361

Competent Authority
Office of the Solicitor
General of the Philippines
134 Amoorsolo Street
Legaspi Village
Makati City, Philippines

SRI LANKA

Geography: An island republic at the tip of the Indian subcontinent covering 25,332 square miles

Capital: Colombo (551,200)

Demography: 12,300,000

Languages: Sinhalese, Tamil, English

Currency: Sri Lankan Rupee (LKR)

Major Religions: Buddhism, Hinduism, Christianity

Orphans Admitted into the United States
Fiscal year 1995: 8   Fiscal year 1997: 5
Fiscal year 1996: 4   Fiscal year 1998: 2

Adoption Information: Formal application to adopt in Sri Lanka by non-residents should be made to the district court of Colombo or such courts with jurisdiction.

Central Adoption Authority
    Commissioner
    Department of Probation and
        Child Care Services
    P.O. Box 546
    Chatham Street
    Colombo 1, Sri Lanka

U.S. Embassy/Visa Issuing Post
    U.S. Embassy
    210 Galle Road
    Colombo 3
    P.O. Box 106
    Colombo, Sri Lanka
    Tel: [94] (1) 448-007
    Fax: [94] (1) 437-345

TAIWAN

Geography: An island off the coast of China, which is claimed by China as a "renegade province"

Capital: Taipei (1,604,543)

Demography: 14,577,000

Languages: Mandarin Chinese, Taiwanese, Formosan, and Hakka dialects

Currency: New Taiwan Dollar

Major Religions: Confucianism, Buddhism, Taoism, Christianity

Orphans Admitted into the United States
Fiscal year 1995: 2   Fiscal year 1997: 19
Fiscal year 1996: 19   Fiscal year 1998: 30

Adoption Information: Since the United States recognized the People's Republic of China as the official government of all China, we no longer have consular representation. The American Institute in Taiwan (A.I.T.) acts as a U.S. liaison office. Childless couples or those with one child who have been married three years and are under 42 years of age may apply for adoption. Either a guardianship or final adoption decree is issued.

The American Institute in Taiwan
    7 Lane 134
    Hsin Yi Road, Section 3
    Taipei, Taiwan
    Tel: [886] (2) 709-2000
    Fax: [886] (2) 702-7675

Private Agencies in Taiwan arranging adoptions:
Catholic Welfare Services (Cathwell)
2 Chung Shan North Road, Section 1
Taipei, Taiwan
Tel: [886] (2) 311-0223

Christian Salvation Service
397 Hsin Yi Road, Section 4
Taipei, Taiwan
Tel: [886] (2) 311-0223

The Pearl Buck Foundation
2 Chung Shan North Road, Section 1
Taipei, Taiwan
Tel: [886] (2) 331-8690

U.S. Embassy/Visa Issuing Post
American Consulate General
26 Garden Road, Box 30
Hong Kong
Tel: [852] 2841-2412
(no city code is needed for Hong Kong)
Fax: [852] 2845-1598

Mailing Address
American Consulate General
FPO AP 96522-0002

*Check with the Office of Children's Issues or the Visa Office of the U.S. Department of State for visa issuing information.

THAILAND

Geography: A kingdom in Southeast Asia on the gulf of Siam. This country, which was formerly named Siam, covers 198,445 square miles.

Capital: Bangkok (2,000,000)

Demography: 55,700,000 persons of Thai and Chinese descent

Languages: Thai, Lao, Chinese, Khmer, Malay

Currency: Thai Baht

Major Religions: Buddhism, Islam, tribal religions

Orphans Admitted into the United States
Fiscal year 1995: 53   Fiscal year 1997: 63
Fiscal year 1996: 55   Fiscal year 1998: 84

Adoption Information: The Minor Adoption Act of 1979 stipulates strict requirements. The adoptive couple must be over 30 years of age, married at least five years, and be 15 years older than the child. Both prospective parents must travel to Thailand for a stay of about two weeks until a final decree is issued and the child's visa is obtained. Documents must be submitted via an approved agency. All adoptions in Thailand are managed by the Department of Public Welfare. The first step in the process is direct communication with that office. For complete information and appropriate forms, write to the address below.

Adoption Authority
Child Adoption Center
Department of Public Welfare
Rajvithee Road
(Rajvithee Home for Girls)
Bangkok 10400, Thailand

U.S. Embassy/Visa Issuing Post
American Consulate
120-122 Wireless Road
Bangkok 10330 Thailand
Tel: [66] (2) 250-4000
Fax: [66] (2) 254-2990

Mailing Address:
American Consulate, Bangkok
APO AP 96546

VIETNAM

Geography: A country in Southeast Asia of 329,566 square miles that shares borders with China, Laos, and Cambodia

Capital: Hanoi

Demography: Population of approximately 66,693,000

Languages: Vietnamese, Thai, Muong, Chinese, Khmer, French, and local dialects

Currency: Dong. The U.S. dollar is also widely accepted and used in large cash transactions.

Major Religions: Buddhism, Taoism, Confucianism, Roman Catholicism

Orphans Admitted into the United States
Fiscal year 1995: 315   Fiscal year 1997: 425
Fiscal year 1996: 354   Fiscal year 1998: 603

Adoption Information: Adoption Authority rests with the Department of Justice in each province, the local People's Committee, and the welfare centers in the province. Procedures may vary from province to province. A final adoption decree is issued after the "Giving and Receiving Ceremony." The medical examination of the child is now done in Ho Chi Minh City (formerly Saigon) and the interview for the U.S. visa is conducted by the Orderly Departure Program (ODP), which is also in charge of family reunions. This is also done in Ho Chi Minh City. Visas are now issued by the U.S. Consulate General in Ho Chi Minh City.

Usually, funding of humanitarian projects within the province is required in order to obtain permission to place the children. Thus, U.S. adoption agencies working with Vietnam typically sponsor humanitarian projects. A law change in February 1999 removed humanitarian projects by non-governmental organizations (or nonprofit organizations) from the People's Aid Coordinating Committee and gave the authority of projects under $200,000 to the Provincial People's Committees and the National Ministry of Finance. These projects need not be connected to children, but could be community services in the district and province.

U.S. Embassy

7 Lang Ha Road
Ba dinh District
Hanoi, Vietnam
Tel: [84] (4) 843-1500
Fax: [84] (4) 835-0484

Mailing Address:
U.S. Embassy, Hanoi
PSC 461
FPO AP 96521-0002

Visa Issuing Post

U.S. Consulate General
#4 Le Duan Street
District 1
Ho Chi Minh City, Vietnam
Tel: [84] (8) 822-9443
Fax: [84] (8) 825-0938

Orderly Departure Program

*Assists in clearance for U.S. orphan visa
184 bis Pasteur
District 1
Ho Chi Minh City, Vietnam
Tel: [84] (8) 824-4622
Fax: [84] (8) 829-7665

Europe

As sources have opened in Eastern European countries and as new U.S. embassies are being established, new possibilities for international adoption have appeared. We are listing countries where information has become available. Please note that although some of the countries formally a part of the Soviet Union and now part of the Commonwealth of Independent States (CIS) are located in Asia, they are listed here because orphan visas for these countries will still be issued by the U.S. Embassy in Moscow. However, visas for Latvia, Lithuania, Belarus, and Ukraine will be issued by the U.S. Embassy in Warsaw, Poland. Visas for Estonia will be issued by the U.S. Embassy in Helsinki, Finland, and visas for Moldova are issued in Bucharest, Romania.

ALBANIA

Geography: A small Balkan country bordering the former Yugoslavia and Greece

Capital: Tirana

Demography: 3,200,000 mainly descendants of the Illyrians of Central Europe. The rest are Greek.

Language: Albanian (Tosk and Gheg)

Currency: Lek

Major Religions: Islam, Eastern Orthodox, Roman Catholic

Orphans Admitted into the United States
Fiscal year 1995: 3   Fiscal year 1997: 12
Fiscal year 1996: 7   Fiscal year 1998: 10

Adoption Information: A law passed in January 1993 regulates all foreign adoptions, which are overseen by the Albanian Adoption Committee (AAC). The authority of this committee began in July of 1995. A register of children eligible for adoption exists. For the first six months, children on the register are available for adoption by Albanian citizens residing in Albania. After six months, they become eligible for international adoption. Adoptions can only be handled through a foreign agency licensed by the Albanian Adoption Committee. Prospective adoptive families are not allowed to go to an orphanage to select a child without authorization by the committee. In general, the Adoption Committee will work through a licensed foreign agency. Bethany Christian Service in Grand Rapids, Michigan, is recognized by the Adoption Committee. Contact the U.S. Consulate or the U.S. State Department for names of other U.S.-based international agencies working in Albania.

Adoption Authority	*U.S. Embassy/Visa Issuing Post*
Albanian Adoption Committee (AAC)	U.S. Embassy, Consular Section
Ms. Ilmije Mara	Rruga E. Labinoti 103
Komiteti Shqiptar I Biresimeve	Tirana, Albania
Kryeministria	Tel: [355] (42) 32875
Tirana, Albania	Fax: [355] (42) 32222

U.S. Agencies Accredited by the AAC	*Mailing Address:*
Bethany Christian Service	Consular Section
901 Eastern Avenue, N.E.	U.S. Embassy, Albania
Box 294	PSC 59
Grand Rapids, MI 49501-0294	Box 100 (A) or
Tel: 1-800-652-7082	APO AE 09624
Fax: (616) 224-7585	

BULGARIA

Geography: A Balkan country of 110,911 square kilometers

Capital: Sofia

Demography: 9,000,000. The majority of the population consists of ethnic Bulgarians; ten percent are mainly Turk, with lesser minorities of Macedonians and Gypsies.

Languages: Bulgarian and Turkish

Currency: Lev

Major Religion: Eastern Orthodox

Orphans Admitted into the United States
Fiscal year 1995: 110   Fiscal year 1997: 148
Fiscal year 1996: 163   Fiscal year 1998: 151

Adoption Information: Adoptive parents must be at least 15 years older than the child. Parent-initiated and agency-initiated adoptions are permitted. In addition to the documentary requirements, there are other conditions of foreign adoptions in Bulgaria to keep in mind. Bulgarian regulations prohibit foreign adoptions of orphans under one year of age or by parents who have previous natural or adopted children. The Ministry of Justice can waive these prohibitions, but prospective adoptive parents should not count on waivers. In practice, most children adopted by Americans are three or four years old. For children under three, the orphanage must certify that three Bulgarian families have declined to adopt the child before it can be placed with a foreign parent.

There are many orphanages in Bulgaria, and there is no central organization for identifying available children through photographs or videotapes. Adoptive parents must meet an orphan in person. Adoptive parents should plan on making two trips to Bulgaria or delegating power of attorney to a lawyer or agent in Bulgaria to complete the case, as the process always takes at least six months.

After the child has been identified and the U.S. preadoption requirements have been met, a packet containing all of the documents is submitted simultaneously to the Bulgarian Ministry of Justice and the Ministry of Health (for children 0-3 years old) or the Ministry of Education (for children 3-6 years old). The Ministry of Justice must give permission for the adoption to take place, with only advisory opinions from the other ministries. When the Ministry of Justice has given approval, the case is turned over to the court for the final adoption decree and the amendment of the birth record. Foreign adoptive parents must retain a Bulgarian lawyer for the court case.

Adoption Authority

    The Ministry of Public Health (children ages 0-3)
    The Ministry of Education (children over 3)
    The Ministry of Justice (approves all adoptions)

All three ministries are located at the district center of each town and at the district center for Sofia.

U.S. Embassy/Visa Issuing Post

U.S. Embassy, Consular Section
1 Saborna Street
Sofia, Bulgaria
Tel: [359] (2) 980-5241
Fax: [359] (2) 963-2859

Mailing Address:
Consular Section
U.S. Embassy, Bulgaria
Unit 25402
APO AE 09213

ESTONIA

Geography: A Baltic republic of 45,100 square kilometers, which was part of the former Soviet Union. Estonia is now independent.

Capital: Tallinn

Demography: 1,600,000 of Finno-Ugric ancestry. Two-thirds of the population is Estonian, one-fourth is Russian, and the remaining population is made up of

Ukrainian, Finnish, and Belarussian minorities.

Languages: Estonian, Russian

Currency: Ruble, Kroon

Major Religions: Eastern Orthodox, Protestant

Orphans Admitted into the United States

Fiscal year 1995: 0   Fiscal year 1997: 0

Fiscal year 1996: 6   Fiscal year 1998: 6

Adoption Information: A U.S. citizen wishing to adopt a child in Estonia must first contact an approved U.S agency or organization. A list of approved agencies and organizations can be obtained from the Estonian Ministry of Social Affairs (MSA). The agency will prepare the application, assist the applicants with their legal prerequisites, obtain all the necessary civil documents, and forward them to the MSA. The MSA has a list of children in Estonia who are currently available for international adoption. A commission from the MSA will identify a child on that list and offer the prospective parent(s) the choice of adopting that particular child. If a prospective parent declines three successive offers, his or her application will be terminated. MSA will not accept applications directly from nonresident prospective parents. These are only accepted through an agency that has been approved and signed an agreement with the MSA.

U.S. Embassy	U.S. Visa Issuing Post
U.S. Embassy	U.S. Consular Section
Kentmanni 20	Itainen Puistotie 14A
Tallinn 15099, Estonia	FIN-00140 Helsinki
Tel: [372] (6) 312-021	Finland
Fax: [372] (6) 312-025	Tel: [358] (9) 171-931
Visa Information Line:	Fax: [358] (9) 174-681
[372] (6) 466-521	

GREECE

Geography: A republic of 131,955 square miles in the southern part of the Balkans, including the islands of Crete, the Aegean, and Dodecanese Islands. Greece is bordered by Turkey, Bulgaria, Macedonia (former Yugoslavia), and Albania.

Capital: Athens (627,564)

Demography: 10,000,000 persons of European descent

Languages: Greek, Turkish

Currency: Drachma

Major Religion: Greek Orthodox

Orphans Admitted into the United States

Fiscal year 1995: 8   Fiscal year 1997: 1

Fiscal year 1996: 9   Fiscal year 1998: 3

Adoption Information: Greek children can only be adopted by persons who are either Greek citizens or of Greek origin and residents in Greece. Exceptions are made for children with health problems at the discretion of the institution sheltering the child. The only condition in such a case is that the adoptive parents be the same religion as the child. A Greek lawyer is needed to obtain a final adoption decree. There is no central adoption authority.

Greek Orphanages

Metera Foster Home
65 Democratias Street
GR-131 22 Athens
Greece
Tel: [30] (1) 262-7156

Demotrika Vrefokomeion
(Municipal Home for Foundlings)
135 Sevastunpoleos St.
Ambelokipi
GR-151 26 Athens
Greece
Tel: [30] (1) 691-0193

Patriotic Institution for Social
   Welfare and Assistance
   (PIKPA)
5 Tsoha Street
Ambelokipi
GR-151 21 Athens
Greece
Tel: [30] (1) 642-7856

U.S. Embassy/Visa Issuing Post

U.S. Embassy, Consular Section
91 Vasilissis Sophias Avenue
101 60 Athens
Greece
Tel: [30] (1) 721-2951 or 721-8407
Fax: [30] (1) 645-6282

Mailing Address:
Consular Section
U.S. Embassy, Greece
PSC 108
Box 56, or
APO AE 09842

HUNGARY

Geography: A landlocked country covering 25,000 square miles, bordered by Romania, Moldova, the Czech Republic, Austria, and the former Yugoslavia

Capital: Budapest

Demography: 10,600,000 people of Hungarian and Gypsy heritage

Language: Hungarian

Currency: Forint

Major Religion: Christian

Orphans Admitted into the United States
Fiscal year 1995: 28   Fiscal year 1997: 72
Fiscal year 1996: 51   Fiscal year 1998: 34

Adoption Information: Parent-initiated and agency-initiated adoptions are permitted. Children in Hungary are available for adoption from institutions. Nineteen such institutions are located in Hungary. The U.S. Embassy can provide a list. Adoption from private sources (from parent to parent) is no longer possible. People who are interested in adopting a child from Hungary should write to one of the Children Care and Welfare Institutes (GYIVI) for information. The GYIVI provides information in writing regarding the procedure and the documentary requirements for adoption. Listings are available by request from the U.S. Embassy in Budapest.

Once a request for adoption with the supporting documents is received, the GYIVI enters the request on a waiting list and the adopting parents must wait until a child becomes available. This waiting period might be five to six years because the demand for children (especially under age 3) is much higher than the number of children available for adoption in Hungary. However, the waiting period for older children or those of non-ethnic Hungarian background is much shorter, perhaps six months to two years.

When the desired child or children are located, the GYIVI notifies the prospective parents, and the parents must come to Hungary to see the child. If they accept the offered child, the GYIVI makes an official record of intention to adopt. At the same time, up-to-date documents must be presented if the original documents, which are generally required, were submitted more than a year earlier (see below). Original documents and/or certified copies with Hungarian translations are required. If translations are done in the United States, the Hungarian Embassy in Washington, D.C. must authenticate the official translations.

Although there are no fees for the adoption itself, expenses for obtaining documents and translations and paying lawyers, if any, can be high. The embassy usually advises adoptive parents to seek the assistance of a lawyer if no friends or relatives are available to help in Hungary since the adoption procedure is time consuming and complex.

Adoption Authority
Children's Care and Welfare Institute (GYIVI)
There are 19 such institutions in Hungary.
Contact the U.S. Embassy in Budapest for a list.

U.S. Embassy/Visa Issuing Post
U.S. Embassy
Consular Section
V. Szabadsag ter 12
H-1054 Budapest
Hungary
Tel: [36] (1) 475-4400
Fax: [36] (1) 475-4764

Mailing Address:
U.S Embassy, Hungary
Unit 25402
APO AE 09213

LATVIA

Geography: A small Baltic republic of 63,700 square miles, which was part of the former Soviet Union. Latvia is now independent.

Capital: Riga

Demography: Approximately 2,700,000. More than half are ethnic Latvians; the rest are Lithuanians and ethnic Russians.

Languages: Latvian, Russian

Currency: Ruble, Lat

Major Religions: Catholic, Protestant, some Eastern Orthodox

Orphans Admitted into the United States
Fiscal year 1995: 59   Fiscal year 1997: 108
Fiscal year 1996: 82   Fiscal year 1998: 76

Adoption Information: Latvia's intercountry adoption law has been in effect since July 1, 1992. Pursuant to the law, the Ministry of Justice and the Ministry of Welfare will be jointly responsible for administering intercountry adoptions.

Adoption of Latvian children is allowed by singles and couples if: The persons adopting are relatives of the child; or the child is ill and will receive medical treatment that is unavailable in Latvia; or no Latvian citizens have expressed a willingness to adopt the child during the first three months of its life (applies only to children available for adoption from birth); or the child has been rejected by at least two persons who had applied for adoption (applies to children available for adoption for one year). The fact that the child was rejected twice must be verified by records in the child's adoption file.

Adoption Authority	**U.S. Embassy**
The Ministry of Welfare	U.S. Embassy, Consular Section
Orphans Department	Raina Boulevard 7
28 Skolas Street	LV-1510 Riga
Riga, LV 1050	Latvia
Latvia	Tel: [371] (7) 210-005
Tel: [371] (2) 277-468	Fax: [371] (7) 820-047
Contact: Ms. Norina Meksa	* Visas are issued by the U.S.
	Embassy in Warsaw, Poland.

Foreigners interested in adopting a Latvian child should also express their interest in writing to the Ministry of Justice of Latvia at the following address:

Civil Registration Department
Latvian Ministry of Justice
Kalku Iela
24 Riga
Latvia LV1050

LITHUANIA

Geography: A Baltic republic of 65,200 square kilometers, which was part of the former Soviet Union. Lithuania is now independent.

Capital: Vilnius

Demography: 3,700,000, Eastern Baltic people of Lithuanian and Russian descent

Languages: Lithuanian, Russian

Currency: Ruble, Litas

Major Religions: Roman Catholic, Eastern Orthodox

Orphans Admitted into the United States

Fiscal year 1995: 96   Fiscal year 1997: 78
Fiscal year 1996: 78   Fiscal year 1998: 72

Adoption Information: Agency-initiated and parent-initiated adoptions are allowed. Beginning in 1995, the Children's Rights Protection Service (Vaiku teisiu apsaugos tarnyba) created a register of foreign families wishing to adopt in Lithuania. Prospective parents must register on this list before beginning any adoption proceedings. As children become available, the CRPS contacts parents according to their position on the list. Prospective parents may register with the CRPS in person or in writing at the address listed below. Representatives of prospective adoptive parents may register on their behalf if they have a power of attorney. Applicants should also provide a statement in which they specify the age, health, sex, or other qualities they are seeking in an adopted child. Along with the statement, prospective adoptive parents must present to the Children Rights Protection Service the documents generally required. All documents must be accompanied by certified and authenticated Lithuanian translations.

Adoptive parent(s) or their representative must present the documents to
    Mr. Ramelis
    Chairman of Civil Cases Department
    Vilnius District Court
    Domaseviciaus Street 9
    Tel: [370] (2) 614-923

There is a 20-day waiting period after the adoption hearing. During that time, the child remains in the institution.

Adoption Authority

    Children's Rights Protection Service
    (Vaiku teisiu apsaugos tarnyba)
    Juozapavicias 10A
    Vilnius, Lithuania

U.S. Embassy

U.S. Embassy, Consular Section
Akmenu 6 232600
Vilnius, Lithuania
Tel: [370] (2) 223-031
Fax: [370] (2) 222-779

Mailing address:
U.S. Embassy, Vilnius
PSC 78, Box V
APO AE 09723

*Visas are issued by the U.S. Embassy in Warsaw, Poland.

POLAND

Geography: Eastern European Republic occupying 120,725 square miles, bordering Germany, the Czech and Slovak Republics, the Ukraine, Belarus, Lithuania, and the Russian region of Kaliningrad

Capital: Warsaw

Demography: 38,400,000. Most of the population are ethnic Poles; two percent are European minorities from bordering countries, as well as Jews and Gypsies.

Language: Polish

Currency: Zloty

Major Religion: Roman Catholic

Orphans Admitted into the United States
Fiscal year 1995: 30   Fiscal year 1997: 78
Fiscal year 1996: 64   Fiscal year 1998: 77

Adoption Information: Poland declared that the adoption of children from Poland may take place only if the functions of the Central Authority in the receiving country are performed in accordance with Article 22, paragraph 1 of the Hague Convention.

Central Adoption Authority
Ministry of National Education
Al. Szucha 25
00-918 Warszawa 7
Poland
Tel: [48] (2) 621-1075

Competent Authority
Krajowy Osrodek
  Adopcyjno-Opiekunvzy
TPD-ul. Jasna 26
06-950 Warzawa
Poland

U.S. Embassy/Visa Issuing Post
U.S. Embassy, Consular Section
Al. Ujazdowskie 29/31
00-054 Warsaw
Poland
Tel: [48] (2) 628-3041
Fax: [48] (2) 628-8298

Mailing Address
U.S. Embassy, Warsaw
APO AE 96553

*Visas for Belarus, Ukraine, Latvia, and Lithuania are also issued here.

PORTUGAL

Geography: A republic of western Europe covering 35,441 square miles and occupying the western part of the Iberian peninsula as well as the Azores Islands

Capital: Lisbon (828,000)

Demography: The population of 10,300,000 is one of the most homogenous populations in Europe. Almost everyone is of Mediterranean heritage.

Language: Portuguese

Currency: Escudo

Major Religion: Roman Catholic

Orphans Admitted into the United States

Fiscal year 1995: 1   Fiscal year 1997: 4
Fiscal year 1996: 3   Fiscal year 1998: 11

Adoption Information: In the case of infant placements, preference is given to young couples. Adopters must be personally interviewed. The adoption agency will maintain contact with the adoptive parents and the child. Applicants must be over 35 years of age, married 10 years, and childless.

Portuguese law does not prohibit adoption by foreigners, but in practice it is not easy since waiting lists for adoptive children exist and preference is given to Portuguese citizens. Portugal grants a formal final adoption decree or a simple adoption. The simple adoption does not qualify a child for an orphan visa under the United States immigration laws.

Adoption Authority
Ministerio da Justica
Direccao-Geral dos Servico
  Tutelares de Menores
Praca do Comercio
1100 Lisbon, Portugal

Adoption Agencies
Instituto da Familia
  e Accao Social
Largo do Rato
Lisbon, Portugal

The Instituto has about 200 small agencies in Portugal and is under the Ministry of Social Affairs.

U.S. Embassy/Visa Issuing Post
U.S. Embassy, Consular Section
Avenida das Forcas Armadas
1600 Lisbon, Portugal
Tel: [351] (1) 727-3300
Fax: [351] (1) 727-9109

ROMANIA

Geography: A country bordered by the Black Sea, Moldova, Hungary, the former Yugoslavia, Ukraine, and Bulgaria

Capital: Bucharest

Demography: 23,300,000, the majority of whom trace their origins to the early Romans. About 10 percent are minorities of Magyars, Szeklers, and Gypsy descent.

Languages: Romanian, Hungarian

Currency: Leu

Major Religion: Eastern Orthodox

Orphans Admitted into the United States
Fiscal year 1995: 275   Fiscal year 1997: 621
Fiscal year 1996: 565   Fiscal year 1998: 406

Adoption Information: An adoption law passed in 1997 gave control of all adoptions to the Romanian Committee for Adoption. The committee assigns children to more than 100 Romanian nonprofit foundations. These foundations have to carry out social service functions to earn points; an accumulated number of points allows the assignment of children for international adoption to these foundations. Foreign agencies also have to be approved by the Romanian Adoption Committee.

A list of accredited foundations is available from the U.S. Embassy; however, U.S. citizens wishing to adopt cannot go directly through an accredited foundation. They must first go through a U.S. agency approved by the Romanian Adoption Committee. Those agencies approved to work in Romania have existing agreements with child-placing foundations.

Romanian requirements for adoption are quite flexible and are interpreted by the presiding judges. In general, however, Romanian requirements for international adoption state that the couple must be married for three years and that the mother can be no more than 35 years older than the child and the father no more than 40. In addition, there can be no more than two children in the adoptive family. Single women may be considered for handicapped or special needs children.

At least one parent must travel to Romania for two weeks to obtain a final adoption decree.

Central Adoption Authority
Romanian Committee for
   Adoption (RCA)
Piata Victoriei Nr. 1 Bucharest
Sector 1
Bucharest

U.S. Embassy/Visa Issuing Post

U.S. Embassy, Consular Section   *Mailing address:*
Strada Tudor Arghezi 7-9   U.S. Embassy, Bucharest
Sector 1   Unit 25402
Bucharest, Romania   APO AE 09213
Tel: [40] (1) 210-4042
Fax: [40] (1) 211-3360

RUSSIA, COMMONWEALTH OF INDEPENDENT STATES (CIS)

Other members of the Commonwealth of Independent States are marked with an asterisk and include Armenia, Belarus, Georgia, Kazakhstan, Moldova, Ukraine, and Uzbekistan. CIS countries not listed in the Compendium either do not allow international adoption or did not respond to requests for information on international adoption.

Geography: With 17,025,000 square kilometers, Russia is the largest of the former republics of the Soviet Union and is now part of the Commonwealth of Independent States. Russia reaches from the Baltic republics, Belarus, and the Ukraine in the west, to the Pacific Ocean in the east, and borders Finland in the north, and Georgia and Kazakhstan to the south.

Capital: Moscow

Demography: 147,386,000. The majority call themselves "Great Russians" (Caucasians). The rest are Mongols, Jews, Kazakhis, and other ethnicities from the former Soviet Union.

Languages: Russian, plus many of the languages of the other republics

Currency: Ruble

Major Religions: Russia has been officially atheist for more than 70 years; however, the Eastern Orthodox church, some Protestant religions, and Judaism are experiencing a revival. There are some Muslim temples, as well.

Orphans Admitted into the United States
Fiscal year 1995: 1,896   Fiscal year 1997: 3,816
Fiscal year 1996: 2,454   Fiscal year 1998: 4,491

Adoption Information: At the time of writing, the Russian Federation was still working on implementation legislation and regulations to a law passed in June of 1998 regarding intercountry adoptions. What is known, but has not yet been put into effect, is that U.S. agencies will need to be accredited (approved) by a commission. Agency representatives in Russia have yet to be disclosed.

The actual process for adoption will probably change very little. Children will still be entered into a data bank and will be available only to Russian citizens for a certain number of months, after which the child may be placed through an international adoption. The adoptive parent(s) must travel to Russia by invitation for a court data. The court date is needed to obtain an entry visa. They will meet the child and, if they accept the child, will proceed with the court hearing. Prospective parents should plan to stay in Russia about two weeks.

Regardless of the region in which the adoption took place (there are 90 regions in Russia, although not all permit intercountry adoption), the parent and child will have to return to Moscow for issuance of the child's visa. The medical exam required for the U.S. visa will also be administered in Moscow by a doctor appointed by the U.S. Embassy. In addition, a consular officer will also review English translations of the adoption documents.

Visas for children adopted from most other CIS countries will also be issued in Moscow; however, visas for children adopted from Ukraine, Belarus, Latvia, and Lithuania will be issued in Warsaw, Poland. Visas for children adopted from Estonia will be issued by the U.S. Embassy in Finland.

Adoption Authority

There is no central adoption authority at this time. The only central aspect of the process is the data bank of waiting children. It is possible that the authority will be broadened once accreditation becomes mandatory.

U.S. Embassy/Visa Issuing Post

U.S. Embassy, Consular Section
Section IV, Immigrant Visa
Novinsky Bul'var 19/23
121099 Moscow, Russia
Tel: [7] (095) 956-4225
Fax: [7] (095) 956-4079

Mailing Address:
U.S. Embassy, Moscow
Consular Section
PSC 77
APO AE 09213

ARMENIA   (CIS)

Geography: Small republic of 29,800 square kilometers, bordered by Georgia, Azerbaijan, Turkey, and Iran

Capital: Yerevan

Demography: 3,283,000 Armenians and Russians

Languages: Russian, Armenian

Currency: Ruble

Major Religion: Eastern Orthodox

Orphans Admitted into the United States

Fiscal year 1995: 4   Fiscal year 1997: not available
Fiscal year 1996: 5   Fiscal year 1998: not available

Adoption Information: Orphans fall under the jurisdiction of the Ministry of

Education. There is no child-placing authority. The Ministry of Education and the President of the Republic must approve adoptions by foreigners.

U.S. Embassy
> U.S. Embassy, Consular Section
> 18 General Bagramian Avenue
> Yerevan, Armenia
> Tel: [374] (2) 151-551
> Fax: [374] (2) 151-550

*Visas are issued by the U.S. Embassy in Moscow, Russia.

*BELARUS (CIS)

Geography: Republic of 207,600 square kilometers bordered by Lithuania, Poland, Latvia, Ukraine, and Russia

Capital: Minsk

Demography: Population of 10,200,000.

Languages: Russian and White Russian (a dialect)

Currency: Ruble

Major Religion: Eastern Orthodox

Orphans Admitted into the United States
Fiscal year 1995: 7   Fiscal year 1997: 49
Fiscal year 1996: 36   Fiscal year 1998: 2

Adoption Information: A new process is under discussion according to the Department of State. The Ministry of National Education in Minsk is responsible for foreign adoptions, but little detailed information is now available.

Located north of the Ukraine, Belarus bore the brunt of the Chernobyl nuclear explosion. Radiation-related illnesses have affected a large part of the population.

U.S. Embassy
> U.S. Embassy, Consular Section
> Starovilenskaya 46-220002
> Minsk, Belarus
> Tel: [375] (172) 315-000
> Fax: [375] (172) 347-853

*Visas are issued by the U.S. Embassy in Warsaw, Poland.

GEORGIA (CIS)

Geography: A small republic on the Black Sea bordered by Russia, Armenia, and Azerbaijan

Capital: Tbilisi

Demography: 5,449,000 people of Georgian and Russian descent

Languages: Georgian and Russian

Currency: Ruble

Major Religion: Eastern Orthodox

Orphans Admitted into the United States
Fiscal year 1995: 52   Fiscal year 1997: 21
Fiscal year 1996: 77   Fiscal year 1998: 6

Adoption Information: President Shervardnadze signed a new law governing international adoption in 1997 after a long de-facto moratorium. Unfortunately, the language of the new law is vague, and uncertainty over the procedures and the responsibilities of the various ministries have delayed its implementation.

Procedures have recently been clarified as well as the various Ministries' responsibilities for international adoptions under the new law. The Ministry of Justice, through its court system, adjudicates international adoptions. The Ministry of Education registers children for adoption and creates a central registration databank of all orphaned and abandoned Georgian children. Healthy children are placed on the Ministry of Education's databank for six months during which time they are eligible to be adopted by Georgian citizens only. In cases in which the child's health is in danger, the Ministry of Education may request the court waive the six month waiting period and allow a foreign adoption immediately.

Contact the U.S. Department of State's office of Children's Issues (202-736-7000) in Washington, D.C., for additional information.

Adoption Authority
   The Ministry of Justice
   The Ministry of Education

U.S. Embassy
   U.S. Embassy, Consular Section
   #25 Antoneli St.
   380026 Tbilisi, Georgia
   Tel: [995] (32) 989-967
   Fax: [995] (32) 933-759

   *Visas are issued by the U.S. Embassy in Moscow, Russia.

*KAZAKHSTAN (CIS)

Geography: A large republic of 2,717,300 square miles bordered by Russia, China, Kyrgyzstan, Uzbekistan, and Turkmenistan

Capital: Almaty

Demography: Population of 16,538,000 Kazakhs and Russians

Languages: Russian and Kazakh

Currency: Ruble

Major Religions: Islam and Eastern Orthodox

Orphans Admitted into the United States
Fiscal year 1995: 16   Fiscal year 1997: 26
Fiscal year 1996: 1   Fiscal year 1998: 54

Adoption Information: Until recently, the adoption of Kazakhstani children by foreigners was expressly forbidden by law. However, in June of 1998 the Lower House passed a new Code of Marriage and Family, which impacts adoption. Unfortunately, finalization of the law has been stalled for many months in the Upper House, and no intercountry adoptions will be allowed until implementing regulations for the country's new family law are approved. As late as the fall of 1999, no details were available on when this might occur. However, visas have been issued in 1999 according to the U.S. Embassy in Moscow, and a process of agency approval has commenced.

Adoption Authority
Ministry of Education of the Republic of Kazakhstan
Almaty 4800100
25 Dzambul Street

U.S. Embassy
U.S. Embassy, Consular Section
Furmanova Street
Alma Ata, Kazakhstan
Tel: [7] (3272) 63-39-21
Fax: [7] (3272) 63-38-83
*Visas are issued by U.S. Embassy in Moscow, Russia.

*MOLDOVA (CIS)

Geography: A small republic of 33,700 square kilometers bordered by the Ukraine and Romania

Capital: Chisinau (Kishinev)

Demography: Approximately 4,341,000, the majority of whom are Moldovans of Russian and Romanian descent

Languages: Moldovan, Russian, Romanian

Currency: Ruble

Major Religion: Eastern Orthodox

Orphans Admitted into the United States

Fiscal year 1995: 40   Fiscal year 1997: 43

Fiscal year 1996: 44   Fiscal year 1998: 46

Adoption Information: In order to be eligible for adoption, a Moldovan child must first be registered on the official list of orphaned or abandoned children. Moldovan citizens are given first priority in adopting children; if after six months the child has not been adopted by a Moldovan family, he or she is then eligible to be adopted by foreign parents working through a registered adoption agency. In practice, it is impossible for a foreigner to adopt a child who is less than six months old. All adoption agencies that wish to operate in Moldova must register with the Committee for Adoption by presenting credentials that establish the agency's right to operate in its country of origin. Once an agency has successfully registered with the Committee, it will be allowed to petition to adopt eligible Moldovan children. Only registered agencies will be given permission to visit these children in orphanages and/or hospitals.

Once an agency has matched a prospective family with an eligible child, the agency must submit documentation to the Committee showing that the family has met all legal requirements for adoption in their own country. The Committee will then review all documentation and make a final decision on the adoption. The Committee will meet on an as-needed basis to consider cases. Those approved to adopt a Moldovan child must pay $1,000.00 and the equivalent of a round-trip ticket to the adoptive country so that Moldovan authorities would be able to visit the child to monitor the home environment, should the need arise.

In 1993, the Moldovan Parliament created the Committee of the Republic of Moldova for Adoption, which is responsible for overseeing and approving all adoptions by foreigners. The Committee is a division of the Ministry of Science and Education and, as chairperson of the Committee, the Vice Minister of Science and Education has the sole authorization to sign documents of adoption. In addition to the permanent staff of five people, the Moldovan State Chancery and the Ministries of Health, Justice, Internal Affairs, and Foreign Affairs are represented on the Committee. Adoptions will be approved or rejected by a majority of votes.

Adoption agencies already registered or seeking registration, along with prospective adoptive parents, should know the following: Every U.S. notarized document submitted in support of an application to adopt a Moldovan child must be authenticated. Authentication of U.S. notarized documents is a time-consuming process that can only be accomplished in the United States. The Embassy in Moldova cannot authenticate U.S. notarized documents.

Arriving in Moldova without notarized and authenticated U.S. documents may mean a long and costly trip to Moldova in vain.

Adoption Authority
    Ministry of Science and Education
    1 Piata Marii Adunari Nationale
    Kishinev, Moldova MD-2033

U.S. Embassy
    U.S. Embassy
    103 Mateevici Street
    Kishinev, Moldova MD-2014
    Tel: [373] (2) 233-772
    Fax: [373] (2) 233-0-44
    *Visas are issued by the U.S. Embassy in Bucharest, Romania.

*UKRAINE (CIS)

Geography: A republic of 603,700 square kilometers bordered by Poland, Belarus, Slovakia, Romania, Russia, and Moldova

Capital: Kiev (Kiyeu)

Demography: 51,704,000, ethnic Ukrainians and Russians

Languages: Ukrainian, Russian

Currency: Ruble

Major Religion: Eastern Orthodox

Orphans Admitted into United States
Fiscal year 1995: 5   Fiscal year 1997: 59
Fiscal year 1996: 10   Fiscal year 1998: 180

Adoption Information: On January 28, 1996, the Rada (Ukrainian parliament) amended the Family and Marriage Code of Ukraine, thereby lifting the moratorium on adoption of Ukrainian children (orphaned or abandoned) by foreign nationals, effective April 1, 1996. The amended law places new burdens on prospective adopting families and bars the use of third-party adoption facilitators.

Citizens of foreign countries may adopt Ukrainian children after those children have been registered with the Adoption Center for one year and if within this year no Ukrainian family expresses a desire to adopt them or become their guardians. If citizens of the foreign countries are relatives of the child, the one-year requirement may be waived. If the child is suffering from a disease (the Ministry of Health protection has a list of those diseases), the one-year requirement may also be waived. Citizens of foreign countries may adopt Ukrainian children only if they have permission from the Adoption

Center (a new structure with the Ministry of Education of Ukraine). Citizens of countries that have signed bilateral agreements on adoption have priority.

Under the new law, a hospital, orphanage, or any other place that keeps or has information about the orphan or abandoned child must notify the local guardianship board about this within one week. Orphans or abandoned children, who may be adopted, as well as citizens of Ukraine willing to adopt, should be registered with local guardianship boards and the Adoption Center. Citizens of foreign countries willing to adopt Ukrainian children should also register with the adoption center.

Citizens of foreign countries interested in adopting a child residing in Ukraine should submit their request to the Adoption Center of the Ministry of Education of Ukraine. International adoptions must by law be open adoptions.

Adoption Authority

Adoption Center
27 Taras Shevchenko
Kiev, Ukraine 252032
Contact: Ms. Tamara Kunko, director
Tel: [380] (44) 246-5431
Fax: [380] (44) 246-5452

Translation Centers

16/22 B Khmelnystky Street
#420
Kiev 252030, Ukraine
Tel: [380] (44) 224-0470

Kiev Translation Center
180 vul. Gorkoho
Kiev 252171, Ukraine
Tel: [380] (44) 268-2574, or
[380] (44) 268-2179

1st Notary Public Office
Department of Translation and
  Certification of Documents
12 Mikhail Kotsubinskiy Street
Kiev, Ukraine
Tel: [380] (44) 246-4805
Or   [380] (44) 224-9996

U.S. Embassy

U.S. Embassy, Consular Section
10 Yuria Kotsyubinskovo
Kiev 254053
Ukraine
Tel: [380] (44) 246-9750
Fax: [380] (44) 244-7350

*Visas are issued by the U.S. Embassy in Warsaw, Poland.

*UZBEKISTAN (CIS)

Geography: A republic of 447,400 square kilometers bordered by Kazakhstan, Turkmenistan, Tajikistan, Kyrgyzstan, and Afghanistan

Capital: Tashkent

Demography: Population of 19,906,000 Uzbekis and Russians

Languages: Uzbeki and Russian

Currency: Ruble

Major Religion: Islam

Orphans Admitted into the United States
Fiscal year 1995: 47   Fiscal year 1997: 3
Fiscal year 1996: 14   Fiscal year 1998: 1

Adoption Information: The government office responsible for adoptions in Uzbekistan is the Ministry of Education. Parent-initiated and agency-initiated adoptions are permitted.

The following steps outline the Uzbeki adoption process:
An agent or the prospective parents select a child from an orphanage;

They present the child's documents to the adoption inspector of the regional Department of Education (Rayonniy Otdel Narodnovo Obrazovaniya, or RAYONO) for review;

The inspector passes the documents to the city's mayor's office (Hokimiste) for approval;

The city Hokimiste sends approval to a local district (Hokimiate), which grants final authority for the adoption;

The local ZAGS (registration office of civil acts) issues a certificate of adoption based on the local Hakimiate's decision (Note: the certificate can also legalize a name change based on the adopting parents' wishes.);

UVVG (the Administration for Exit, Entry, and Citizenship, formerly known as OVIR) issues a passport to the child based on the local Hokimiate's permission, the ZAGS certificate, and a notarized invitation for permanent residence abroad.

Adopted orphans retain their Uzbekistan citizenship until they reach the majority age of sixteen. In order to monitor the rights of its citizens adopted overseas, in 1992 the Cabinet of Ministers officially delegated this responsibility to the Red Crescent Society (an Islamic version of the Red Cross). The Red Crescent Society, in turn, delegated this responsibility to a sub-organization called Tayanach.

Tayanach, a not-for-profit organization, has become an active participant in the process of foreign adoptions. Although it has no official authority to do so, this organization has been accepting the documents and bona fides of various adoption agencies and granting them permission to operate in

Uzbekistan. Since it works to ensure that children adopted from Uzbekistan have good living conditions and receive necessary medical treatment once overseas, it also requests regular reports about the children's life and health abroad during the first five years after adoption.

Adoption Authority
Ministry of Education
Tashkent, Uzbekistan

U.S. Embassy

U.S. Embassy, Consular Section	*Mailing Address:*
82 Chilanzarskaya	U.S. Embassy, Uzbekistan
Tashkent, Uzbekistan	U.S. Department of State
Tel: [7] (3712) 771-407	Washington, DC 20521-5850.
Fax: [7] (3712) 406-335	

*Visas are issued by the U.S. Embassy in Moscow, Russia.

YUGOSLAVIA

Now less than half its original size, this newly reshaped Balkan country is now referred to as Serbia-Montenegro and consists of the republics of Serbia and Montenegro, as well as Kosovo. The former republics of Croatia, Slovenia, Macedonia, and Bosnia and Herzegovina are now independent countries.

* BOSNIA AND HERZEGOVINA

Geography: A newly formed republic of southeastern Europe that borders Croatia and Serbia-Montenegro. Bosnia and Herzegovina (the Bosnian abbreviation is "BIH") is divided into two entities — the Republika Srpska (RS) and The Federation of Bosnia and Herzegovina.

Capital: Sarajevo

Demography: Population of approximately 3,594,000

Languages: Croatian, Serbian, Bosnian

Currency: BH Dinar

Major Religions: Islam, Roman Catholic, and Eastern Orthodox

Orphans Admitted into the United States
Fiscal year 1995: 0   Fiscal year 1997: 0
Fiscal year 1996: 0   Fiscal year 1998: 0

Adoption Information: Both the Republika Srpska (RS) and The Federation of Bosnia and Herzegovina have inherited the old family law of the former

Yugoslavia, which, among other things, regulates adoption. While there is nothing in the Bosnian law that specifically prohibits foreigners from applying to adopt a Bosnian child, the law stresses that there has to be overwhelming justification and exceptionally compelling reasons for a foreigner to be able to adopt a Bosnian child. Just what an "overwhelming justification" might be is judged on a case-by-case basis.

Foreign adoption is a particularly sensitive subject to Bosnian authorities and to the people of Bosnia. Having lost so many lives in the recent war, Bosnians have strong feelings against permitting Bosnian children to be removed from their homeland. Therefore, Bosnian law gives absolute priority to adoptions by Bosnian citizens. There are no indications that either the RS or the Federation is considering liberalizing their adoption laws to make foreign adoptions easier.

Adoptions by foreigners must be approved by the Ministry of Social Policy, which is not the case for adoptions by local Bosnian citizens. In practice, it is extremely difficult or almost impossible to obtain this approval. The main reason is the fact that neither the government of the Federation nor that of the RS considers it beneficial for native-born children to be uprooted, to lose contact with other relatives, or to lose their identity through losing their citizenship. Furthermore, in a country that is still recovering from a long and brutal conflict, it can be extremely difficult to determine if the whereabouts of a parent is simply unknown or if the child is truly an orphan. In fact, relatively few of the children in Bosnian orphanages or children's homes are true orphans in the sense of having lost both parents. Many are the children of parents who are unable to care for them at home, but continue to take an interest in their welfare

Adoption Authority
Ministry of Social Policy (for foreign adoptions)

U.S. Embassy/Visa Issuing Post
U.S. Embassy, Consular Section
Alipasina 43
71000 Sarajevo
Bosnia and Herzegovina
Tel: [387] (71) 445-700
Fax: [387] (71) 659-722

*CROATIA

Geography: Large republic split off from former Yugoslavia bordered by Slovenia, Hungary, Romania, Bosnia and Herzegovina, and Serbia

Capital: Zagreb

Demography: Approximately 1,700,000 Croatians and Serbs

Languages: Croatian, Serbian, Slovenian

Currency: Kuna

Major Religions: Eastern Orthodox, Roman Catholic

Orphans Admitted into the United States
Fiscal year 1995: 0   Fiscal year 1997: 2
Fiscal year 1996: 2   Fiscal year 1998: 3

Adoption Information: Under normal circumstances, only Croatian citizens may adopt children from Croatia. In some "extraordinary circumstances" persons of Croatian ethnic origins who have lived in Croatia for some time or persons willing to adopt children with special needs have been allowed to adopt. No more than three or four orphan visas have been issued per year.

Adoption Authority
Minisarstvo Radai Socijalne Skrbi Hrvatske
(Croatian Ministry of Labor and Social Service)
10000 Zagreb
Prisculje4 Zagreb
Attn. Ms. Helena Ujevic

U.S. Embassy/Visa Issuing Post
U.S. Embassy, Consular Section
Andrije Hebrangar
Zagreb, Croatia
Tel: [385] (1) 455-5500
Fax: [385] (1) 455-8585

Mailing Address:
Consular Section
U.S. Embassy, Croatia
APO, AE 09213-1345

*MACEDONIA

Geography: A former republic of Yugoslavia bordering Albania, Greece, Bulgaria, and Kosovo

Capital: Skobje

Demography: Approximately 1,500,000 Macedonians of Serbian, Greek, and other minorities

Languages: Serbian, Greek, Albanian

Currency: Macedonian Dinar

Major Religions: Greek Orthodox, Roman Catholic, and Muslim

Orphans Admitted into the United States
Fiscal year 1995: 0   Fiscal year 1997: 3
Fiscal year 1996: 0   Fiscal year 1998: 8

Adoption Information: The waiting list of qualified Macedonian couples seeking to adopt Macedonian children far exceeds the availability. In fact, in recent times, the only foreign couples who have successfully adopted Macedonian children have been persons holding dual nationality (Macedonian and another) and who have long-standing family and ethnic ties to Macedonia. Nonetheless, responsible officials are not totally closed to the possibility of adoption by foreigners, but are considering future procedures and revision to law in order to ensure the best interests of those few children who may become available for intercountry adoption. Among options presently under consideration by the Ministry of Labor and Social Affairs is the designation of a sole U.S. agency for U.S. adoptions.

Adoption Authority	*U.S. Embassy/Visa Issuing Post*
Mr. Ilija Rajcinovski	U.S. Embassy, Consular Section
Ministry of Labor and Social Affairs	Bul, Ilinden bb/
91000 Skobje	9100 Skobje
F.Y.R.O. Macedonia	Macedonia
	Tel: [389] (91) 116-180
	Fax: (389) (91) 117-103

*SERBIA-MONTENEGRO

Geography: The largest of the former Yugoslavia republics, Serbia also still controls Kosovo, Montenegro, and Vojvodina.

Capital: Belgrade

Demography: Approximately 10,800,000 Serbs, Kosovans, Montenegrins, and Vojvodinans

Languages: Serbian, Croatian, Slovenian, and other languages and dialects of former Yugoslavia

Currency: Dinar

Major Religions: Eastern Orthodox, Roman Catholic

Orphans Admitted into the United States
Fiscal year 1995: not available   Fiscal year 1997: 10
Fiscal year 1996: not available   Fiscal year 1998: 4

Adoption Information: An excerpt from a U.S. Consulate report states that according to the Law of Marriage and Marital Affairs, adoption of orphans by foreign citizens is only allowed under unusual circumstances. For example, a few exceptions may be made for diplomats and foreign citizens of Yugoslav origin or dual nationals when an adoptive parent is not found within national boundaries.

U.S. Embassy/Visa Issuing Post
U.S. Embassy, Consular Section
Kneza Milosa 50
11000 Belgrade
Serbia-Montenegro
Tel: [381] (11) 645-655
Fax: [381] (11) 645-332

*SLOVENIA

Geography: Formerly a part of Yugoslavia, this republic became independent and, for the most part, escaped the civil war that followed the break-up. Slovenia shares a border with Italy, Austria, Croatia, and Hungary.

Capital: Ljubljana

Demography: 1,625,000 people of Slovenian, Italian, and Croatian ethnicity

Languages: Slovenian, Serbian, Croatian

Currency: Slovenian Dinar

Major Religion: Roman Catholic

Orphans Admitted into the United States

Fiscal year 1995: 5	Fiscal year 1997: 0
Fiscal year 1996: 0	Fiscal year 1998: 0

Adoption Information: Usually only Slovenians can adopt children who have been relinquished to a "competent body." There are no central institutions for adoption, rather 52 centers of social work carry out social services. Approximately 200 Slovenian couples are waiting to adopt — a high number for a relatively small population.

U.S. Embassy/Visa Issuing Post

U.S. Embassy, Consular Section
P.O. Box 254
Prazakova 4
61000 Ljubljana
Slovenia
Tel: [386] (61) 301-427
Fax: [386] (61) 301-401

Mailing Address:
Consular Section
U.S. Embassy, Belgrade
APO AE 09213-1310

TURKEY

Geography: A nation located between southwestern Europe and the Middle East Peninsula

Capital: Ankara

Demography: 55,900,000 persons of Mediterranean, Caucasian, and Mongoloid heritage

Language: Turkish

Currency: Turkish Lira

Major Religion: Islam

Orphans Admitted into the United States
Fiscal year 1995: 9   Fiscal year 1997: 1
Fiscal year 1996: 1   Fiscal year 1998: 2

Adoption Information: Adoptions are governed by the Turkish Civil Code, which requires the adopting parents to be at least 40 years of age, at least 18 years older than the child to be adopted, and have no biological children. The final adoption decree is issued in court.

Government Authority in Charge of Adoptions
General Directorate of Social Services
and Child Protection Agency
Anafartalar Caddes i, No. 70
Ankara, Turkey

U.S. Embassy/Visa Issuing Post
U.S. Embassy, Consular Section
110 Ataturk Blvd.
Kavaklidere
Ankara 06100, Turkey
Tel: [90] (312) 468-6110
Fax: [90] (312) 467-0019

Mailing Address:
Consular Section
U.S. Embassy, Turkey
PSC 93
Box 5000
APO AE 09823

Latin America

The geographic designation of Latin America includes Mexico, the countries of Central and South America, and the Caribbean Islands.

ARGENTINA

Geography: Argentina, the eighth largest country in the world, forms the southeastern part of South America.

Capital: Buenos Aires

Demography: Argentina's population of 32,300,000 is made up mainly of people of European descent, including Spanish, Italian, German, French, and other nationalities. In the northern parts of the country about two percent of the people are mestizos; a few Amerindians remain in southern Patagonia, the Chaco, and the northwestern highlands.

Language: Spanish; little English is spoken

Currency: Nuevo Peso Argentino (ARA)

Major Religion: Roman Catholic

Orphans Admitted into the United States
Fiscal year 1995: 1   Fiscal year 1997: 0
Fiscal year 1996: not available   Fiscal year 1998: 0

Adoption Information: Individuals over 35 years of age who have been married for at least five years and who do not have children may adopt in Argentina. Medical evidence of sterility must be presented. Persons over 35 who are widowed, divorced, or single may also adopt. It is extremely difficult for nonresidents to adopt in Argentina.

Another approach to adoption in Argentina is through judges who are willing to arrange guardianships for foreign adopters. The final adoption can then be granted abroad. The law states (Chapter V, Article 32): "The rights and duties of the adopter(s) and the adopted will be ruled by the law of the address of the adopted at the time of the adoption, when granted abroad."

Adoption Authority
Direccion de la Minoridad General
Humberto 1762, Primer piso, 1103 Capital Federal
Buenos Aires, Argentina

Private Adoption Agency
Director por el Equipo de Adopción
Movimiento Familiar Cristiano
Concepción Arenal 3540, 1427 Capital Federal
Buenos Aires, Argentina

U.S. Embassy/Visa Issuing Post
U.S. Embassy
Avenida 4300 Colombia
Buenos Aires 1425, Argentina
Tel: [54] (1) 4777-4533
Fax: [54] (1) 4511-4997

Mailing Address:
U.S. Embassy, Buenos Aires
Unit 4334
APO AA 34034

BAHAMAS

Geography: The Bahamas are made up of about 3,000 coral islands and reefs extending from the Straits of Florida to the northeastern tip of Cuba.

Capital: Nassau

Demography: About 80 percent of the population of 250,000 are descendants of slaves who were brought to the islands by British loyalists after the Revolutionary War; the rest of the people are Caucasian and mulattos (persons of mixed Caucasian and Negro ancestry).

Language: English, Creole

Currency: Bahamian Dollar

Major Religions: Protestant, Anglican

Orphans Admitted into the United States
Fiscal year 1995: 0
Fiscal year 1996: not available
Fiscal year 1997: 0
Fiscal year 1998: 0

Adoption Information: Bahamian law allows adoption by any person with legal status in the Bahamas, including tourists. However, the number of children is very small and the waiting list for prospective adoptive parents is very long. The entire adoption procedure requires a minimum of three months, with the Department of Social Services acting as the representative of the child's interests. A lawyer must guide the process through the Supreme Court of the Bahamas. Children are required to be adopted in the Bahamas, unless the guardian grants permission for a guardianship. While there are no court fees, the lawyers charge a fee for their services (between $400 to $1,000).

Personal contact between adopters and adoption sources is preferable. Private adoptions are arranged by local attorneys, and prospective adopters should contact an attorney recommended by the U.S. Embassy or another reputable person.

Adoption Authority
Department of Social Services

U.S. Embassy/Visa Issuing Post

U.S. Embassy
Mosmar Building, Queen Street
Nassau, Bahamas
Tel: (242) 322-1181 or
 (242) 328-2206
Fax: (242) 328-7838

Mailing Address:
U.S. Embassy
P.O. Box N-8197
Nassau, Bahamas

BARBADOS

Geography: The U.S. Consular district of Barbados also includes Anguilla, Antigua, the British Virgin Islands, Dominica, Grenada, Saint Kitts-Nevis, Saint Lucia, and Saint Vincent. The islands of Barbados, Dominica, Grenada, Saint Lucia, and Saint Vincent are independent nations in the West Indies; the islands of Anguilla, Antigua, and Saint Kitts-Nevis are states in association with Great Britain; the British Virgin Islands is a British possession.

Capital: Bridgetown

Demography: Although the 255,000 people of these islands represent many different races and nationalities, most are blacks whose ancestors were brought to the West Indies as slaves. Other groups include people of Chinese, Danish, Dutch, East Indian, English, French, Portuguese, Spanish, and Carib-Indian heritage.

Languages: English, Spanish, French, and Creole (an English/African patois)

Currency: Barbados Dollar

Major Religion: Anglican, African religions, Roman Catholic

Orphans Admitted into the United States
Fiscal year 1995: 0   Fiscal year 1997: 0
Fiscal year 1996: 1   Fiscal year 1998: 0

Adoption Information: Citizens of countries with which Barbados has diplomatic or consular relations may adopt Barbadian children. This includes U.S. citizens. Adoptive parents who are non-nationals may obtain a final decree if they are domiciled and residing in Barbados. If they live abroad, they must obtain authorization for guardianship with the intent of adopting abroad. The judge must be satisfied that the minor will be lawfully admitted to the adoptive parent's country. Normally it takes non-nationals between six months and a year to adopt a child in Barbados.

In St. Vincent, the Child Care Board makes arrangements for adoptions and carries out investigations. The Adoption Board is chaired by the Senior Magistrate in St. Vincent. The application to the court in St. Vincent for an adoption order shall not be made by the adopter until the expiration of a period of six months from the date the child was delivered into the care and possession of the adopter pursuant to the arrangements made by the Adoption Board.

Any married couple domiciled and resident in St. Vincent and at least 25 years of age may adopt as may any relative of the child at least 21 years old or the mother or father of the child. A married person adopting a child must have the consent of his/her spouse and the parent of the child. All adoptions must take place in St. Vincent. British subjects may obtain a license permitting adoption outside of St. Vincent.

Adoption Authority

Barbados Child Care Board
Cotton Park Complex, Waldron St.
Bridgetown, Barbados, West Indies
General Office: (246) 426-2577
Director's Tel: (246) 429-3691

U.S. Embassy/Visa Issuing Post

U.S. Embassy
Canadian Imperial Bank of Commerce Building
Broad Street
Bridgetown, Barbados, West Indies
Tel: (246) 436-4950
Fax: (246) 429-5246

Mailing Address:
U.S. Embassy
P.O. Box 302
Bridgetown, Barbados, West Indies

or U.S. Embassy
CMR 1014
Bridgetown, Barbados
FPO AA 34055

BELIZE

Geography: Located on the east coast of Central America, Belize is about the size of Massachusetts and is bordered by Mexico and Guatemala. A former British colony known as British Honduras, Belize gained its independence in 1981.

Capital: In 1975, the capital was moved from Belize City, which is on the coast, inland to Belmopan, which offers more protection from hurricanes. The U.S. Consulate is still located in Belize City (40,000).

Demography: The population of about 187,000 is made up of Creole (African/English), Mestizo, Maya, and Carib-Indian groups, as well as East Indian, African, Asian, and Caucasian minorities

Languages: English, Spanish, and Mayan

Currency: Belizean dollar

Major Religion: Anglican

Orphans Admitted into the United States
Fiscal year 1995: 1   Fiscal year 1997: 3
Fiscal year 1996: 7   Fiscal year 1998: 4

Adoption Information: Belizean adoption law is not fully delineated and is in the process of revision. While U.S. citizens may adopt in Belize, Belizean adoption law requires that both the adoptive parents and the child reside in Belize. However, Belizean law does not specify residence requirements, which have often been liberally interpreted to mean being physically present long enough to accomplish the adoption. Adoptive parents must be at least 25 years of age and 21 years older than the child. The process of adoption in Belize can take as long as two years. Cases are processed by the Belize Supreme Court and do not require the services of a private attorney.

U.S. Embassy/Visa Issuing Post
U.S. Embassy   *Mailing Address:*
29 Gabourel Lane   U.S. Embassy, Belize
Belize City, Belize   P.O. Box 286
Tel: [501] (2) 35321   Unit 7401
Fax: [501] (2) 30802   or APO AA 34025

BERMUDA

Geography: Britain's oldest self-governing colony, Bermuda consists of a group of about 365 islands, of which 16 are inhabited.

Capital: Hamilton

Demography: 58,000, the majority of whom are either of African descent or biracial. There is a minority of Anglo-Saxons.

Language: English

Currency: Bermuda Dollar

Major Religion: Anglican

Orphans Admitted into the United States
Fiscal year 1995: 0   Fiscal year 1997: 0
Fiscal year 1996: 0   Fiscal year 1998: 0

Adoption Information: Private adoptions in Bermuda are handled through lawyers.

Adoption Authority
   Ministry of Health, Social
     Services, and Housing
   Old Hospital Building
   7 Point Finger Road
   Paget DV 04,
   P.O. Box HM 380
   Hamilton HM BX, Bermuda

U.S. Embassy/Visa Issuing Post
   U.S. Consular General
   Crown Hill, 16 Middle Road
   Devonshire
   P.O. Box HM325
   Hamilton HMBX, Bermuda
   Tel: (441) 295-1342
   Fax: (441) 295-1592

   Mailing Address:
   Consular General
   U.S. Embassy, Bermuda
   PSC 1002

BOLIVIA

Geography: Bolivia is the fifth largest country in South America. It is bordered by Brazil on the north and east; Paraguay on the southeast; Argentina on the south; and Chile and Peru on the west.

Demography: More than half of Bolivia's 7,300,000 people are Amerindians; the rest are mestizos and people of European descent.

Capital: La Paz

Languages: Although Spanish is the official language, Aymará and Quechuan are more widely used. Little English is spoken.

Currency: Bolivian Peso

Major Religion: Roman Catholic

Orphans Admitted into the United States
Fiscal year 1995: 21   Fiscal year 1997: 77
Fiscal year 1996: 33   Fiscal year 1998: 73

Adoption Information: Regulations by the Bolivian Minor Courts and the Regional Directorates for Minors concerning adoptions represent the changes in the law. The decentralization of the social services in 1996 appointed each Department of Prefectura (equal to a state office) as the advisor on the suitability for the decision to place a child with adoptive parents. The departments conduct psychological and special studies for the courts and must grant approval for a child to leave the country.

Several U.S. adoption agencies are approved to process Bolivian adoptions. A list can be obtained from the Asuntos Genero Generacionales y Familia. The agencies work with Bolivian attorneys who are responsible for ensuring that the adoption meets the requirements of Bolivian and U.S. law. Key provisions in the law state that foreigners who wish to adopt a Bolivian child must work through organizations legally authorized, accredited, and registered with the Bolivian government. Requests for a Personeria Juridica or Carta de Intenciones should be addressed to the Adoption Authority.

The U.S. agencies are also responsible for conducting postadoption evaluations on a periodic basis for five years after the adoptive family leaves Bolivia.

Adoption Authority

Vice Ministerio de Asuntos de Genero Generacionales y Familia
Dr. Pablo Metzelar, Aseroria Juridica
Casilla 5960
La Paz, Bolivia
Tel: [591] (2) 376-862
Fax: [591] (2) 366-763

U.S. Embassy/Visa Issuing Post

U.S. Embassy, Consular Section
Avenida Arce No. 2780
Esquina Cordero
La Paz, Bolivia
Tel: [591] (2) 430-120 (Embassy)
Fax: [591] (2) 433-900 (Embassy)
Tel: [591] (2) 433-854 (Consulate)

Mailing Address:
U.S. Embassy, La Paz
APO AA 34032

BRAZIL

Geography: Colossal Brazil is the largest country in Latin America and the fifth largest country in the world. Its 21 states, four territories, and federal district are slightly larger than the 48 continental United States.

Capital: Brasília

Demography: 150,400,000. About 60 percent of the Brazilian people have European ancestry (Italian, Portuguese, Spanish, and German); more than 25 percent are of mixed ancestry (European, African, and Indian). About 10 percent of the people are black, and one percent are Amerindian. Most of the people who live in northern, northwestern, and central Brazil are Indians; those in the northeastern coastal area are of African ancestry; those in the southeastern area are of European ancestry; and those within the triangle formed by Brasília, Sao Paulo, and Rio de Janeiro are mixed. Brazil's estimated population of 150 million is about half of the entire population of Latin America. One-half of all Brazilians are less than 25 years of age.

Languages: Portuguese; some English is spoken in major cities.

Currency: Real (BRC)

Major Religion: Roman Catholic

Orphans Admitted into the United States

Fiscal year 1995: 146   Fiscal year 1997: 91
Fiscal year 1996: 103   Fiscal year 1998: 103

Adoption Information: Persons over 21 years of age may adopt as long as they are at least 16 years older than the child. A final adoption decree has to be issued in order for the child to leave Brazil. Adoptions can be arranged either directly between the court and the adopters or through approved U.S. adoption agencies. There is a great variance between the exercise of the adoption authority at municipal, state, and federal levels. Brazilian judicial authorities maintain a register of children available for adoption and a second register for persons wishing to adopt.

Each state in Brazil has a Department of Social Service (or Febem) responsible for adoptions. The national Febem is located in Brasilia.

Adoption Authority
　　Febem, E. IRB-11
　　Andai, Sector Bancario-SBS
　　CEP 7000, Brasilia-DF
　　Brazil

U.S. Embassy/Visa Issuing Post
　　U.S. Consul General
　　Avenida Presidente Wilson
　　147 — Castelo
　　20030-020 Rio de Janeiro RJ
　　Brazil
　　Tel: [55] (21) 292-7117
　　Fax: [55] (21) 220-0439

　　Mailing Address:
　　U.S. Embassy, Brazil
　　APO AA 34030

CHILE

Geography: Chile is the southernmost country of Latin America. It occupies a long, narrow ribbon of land between the Pacific Ocean and the Andes Mountains.

Capital: Santiago

Demography: About one-third of Chile's 13.2 million people are mestizos; two percent are Araucanian Indians; and most of the rest are descended from Spanish or other European settlers.

Languages: Spanish; some English is spoken in the cities.

Currency: Peso

Major Religion: Roman Catholic

Orphans Admitted into the United States

Fiscal year 1995: 90   Fiscal year 1997: 41
Fiscal year 1996: 63   Fiscal year 1998: 26

Adoption Information: Couples must be 20 years older than the child to be adopted and married for at least three years. Singles are seldom accepted, even for older children. To be adopted, a child with a living parent must be declared abandoned by a family court with jurisdiction over the child's place of residence. Such a declaration is based on the mother's irrevocable and final release of the child to the court or to the prospective adoptive parents.

Because non-resident foreigners may not adopt, they are given guardianship and authority to take the child out of Chile. This authority is transmitted through a court order. A huge disparity in fees is the result of a system dominated entirely by private attorneys. SENAME, the Chilean Child Welfare Service, has been appointed to handle all applications before presentation in court.

The Chilean Consul with jurisdiction over your state must issue a certificate that all state and U.S. preadoption requirements have been met before a dossier is accepted by SENAME. The adopting parents must appear personally before a judge in Chile. Married couples may request the judge to require the presence of only one spouse. The adoptive parent usually stays in Chile about two weeks in order to obtain the guardianship and emigrate the child. A new law is under discussion to change from guardianships to final decrees.

Adoption Authority

SENAME
Avenida Pedro de Valdivia #40-70
Santiago, Chile

U.S. Embassy/Visa Issuing Post

U.S. Embassy
Avda. Andrés Bello 2800
Las Condes
Santiago, Chile
Tel: [56] (2) 232-2600
Fax: [56] (2) 330-3160

Mailing Address:
U.S. Embassy, Chile
APO AA 34033

COLOMBIA

Geography: Colombia is the fourth largest country in South America, with coastlines on both the Atlantic and Pacific oceans. Colombia shares a border with Panama.

Capital: Bogotá

Demography: Of Colombia's 33,000,000 population, about 40 percent are mestizos; 30 percent whites, mostly of Spanish descent; 15 percent mulattos; seven percent Amerindians (Colombia has 398 distinct tribes); and five percent are of African descent. Bogotá has a high percentage of mestizos, while Medellín has a high percentage of people with European ancestry, and Cali has a tri-ethnic mixture of mestizos, and people of African or European descent.

Languages: Spanish; English is spoken in major cities.

Currency: Peso

Major Religion: Roman Catholic

Orphans Admitted into the United States
Fiscal year 1995: 350   Fiscal year 1997: 233
Fiscal year 1996: 255   Fiscal year 1998: 351

Adoption Information: Singles are accepted, although couples are preferred. For married couples, at least one of the adopting parents must be over 25 years of age and be physically, emotionally, and economically capable of supporting a child. In practice, newborns are assigned to younger couples, and older children are assigned to older couples. The child to be adopted must not be over 16 years of age.

The law establishes that only sources licensed by the ICBF (Instituto Colombiano de Bienestar Familiar (or Colombian Institute of Family Welfare) and licensed Colombian adoption agencies can offer children for adoption. A short waiting period for orphaned, abandoned, and relinquished children takes place while relatives are sought. If none appear, a certificate of abandonment is issued by the court. Then when the child is placed, a final adoption decree is soon issued, which negates the possibility of the birth parents or adoptive parents overturning the adoption.

Private adoption agencies shelter abandoned children and some wards of the ICBF. Wards of the family welfare institute are usually housed in government orphanages. Since government orphanages usually provide minimal care, adopters may find it possible and desirable to arrange foster care for a child who has been assigned to them.

The ICBF, as well as most of the private agencies, works with adoption agencies rather than individuals. The exception is Casa de la Madre y el Niño, which will only place children directly with couples.

Central Adoption Authority
Instituto Colombian de Beinestar Familiar (ICBF)
Division de Adopciones
Avenida 68, numero 64-01
Santa Fe de Bogotá, Colombia
Tel: [57] (1) 231-4558
Fax: [57] (1) 310-8574

Competent Adoption Authorities

Asociacion Amigos del Nino
(Ayudame)
Calle 128, numero 8-53
Santa Fe de Bogotá, D.C.
Cundinamarca, Colombia
Tel: [57] (1) 258-3390

Casa de la Madre y el Niño
Calle 48, numero 28-30
Santa Fe de Bogota, D.C.
Colombia
Tel: [57] (1) 268-7400
Fax: [57] (1) 268-1008

Casa de Maria y el Nino
Calle 9 Sur, numero 24-422
Medellin, Antioquia
Colombia
Tel: [57] (4) 268-6112
Fax: [57] (4) 266-6771

Casita de Nicolas
Carrera 50, numero 65-23
Medellin, Antioquia
Colombia
Tel: [57] (4) 263-8086
Fax: [57] (4) 211-4240

Centro de Rehabilitacion
para la Adopcion de la Ninez
Abandonado (CRAN)
Transversal 66, numero 164-30
Santa Fe de Bogotá, D.C.
Cundinamarca, Colombia
Tel: [57] (1) 681-3599
Fax: [57] (1) 684-7404

Chiquitines (Babies)
Avenida Lucio Velasco,
numero 15-325
Cali, Valle
Colombia
Tel: [57] (2) 880-7496
Fax: [57] (2) 889-8175

Fundacion Los Pisingos
Avenida 7, numero 157-91
Santa Fe de Bogotá, D.C.
Cundinamarca, Colombia
Tel: [57] (1) 671-8591
Fax: [57] (1) 672-9793

Fundacion para la Adopcion de la
Ninez Abandonada (FANA)
Carrera 96, numero 156B-10
Municipio de Suba
Cundinamarca, Colombia
Tel: [57] (1) 681-5037
Fax: [57] (1) 686-0324

U.S. Embassy/Visa Issuing Post
U.S. Embassy, Consular Section
Calle 22D-bis #47-51
Bogotá, Colombia
Tel: [57] (1) 315-0811
Fax: [57] (1) 315-2197

Mailing Address:
U.S. Embassy, Bogota
APO AA 34038

COSTA RICA

Geography: Costa Rica is a small, mountainous country in Central America with coastlines on both the Atlantic and Pacific oceans.

Capital: San José

Demography: More than 97 percent of Costa Rica's population of 3,015,000 are either mestizos or whites of European ancestry. Amerindians and blacks make up two small minority groups.

Languages: Spanish; some English is spoken in the larger cities.

Currency: Colón

Major Religion: Roman Catholic

Orphans Admitted into the United States
Fiscal year 1995: 11   Fiscal year 1997: 22
Fiscal year 1996: 20   Fiscal year 1998: 7

Adoption Information: Patronanto Nacional de la Infancia (PANI) requires that adoptive couples must be between 25 and 60 years of age and at least 15 years older than the adopted child. Children four years old or more may be adopted. They may be younger than four if they are part of a sibling group adopted together. Both spouses must travel to Costa Rica. Adoptions are processed through PANI.

Once a child is assigned, the couple must stay in Costa Rica for two weeks to initiate the adoption. Then, the child can be placed in foster care and both spouses can return home, or one can stay and care for the child. One spouse must return in 45 to 60 days for the final adoption decree and to obtain the child's U.S. visa before immigrating the child.

The Patronato does not charge a fee for child care or legal work. Excellent medical and psychological evaluations on each child are provided at the time of assignment. Adoptions through private attorneys or agencies must be authorized by the Patronato.

Central Adoption Authority
Patronato Nacional de la Infancia (PANI)
Apartado 5000
San José, Costa Rica

U.S. Embassy/Visa Issuing Post
U.S. Embassy, Consular Section
Calle 120 Avenida 0
Pavas, San José
Costa Rica
Tel: [506] 220-3939
Fax: [506] 220-2305

Mailing Address:
U.S. Embassy, Costa Rica
APO AA 34020

DOMINICAN REPUBLIC

Geography: The Dominican Republic makes up the eastern two-thirds of the island of Hispaniola in the Caribbean Sea; Haiti occupies the western third of the island.

Capital: Santo Domingo

Demography: About 65 percent of the 7,170,000 population are biracial, 20 percent are blacks, and 15 percent are whites.

Language: Spanish

Currency: Peso

Major Religion: Roman Catholic

Orphans Admitted into the United States
Fiscal year 1995: 15   Fiscal year 1997: 19
Fiscal year 1996: 13   Fiscal year 1998: 140

Adoption Information: Consent of the biological parents is required under the Dominican law to adopt a minor child. If the parents are separated or divorced, the consent of the parent having custody is essential and the noncustodial parent must be notified of the impending adoption. In the case of abandonment, the legal representative can give the consent. The representative is appointed by the Secretaria de Estado Salud or by a judicial authority.

Under Dominican law, a single individual, married couple, or unmarried couple may adopt a child. A single individual must be at least 25 years old and at least 15 years older than the child. A married couple may adopt a child if one of the spouses is at least 25 years old.

Adoption Authority
Secretaria de Estado de Salud Publica y Asistencia Social
Avenida San Cristobal esq. Avenida Tiradentes
Ensanche La Fe
Santo Domingo, Dominican Republic
Tel: [809] 565-3218

U.S. Embassy/Visa Issuing Post
U.S. Embassy
Corner of Calle Cesar Nicolas Penson
& Calle Leopoldo Navarro
Santo Domingo, Dominican Republic
Tel: [809] 221-2171
Fax: [809] 686-7437

Mailing Address:
U.S. Embassy, Santo Domingo
APO AA 34041-0008

ECUADOR

Geography: A small, mountainous country in South America that lies on the west coast of the continent between Colombia to the north and Peru to the south

Capital: Quito. The largest city is Guayaquil, where the U.S. Consulate is located.

Demography: The population of 10,600,000 consists of about 40 percent mestizos, about 40 percent Amerindians, and about 10 percent whites of European ancestry.

Languages: Spanish; some English is spoken in the cities.

Currency: Sucre

Major Religion: Roman Catholic

Orphans Admitted into the United States
Fiscal year 1995: 67   Fiscal year 1997: 43
Fiscal year 1996: 51   Fiscal year 1998: 55

Adoption Information: Husbands must be between 30 and 50 years of age, and wives must be between 25 and 40. No prior divorce is permitted, and the couple must be married at least five years. Childless couples are given preference. If the couple has a biological child, they must present a statement of infertility in order to adopt a child of the opposite sex to the one they already have. If they have an adopted child, they may adopt a child of either sex. Some exceptions may be made for couples wishing to adopt a special needs child.

The wait between the assignment of the child and the adoption trip is about one week. Both spouses travel to Ecuador for a stay of about two weeks in Guayaquil. They receive custody during their stay. The final decree is issued five to six weeks later. Children can only be placed in Ecuador through licensed Ecuadorian agencies or the Ministerio de Bienestar Social who, in turn, licenses U.S. adoption agencies to place children.

Central Adoption Authority
Corte Nacional de Menores
Calle Veintimilla y Reina Victoria
Edificio Wandenberg, 6to piso
Quito, Ecuador

U.S. Embassy/Visa Issuing Post
U.S. Consulate General
9 de Octubre y Garcia Moreno
Guayaquil, Ecuador
Tel: [593] (4) 323-570
Fax [593] (4) 320-904

Mailing Address:
Consulate General
U.S. Embassy, Quito
APO AA 34039

* Although the U.S. Embassy is in Quito, immigrant visas are processed at the U.S. Consulate General in Guayaquil.

EL SALVADOR

Geography: Located on the Pacific coast between Guatemala and Honduras, El Salvador is the smallest and most densely populated country in Central America.

Capital: San Salvador

Demography: About 92 percent of El Salvador's 5,300,000 people are mestizos; nearly five percent are whites of European ancestry, and three percent are U.S. citizens.

Language: Spanish; some English is spoken in the major cities.

Currency: Colon

Major Religion: Roman Catholic

Orphans Admitted into the United States

Fiscal year 1995: 30   Fiscal year 1997: 5
Fiscal year 1996: 17   Fiscal year 1998: 13

Adoption Information: Adopters must be more than 25 years old, and couples must be married at least two years. Generally, an orphan's birth documents are sent to preadoptive parents shortly after the child is assigned to them. Only one spouse is required to travel to El Salvador to obtain custody of the child; adopters stay in the country about one week.

The Central Authority included in the ratification of the Convention states that only residents of countries who ratified the convention and have established a central authority will be approved for an adoption.

Central Adoption Authority

La Procuradoria
General de la Republica (PGR)
13 a Calle Poniente
Centro de Gobierno
San Salvador, El Salvador
Tel: [503] 222-3815
Fax: [503] 211-3602

El Instituto de Proteccion al Menor
Colonia Costa Rica, ve.
Ave. Irazu Final
Calle Santa Marta
Complejo "La Gloria"
San Salvador, El Salvador
Tel: [503] 270-4142
Fax: [503] 270-1348

U.S. Embassy/Visa Issuing Post

U.S. Embassy, Consular
  Section
Final Bld., Santa Elena
Antiguo Cuscatlan
San Salvador, El Salvador
Tel: [503] 278-4444
Fax: [503] 278-6011

Mailing Address:
U.S. Embassy, San Salvador
APO AA 34023

GRENADA

Geography: Small island off the coast of Venezuela, consisting of 344 square kilometers

Capital: St. George's

Demography: Population of 85,000, mostly of African and mixed heritage

Languages: English, French patois

Currency: East Caribbean Dollar

Major Religions: Christian, Protestant

Orphans Admitted into the United States

Fiscal year 1995: 1   Fiscal year 1997: 0
Fiscal year 1996: not available   Fiscal year 1998: 3

Adoption Information: Although limited detailed information is available, international adoption is allowed in Grenada.

Adoption Authority
Adoptions are usually handled
   by this law firm:
Renwick & Payne
Church Street
St. George's, Grenada
Tel: [473] 440-2479

U.S. Embassy/Visa Issuing Post
U.S. Embassy
P.O. Box 54
St. George's,
Grenada, West Indies
Tel: [473] 444-1173
Fax: [473] 444-4820

Orphanage
The Queen Elizabeth Home for Children
Tempe Street
St. George's, Grenada
Tel: [473] 440-2327

GUATEMALA

Geography: With 108,888 square kilometers, Guatemala is the third largest of the Central American countries. Guatemala shares a long border with Mexico and has coastlines on both the Atlantic and Pacific oceans.

Capital: Guatemala City

Demography: About 55 percent of Guatemala's 9,200,000 people are mestizos; most of the remaining 45 percent are Amerindians. The infant mortality rate is 95 per 1,000 births; 82 percent of urban children and 95 percent of rural children suffer from chronic malnutrition.

Languages: Spanish and Mayan; some English is spoken in the larger cities.

Currency: Quetzal

Major Religion: Roman Catholic

Orphans Admitted into the United States
Fiscal year 1995: 449   Fiscal year 1997: 788
Fiscal year 1996: 427   Fiscal year 1998: 911

Adoption Information: Couples between 25 and 50, married at least one year, as well as single women over 25, may adopt. Adoptable children must be orphans or, if there is a living parent, must be unconditionally released for adoption through a declaration to a private attorney. Private and church-run agencies may have additional requirements.

Adoptions in Guatemala follow either the public (judicial) or the private (extrajudicial) route, depending on the status of the child to be adopted. Public adoptions, which require a court decree declaring that the child has been abandoned, are only processed when the biological parents are known to have died or deserted the child. This process grants considerable discretion to the judge and normally takes about a year to complete. Public adoptions are under the jurisdiction of the Dirección de Bienestar Infantil y Familiar (see address below).

Under the private adoption procedure, the natural parent makes a declaration of release of the child to an attorney who represents both the natural and the adoptive parents. Guatemalan adoption law requires a document review by the Attorney General's office and a social worker's report on the natural and adoptive parents. The private adoption process usually takes about six months to complete. All Guatemalan children must be adopted there; however, adopters are not required to remain in Guatemala during the entire adoption process.

As of October 1, 1998, the U.S. Embassy requires that all birth mothers and children to undergo DNA testing to ensure that the child is actually the birth mother's offspring. In private adoptions, the private adoption agencies of Guatemala place children through a child-placing contract with several U.S. adoption agencies and help arrange final adoptions or guardianships. Some provide an escort service for orphans from newborn to grade school age.

Adoption Authority
(For abandoned children)
Dirección de Bienestar Infantil y Familiar
81. Ave. y 32 Calle, Zona 11
Guatemala City, Guatemala

Private Guatemalan Adoption Agencies
Alycon Ruth Fleck
Hogar Campestre Adventista "Los Pinos"
(Seventh Day Adventist couples)
15 Avenida 19-62, Zona 13
Apartado 35-C
Guatemala City, Guatemala
Tel: [502] (2) 31-04-76

Joyce Heinlein
Agua Viva
(located at Km. 18,
  Carretera Roosevelt)
Apartado 10
Guatemala, City, Guatemala
Tel: [502] (2) 92-12-07

Luz del Carmen Morales Catalán
  de Paredes
Patronato Contra la Mendicidad
5a Avenida 4-26, Zona 1
Guatemala City, Guatemala
Tel: [502] (2) 58-86-96

Roberto Wer
Asociación Amigos de
  Todos Los Niños
19 Calle 12-57, Zona 11
Guatemala City, Guatemala
Tel: [502] (2) 48-14-23

Sor Jesephina Fumagalli
Mater Orphanorum
Km. 14 and 1/2 Carretera San Juan
Sacatepequez
Guatemala City, Guatemala
Tel: [502] (2) 91-00-87

U.S. Embassy/Visa Issuing Post
U.S. Embassy, Consular Section
7-01 Avenida de la Reforma,
  Zone 10
Guatemala City, Guatemala
Tel: [502] (2) 31-15-41
Fax: [502] (2) 31-88-85

Mailing Address:
U.S. Embassy, Guatemala
APO AA 34024

HAITI

Geography: Haiti occupies the western third of the Caribbean island of Hispaniola, which lies between Cuba and Puerto Rico.

Capital: Port-au-Prince

Demography: Most of Haiti's 6,513,000 people are descendants of Africans who were brought to Haiti as slaves; about five percent are biracial.

Languages: French and Creole (a French/African patois)

Currency: Gourde

Major Religions: Roman Catholic, Voodoo

Orphans Admitted into the United States
Fiscal year 1995: 49   Fiscal year 1997: 142
Fiscal year 1996: 68   Fiscal year 1998: 121

Adoption Information: As of February 1991, Haitian law requires that a completed final adoption decree must be issued in Haiti before a child can leave the country. The adoption process normally takes from two to six months, but can stretch to longer than a year. The host government is involved in two distinct stages. The court issues adoption decrees, and The Ministry of Social Affairs provides adoption authorizations. While it is possible to complete the adoption process without the use of a local attorney, the U.S. Embassy will refer you to competent Haitian counsel.

Adoption Authority
Ministry of Social Affairs

U.S. Embassy/Visa Issuing Post
U.S. Embassy
5 Harry Truman Boulevard
P.O. Box 1761
Port-au-Prince, Haiti
Tel: [509] 222-0200 or
[509] 222-0354
Fax: [509] 223-1641

HONDURAS

Geography: Second largest of the Central American countries, Honduras is bordered by Guatemala and Nicaragua. Honduras has a long coastline on the Caribbean Sea and a small strip of coastline on the Pacific Ocean.

Capital: Tegucigalpa

Demography: 5,138,000 people, of which about 95 percent are mestizos; the rest are small minorities of Amerindians and people of African descent.

Languages: Spanish; some English is spoken in the larger cities.

Currency: Lempira

Major Religion: Roman Catholic

Orphans Admitted into the United States
Fiscal year 1995: 28   Fiscal year 1997: 26
Fiscal year 1996: 28   Fiscal year 1998: 7

Adoption Information: Limited information is available.

Adoption Authority
I.H.N.F.A. (a successor of the Junta Nacional de Bienestar Social)

U.S. Embassy/Visa Issuing Post
U.S. Embassy, Consular Section
Avenida La Paz
Apartado Postal No. 3453
Tegucigalpa, Honduras
Tel: [504] 238-5114
Fax: [504] 236-9037

Mailing Address:
U.S. Embassy, Honduras
APO AA 34022

JAMAICA

Geography: A Caribbean island 480 miles south of Florida

Capital: Kingston

Demography: About 90 percent of Jamaica's population of 2,500,000 are descendants of Africans who were brought to Jamaica as slaves.

Languages: English and Creole (an English/African patois)

Currency: Jamaican Dollar

Major Religions: Protestant, Roman Catholic

Orphans Admitted into the United States

Fiscal year 1995: 45   Fiscal year 1997: 31
Fiscal year 1996: 34   Fiscal year 1997: 38

Adoption Information: Only Jamaicans who have become naturalized U.S. citizens can obtain a final adoption decree. Children adopted need only to meet Jamaica's definition of an orphan — a child who has lost, or been deserted, or abandoned by his or her parents. Adoptions are completed in Jamaica in three to six months. The adoption board oversees a home study and other preadoption requirements, then issues a license to adopt. Next, a court hearing is scheduled and at least one of the adopting parents must appear.

Since the Adoption Board prepares all of the necessary documents, private attorneys are not necessary. At present, there are no official fees for a Jamaican adoption; however, the U.S. Embassy in Kingston expects this policy to change in the future. The only costs borne by prospective parents are payments toward foster care during the processing period.

Adoption Authority	U.S. Embassy/Visa Issuing Post
The Adoption Board	U.S. Embassy, Consular Section
Children's Services	16 Oxford Road
10 Chelsea Ave.	Kingston 5
Kingston 10	Jamaica, West Indies
Jamaica, West Indies	Tel: [876] 929-4850
	Fax: [876] 926-5833

MEXICO

Geography: Mexico is the northernmost country of Latin America. High mountains and rolling plateaus cover more than two-thirds of the country. Mexico also has tropical forests, barren deserts, and fertile valleys.

Capital: Mexico City

Demography: More than 70 percent of Mexico's 88.6 million people are mestizos; about 20 percent are Amerindians, and less than 10 percent are people of European ancestry. Maya Indians live mainly in the Mexican states of

Campeche, Quintana Roo, and Yucatán.

Languages: Although Spanish is the official language, more than ninety Amerindian languages are still in use. About one million Indians speak only their native language.

Currency: Peso

Major Religion: Roman Catholic

Orphans Admitted into the United States
Fiscal year 1995: 83   Fiscal year 1997: 152
Fiscal year 1996: 76   Fiscal year 1998: 168

Adoption Information: The adopting parents may be married or single, and male or female. All adopters must be at least 25 years of age and at least 17 years older than the child. In the case of a married couple, only one of the adoptive parents must meet the 17-year seniority requirement. If the child is over 14 years old, he or she must agree to the adoption.

The Mexican government welfare department, Sistema Nacional Para el Delarrollo Integral de la Famila (DIF), in each state is assigned responsibility for determining a child's eligibility for adoption. A child is considered legally abandoned six months after a determination by the public ministry of the municipality in which the child lives. The Foreign Ministry is responsible for approving all documents for adoption.

Contact the U.S. Embassy for a list of DIF offices in each state.

Central Adoption Authority
Sistema Nacional Para el Delarrollo Integral de la Famila (DIF)
Prolongacién Xochialco 960
Colonia Santa Cruz Atoyae
Cochigo Postal 03300
Mexico, DF
Tel: [52] (5) 601-2222 ext. 6031

*Also all DIF Offices in each state.

U.S. Embassy/Visa Issuing Posts
U.S. Consulate General
Paseo de la Reforma 305
Col. Cuauhtémoc O6500 Mexico D.F.
Tel: [52] (5) 209-9100
Fax: [52] (5) 511-9980

Mailing Address:
U.S. Embassy, Mexico
P.O. Box 3087
Laredo TX 78044-3087

Orphan Visa Issuing Post
U.S. Consulate General
Avenida Lopez Mateos
924 Norte
32000 Ciudad Juarez
Chihuahua, Mexico
Tel: [52] (16) 113-000
Fax: [52] (16) 169-056

NICARAGUA

Geography: Nicaragua, the largest of the Central American countries, is bordered by Honduras to the north and Costa Rica to the south.

Capital: Managua (400,000)

Demography: Mestizos make up about 75 percent of the population of 3,871,000; black and Amerindian minorities live in the coastal areas near the Caribbean Sea.

Languages: Spanish; some English is spoken in the larger cities.

Currency: Córdoba

Major Religion: Roman Catholic

Orphans Admitted into the United States
Fiscal year 1995: 10   Fiscal year 1997: 13
Fiscal year 1996: 14   Fiscal year 1998: 16

Adoption Information: The child must either be orphaned or abandoned to qualify for adoption. Parental abandonment must be unconditional and irreversible. According to the law, adopters must either be Nicaraguan citizens or have permanent residence in the country.

Adoption Authority
Nicaragua Social Security and Welfare Institution (INSSBI)
Managua, Nicaragua

U.S. Embassy/Visa Issuing Post
U.S. Embassy
Apartado Postal 327
Kilometro 4-1/2
Carretera Sur
Managua, Nicaragua
Tel: [505] (2) 680-123
Fax: [505] (2) 669-943

Mailing Address:
U.S. Embassy, Nicaragua
Unit 2713, Box 10
APO AA 34021

PANAMA

Geography: The southernmost country in Central America. Panama is divided by the Panama Canal, which runs through the Canal Zone between the Atlantic and Pacific oceans.

Capital: Panama City

Demography: Most of Panama's 2,418,000 people are of mixed European, Indian, and African ancestry; 14 percent are black, nine percent are whites, and seven percent are Amerindians.

Languages: Spanish; English is widely understood.

Currency: Balboa (which is really the U.S. dollar)

Major Religion: Roman Catholic

Orphans Admitted into the United States

Fiscal year 1995: 24   Fiscal year 1997: 18
Fiscal year 1996: 10   Fiscal year 1998: 16

Adoption Information: The Tribunal Tutelar de Menores (Minors' Court) has jurisdiction over the adoption case if the child is an orphan, legally abandoned, or declared a ward of the court. The Juzagados de Circuito (Circuit Courts) have jurisdiction when the child has been voluntarily surrendered by the biological parent(s) to the adopting parent(s). Persons interested in adopting through a Circuit Court should contact the U.S. Embassy to determine if the child meets the definition of orphan, or if the child must reside for at least two years with the adoptive parents in Panama before becoming eligible for an immigrant visa.

If adopting through the Minor's Court, a judge will appoint the prospective adoptive parents as the child's legal guardians for a trial period. At the end of the trial period — which is usually six months or less — the judge will determine if the child's adjustment has been successful. If so, the adoption is finalized. If the judge is concerned about the child's welfare, he or she may extend the trial period, or cancel the adoption process altogether. Cancellation is extremely rare. If adopting through a Circuit Court, no trial period is required.

Adoption Authority

(For abandoned children)
Tribunal Tutelar de Menores
Avenida de los Poetas
Chorillo, Panama

(For relinquished children)
Juzgados Circuitos (Circuit Courts)

U.S. Embassy/Visa Issuing Post

U.S. Embassy, Consular Section
Balboa Ave.
Panama City 5
Republic of Panama
Tel: [507] 27-1777

Mailing Address:
U.S. Embassy, Panama
APO AA 34002

PARAGUAY

Geography: Paraguay is a landlocked country in the heart of South America, bordered by Brazil, Argentina, and Bolivia.

Capital: Asuncion

Demography: Most of the population of 2,804,000 are mestizos; the rest are Guarani Indians.

Languages: Although Spanish is the official language, Guarani, the language of the Guarani Indians, is spoken almost as widely as Spanish.

Currency: Guarani

Major Religion: Roman Catholic

Orphans Admitted into the United States

Fiscal year 1995: 351   Fiscal year 1997: 33
Fiscal year 1996: 258   Fiscal year 1998: 7

Adoption Information: Paraguay suspended new international adoption cases effective September 1995. No new adoptions will take place until the new government Center for Adoptions has been established. (Most of the orphan visas issued in recent years are related to the completion of old adoption cases initiated before the change in law.)

In addition, in connection with the ratification of the Hague Convention, Paraguay has indicated that once the new Center for Adoptions is established, the country will work only with citizens of countries that have also ratified the Hague Convention and have established a central authority.

U.S. Embassy/Visa Issuing Post

U.S. Embassy
1776 Mariscal Lopez Ave.
Asuncion, Paraguay
Tel: [595] (21) 213-715
Fax: [595] (21) 213-728

Mailing Address:
U.S. Embassy, Paraguayu
APO AA 34036-0001

PERU

Geography: Located on the northern half of South America's west coast, Peru has three main land regions: the arid coastal area, the highlands of the Andes Mountains, and the thick rainforests and jungles to the east of the Andes.

Capital: Lima

Demography: About 46 percent of Peru's 21.5 million people are Amerindians; about 43 percent are mestizos, and about 10 percent are whites of European ancestry.

Languages: Spanish and Quechua, the language of the Incas, are the official languages; some highland Indians speak Aymara.

Currency: Neuvo Sol

Major Religion: Roman Catholic

Orphans Admitted into the United States
Fiscal year 1995: 15   Fiscal year 1997: 14
Fiscal year 1996: 17   Fiscal year 1998: 26

Adoption Information: All adoptions are handled through agencies approved by the central authority in Lima.

Central Adoption Authority
Ministerio de Promocion de la
Mujer y el Desarollo Humano (PROMUDEH)
(Ministry for the Promotion of Women and Human Development)
Jefe de Adopciones:
Sr. Matha Patriacia Careres de Villcorta
Jr. Camana 616
Lima 1,Peru
Tel: [51] (12) 428-9800

U.S. Embassy/Visa Issuing Post

U.S. Embassy
Avenida La Encalada cdra. 17 s/n
Surco, Lima 33
Peru
Tel: [51] (1) 434-3000
Fax: [51] (1) 434-3037

Mailing Address:
U.S. Embassy, Lima
P.O. Box 1995
Lima, Peru
or
APO AA 34031-5000

SURINAME

Geography: A small country on the northern coast of South America covered mostly by mountainous rainforests

Capital: Paramaribo (150,000)

Demography: More than one-third of the population of 481,000 are Hindustanis whose ancestors came from India; another third of the people are Creoles who have mixed African and European ancestry.

Languages: Dutch is the official language; English is widely spoken. The lingua franca is Sranang Tongo, also called Taki-Taki.

Currency: Guilder

Major Religions: Christian, Hindu, Islam

Orphans Admitted into United States
Fiscal year 1995: not available   Fiscal year 1997: 0
Fiscal year 1996: not available   Fiscal year 1998: 2

Adoption Information: Although Surinamese nationals are given priority in adopting, U.S. citizens may adopt in Suriname. Most Surinamese children in adoptive placements are from unmarried mothers. Almost ninety percent come from ethnically East Indian mothers.

The adoption process in Suriname begins when a mother declares in writing that she wishes to place her child in adoption. The Suriname government strongly encourages all arrangements be conducted by them. U.S. citizens not resident in Suriname must allow for a six- to eight-week stay in Suriname in order to adopt a Surinamese child. The authorities will release the child into the custody of the new family only after they can demonstrate that the child has permission to travel and to reside in the country of destination. There is no charge for adoption in Suriname.

Adoption Authority	*U.S. Embassy/Visa Issuing Post*
Bureau voor Familie	U.S. Embassy
rechttelijke Zaken	Dr. Sophie Redmondstraat 129
Minstry of Justice and Police	P.O. Box 1821
De Voodijraad	Paramaribo, Suriname
Grote Combeweg, P.O. Box 67	Tel: [597] 472-900
Paramaribo, Suriname	Fax: [597] 410-025
Tel: [597] 475-763	

TRINIDAD AND TOBAGO

Geography: Two islands in the West Indies, located 10 miles from the coast of Venezuela

Capital: Port-of-Spain (250,000)

Demography: More than one-third of the population of 1,281,000 is made up of people of African ancestry and about a third are descendants of people from India. Other groups are Creoles, whites of European ancestry, and people of Chinese heritage.

Languages: English, French, Spanish, Hindi

Currency: West Indian Dollar

Major Religions: Roman Catholic, Protestant

Orphans Admitted into the United States
Fiscal year 1995: 9	Fiscal year 1997: not available
Fiscal year 1996: 4	Fiscal year 1998: not available

Adoption Information: According to the Adoption of Children Ordinance, residents of several years and citizens of Trinidad and Tobago may apply for adoption. Information concerning adoption and residency requirements is available from the Adoption Board at the address below.

Adoption Authority
Ministry of Social Development and Family Services
c/o Mrs. Hyacinth Whiteman, Secretary
Adoption Board, Fourth Floor
Salvation Building, Frederick Street
Port-of-Spain, Trinidad
Tel: (809) 625-1926

U.S. Embassy/Visa Issuing Post
U.S. Embassy, Consular Section
15 Queen's Park West
Port-of-Spain, Trinidad
Tel: (809) 622-6372 or 6376
Fax: (809) 628-5462

Mailing Address:
U.S. Embassy
P.O. Box 752
Port-of-Spain, Trinidad

VENEZUELA

Geography: Located on the north coast of South America, Venezuela is bordered by Colombia, Brazil, and Guyana.

Capital: Caracas

Demography: About two-thirds of Venezuela's 19,700,000 people are of mixed Spanish, African, and Indian ancestry; the rest of the people are whites, blacks, and Amerindians of unmixed ancestry.

Languages: Spanish; English is spoken in the major cities.

Currency: Bolívar

Major Religion: Roman Catholic

Orphans Admitted into the United States
Fiscal year 1995: 6   Fiscal year 1997: 8
Fiscal year 1996: 14   Fiscal year 1998: 6

Adoption Information: There are basically two ways to adopt a child in Venezuela — through the Instituto Nacional de Menores (INAM) or through an "entrega directa." INAM is the Venezuelan child protection service. They deal with adoptions of children over the age of two who have been abandoned by their parents. "Entrega directa" is an adoption in which the mother gives up her child, through the court, directly to the prospective parents.

Venezuelan law does not specifically address completion of an adoption outside of Venezuela but it can be done. Parents may be granted provisional custody of a child by a Venezuelan judge and permission to take the child out of Venezuela. Parents should be sure that the court has made it clear, in writing, that the child may travel to the United States for the purpose of emigration. Once the embassy concludes its investigation and determines that the orphan criteria have been met and that all other legal requirements such as the medical exam and home study are in order, an immigrant visa may be issued.

Venezuelan law mandates a three-month probationary period after custody has been granted. During this time, a home study may be conducted by a social worker in Venezuela. However, home studies that have been completed in the United States and approved by an international service agency may be acceptable to the court. In such cases, the three-month waiting period may take place outside Venezuela.

Central Adoption Authority
Instituto Nacional del Menor (INAM)
Servicio de Colocaciónes Familiares y Adopciónes
Avda. San Martin
Edif. Jta. Beneficencia Pub.
San Martin, Caracas 1020
Venezuela
Tel: [58] (2) 461-7866

U.S. Embassy/Visa Issuing Post
U.S. Embassy
Calle F con Calle Suapure
Urb. Colonias de Valle Arriba
Caracas 1060, Venezuela
Tel: [58] (2) 975-6411
Fax: [58] (2) 977-0843

Mailing Address:
U.S. Embassy
P.O. Box 62291
Caracas 1060-A, Venezuela, or
APO AA 34037

Oceania

The geographic designation of Oceania includes Australia and the Pacific Islands. With the exception of the Marshall Islands, international adoption activity is almost nonexistent in this part of the world.

The total number of orphans admitted into the United States from all of Oceania in recent years is detailed below. Visa information for individual countries in Oceania is not available.

Fiscal year 1995: 9   Fiscal year 1997: 4
Fiscal year 1996: 4   Fiscal year 1998: 4

MARSHALL ISLANDS

Geography: A group of islands in the South Pacific, about halfway between the Continental United States and China. The Marshall Islands are located just across the international dateline.

Capital: Majuro

Demography: Population is mainly Caucasoid related to Polynesians

Languages: English, Marshallese, Japanese

Currency: U.S. Dollar

Major religion: Christianity

Adoption Information: There are two ways to adopt children in the court system, but only the legal adoption is available to non-citizens of the Republic of the Marshall Islands (RMI). These are final adoptions. Prospective adoptive parents must file a petition for adoption with an RMI court through a local attorney. (Lists of local attorneys are available from the U.S. Embassy in Majuro).

Adopters must be at least 18 years of age, married or single (for U.S. adopters, singles have to be at least 25 years of age to qualify for an Orphan Petition), and must be able to support and give love, affection, a home, and education to the child according to community standards. There are no proxy adoptions. Both parents (in the case of couples) must be present to complete the adoption. There are no adoption agencies in the Marshall Islands.

Under the terms of the "Compact of Free Association" between the United States and the Marshall Islands, Marshallese citizens have the right to enter the United States without a visa to live and to work. U.S. adoptive parents who bring a Marshallese child into the United States (either already adopted under Marshallese law or with the intention of adopting the child in the United States after having been granted legal guardianship of the child by a Marshallese court) may encounter problems having the child naturalized as a U.S. citizen.

A Marshallese national who enters the United States without an immigrant visa is not a lawful, permanent resident. Under such circumstances, the INS advises that the adoptive parents have to have the child in their physical and legal custody for a period of more than two years before they can apply for a change of status at the INS office in their District. After this, they can initiate the naturalization process. Persons contemplating this course of action should consult with their INS office before they adopt the child, The adopters should be careful to preserve all documents pertaining to the adoption the child: Certified Adoption Order from the Marshallese court authenticated by the U.S. Embassy in Majuro; authenticated copies of the child's birth certificate; and proof of termination of parental rights of the birth parents.

The U.S. Embassy in Majuro is not a visa issuing post. All immigration matters are referred to the U.S. Embassy in Manila, Philippines. It will be necessary for the adoptive parent(s) and the child to travel to the Philippines for the visa interview and issue. This adds approximately six months to the time and additional travel costs.

More information on adopting from the Marshall Islands or Oceania can be obtained from the U.S. Department of State Office of Children's Issues in Washington D.C. The telephone number is (202)-647-2688.

Appendix
Resources and Contacts

NATIONAL ADOPTIVE PARENT SUPPORT GROUPS

Countless organizations exist throughout the United States. Those listed support foreign as well as domestic adoptions. They also provide information and literature on adoption-related issues.

Adoptive Families of America
Largest nonprofit adoptive family organization in the United States representing both member families and affiliate adoptive family support groups.
> 2309 Como Avenue
> St. Paul, Minnesota 55108
> Toll-free: 800-372-3300
> Tel: (651) 645-9955
> Email: info@adoptivefam.org
> Web Site: http://www.adoptivefam.org

Child Welfare League of America
The league is the largest publisher of child welfare materials in the country. It is also extensively involved in consulting with governmental and voluntary child welfare organizations to promote the well being of children and their families.
> 440 First St. N.W., Third Floor
> Washington, D.C. 20001-2085
> Tel: (202) 638-2952
> Fax: (202) 638-4004
> Web Site: http://www.cwla.org

Joint Council on International Children's Services
Oldest and largest affiliation of licensed, nonprofit international adoption agencies. JCICS membership also includes parent groups, advocacy organizations, and individuals who have an interest in intercountry adoption.

Maureen Evans, Executive Director
7 Cheverly Circle
Cheverly, MD 20785-3040
Tel: (301) 322-1906
Fax: (301) 322-3425
Email: Mevans@jcics.org
Web Site: http://www.jcics.org

National Council for Adoption

Adoption advocacy, research, and education organization for individuals as well as licensed nonprofit agencies.

1930 17th St. N.W.
Washington, D.C. 20009-6207
Tel: (202) 328-8072
Fax: (202) 332-0935
Email: ncfadc@ibm.net
Web Site: http://www.ncfa-usa.org

North American Council on Adoptable Children

Founded in 1974 by adoptive parents, the North American Council on Adoptable Children is committed to meeting the needs of waiting children and the families who adopt them.

970 Raymond Ave., Ste. 106
St. Paul, MN 55114
Tel: (651) 644-3036
Fax: (651) 644-9848
Email: NACAC@aol.com
Web Site: http://members.aol.com/nacac

IMMIGRATION & NATURALIZATION SERVICE (INS) DISTRICT OFFICES

These offices process Form I-600A (Application for Advance Processing) and Form I-600 (Petition to Classify an Orphan as an Immediate Relative) as well as providing other services essential in the international adoption process.

An up-to-date list of INS District Offices can be found on the INS Web Site at http://www.ins.usdoj.gov/graphics/fieldoffices/alphaa.htm.

Alaska, Anchorage
620 East 10th Avenue
Suite 102
Anchorage, AK 99501

Arizona, San Luis (POE)
Highway 95 Marker 0
International Port of Entry
San Luis, AZ 85349

Arizona, Tucson
6431 South Country Club
Tucson, AZ 85706

California, Los Angeles
300 N. Los Angeles St.

California, Sacramento
711 J Street
Sacramento, CA

California, San Francisco
630 Sansome Street
Appraiser's Building
San Francisco, CA 94111

California, San Jose
1887 Monterey Road,
Room 216
San Jose, CA 95112

Colorado, Denver
4730 Paris Street
Denver, CO 80209

Connecticut, Hartford
450 Main Street
Hartford, CT 06103

Florida, Jacksonville
400 West Bay Street
Room G-18
Jacksonville, FL 32202

Florida, Miami
7880 Biscayne Blvd.
Miami, FL 33138

Florida, Orlando
9403 Tradeport Drive
Orlando, FL 32827

Georgia, Atlanta
77 Forsythe Street, SW
Room G-85
Atlanta, GA 30303

Hawaii, Honolulu
595 Ala Moana Blvd.
Honolulu, HI 96813

Illinois, Chicago
10 West Jackson Blvd.
Room 333
Chicago, IL 60604

Indianapolis, IN
950 North Meridian Street
Room 400
Indianapolis, IN 46204

Maine, Portland
176 Gannett Drive
Portland, ME 04106

Maryland, Baltimore
100 South Charles Street
12th Floor
Baltimore, MD 21201

Michigan, Detroit
Mt. Elliot Street
Federal Building
Detroit, MI 48207

Minnesota, Bloomington
2901 Metro Drive
Bloomington, MN 55425

Missouri, Kansas City
9747 North Conant Avenue
Kansas City, MO 64153

Missouri, Helena
2800 Skyway Drive
Helena, MT 59601

Nebraska, Omaha
3736 South 132nd Street
Omaha, NE 68144

New Jersey, Newark
970 Broad Street
Newark, NJ 07102

New Mexico, Albuquerque
P.O. Box 567
Room 1010
Albuquerque, NM 87103

New York, New York
26 Federal Plaza
Room 1402
New York, NY 10278

North Carolina, Charlotte
210 Woodlawn Road
Building 6, Suite 138
Charlotte, NC

Ohio, Cleveland
1240 East 9th Street
Room 1917
Cleveland, OH 44199

Pennsylvania, Pittsburgh
2130 Federal Building
1000 Liberty Avenue
Pittsburgh, PA 15222

Puerto Rico, San Juan
Carlos Chardon Avenue
Room 359
Hato Rey, PR 00918

Rhode Island, Providence
200 Dyer Street
Providence, RI 02903

Tennessee, Memphis
1341 Sycamore View
Suite 100
Memphis, TN 38134

Texas, Dallas
8101 North Stemmons Frwy.
Dallas, TX 75247

Texas, El Paso
1545 Hawkins Blvd.
Suite 167
El Paso, TX 79901

Texas, Harlingen
2102 Teege
Harlingen, TX 78550

Texas, Houston
126 Northpoint
Houston, TX 78550

Utah, Salt Lake City
5272 South College Drive
#100
Salt Lake City, UT

Washington, Spokane
691 US Courthouse Building
920 West Riverside Ave.
Spokane, WA 99201

STATE LICENSING SPECIALISTS

State licensing specialists can provide a list of adoption agencies in each state. They can also tell you if an agency is incorporated, if it has nonprofit status, and how long the agency has been licensed under its current name.

This is also where you can check up on the reliability of an adoption agency. The state licensing specialist or the licensing consultant in the county where the agency is located can tell you how many complaints they have received on the agency and if any complaints are unresolved. If you encounter a problem in dealing with an agency, this is also where you should file a complaint.

For up-to-date information on state licensing specialists, visit http://www.calib.com/naic/databases/nadd/naddatabase.htm.

ALABAMA
Office of Residential Licensing
Alabama Department of Human
Resources
Gordon Person Bldg., Box 30400
50 N. Ripley Street
Montgomery, AL 36130-4000
Tel: (334) 242-9500

ALASKA
Alaska Department of Health and
Social Services
Division of Family and Youth
Services
P.O. Box 110630
Juneau, AK 99811-0630
Tel: (907) 465-2817

ARIZONA
Arizona Department of Economic
Security
P.O. Box 6123
Phoenix, AZ 85005
Tel: (602) 542-2289

ARKANSAS
Arkansas Department of Human
Services
Child Welfare Agency Licensing
Unit
523 S. Louisiana, Slot 626
Little Rock, AR 72203
Tel: (501) 682-9978

CALIFORNIA
California Department of Social
Services
744 P Street, M/S 17-17
Sacramento, CA 95814
Tel: (916) 657-2346

COLORADO
Colorado Department of Human
Services
1575 Sherman St., 1st Floor
Denver, CO 80203-1714
Tel: (303) 866-5961

CONNECTICUT
Connecticut Department of
Children & Families
505 Hudson Street
Hartford, CT 06106
Tel: (806) 550-6385

DELAWARE
Delaware Department of Services
for Children, Youth, and Families
1825 Faulkland Road
Wilmington, DE 19805
Tel: (302) 739-5929

DISTRICT OF COLUMBIA
District of Columbia Department of
Human Services
Department of Health-Licensing
and Regulatory Administration
825 North Capital Street, N.E.
Washington, DC 20002
Tel: (202) 442-5929

FLORIDA
Florida Department of Children
and Family
2811-E Industrial Plaza Drive
Tallahassee, FL 32308
Tel: (850) 487-2383

GEORGIA
Georgia Department of Human
Resources
2 Peachtree Street N.W., Ste. 32-
452
Atlanta, GA 30303-3142
Tel: (404) 657-5562

HAWAII
Hawaii Department of Human
Services
810 Richards Street, Ste. 400
Honolulu, HI 96813
Tel: (808) 586-5698

IDAHO
Idaho Department of Health and
Welfare
Division of Family and Children's
Services
P.O. Box 83720
Boise, ID 83720-0036
Tel: (208) 334-5700

ILLINOIS
Illinois Department of Children and
Family Services
406 East Monroe
Springhill, IL 62701
Tel: (217) 785-2688

INDIANA
Division of Family and Children
402 W. Washington Street
Indianapolis, IN 46204
Tel: (317) 232-3476

IOWA
Iowa Department of Inspections
and Appeals
Lucas State Office Building
Des Moines, IA 50319
Tel: (515) 281-3186

KANSAS
Department of Health and
Environment
Mills Building, Ste. 400C
Topeka, KS 66612
Tel: (785) 296-1270

KENTUCKY
Cabinet for Health Services
275 E. Main Street
Frankfort, KY 40621
Tel: (502) 564-2800

LOUISIANA
Louisiana Department of Social
Services
Office of the Secretary
P.O. Box 3767
Baton Rouge, LA 70821
Tel: (504) 922-0015

MAINE
Maine Department of Human
Services
State House, Station 11
221 State St.
Augusta, ME 04333
Tel: (207) 287-5060

MARYLAND
Maryland Department of Human
Resources
311 W. Saratoga Street
Baltimore, MD 21201
Tel: (410) 767-7903

MASSACHUSETTS
Massachusetts Department of
Social Services
24 Farnsworth Street
Boston, MA 02210
Tel: (617) 727-0900

MICHIGAN
Michigan Department of Social
Services
Family Independence Agency
P.O. Box 30650
Lansing, MI 48909
Tel: (517) 373-8383

MINNESOTA
Minnesota Department of Human
Services
Division of Licensing
444 Lafayette Road
St. Paul, MN 55155
Tel: (612) 296-3971

MISSISSIPPI
Mississippi Department of Human
Services
750 N. State Street
Jackson, MS 39202
Tel: (601) 359-4978

MISSOURI
Missouri Division of Family Services
P.O. Box 88
Jefferson City, MO 65103-0088
Tel: (573) 751-4920

MONTANA
Montana Department of Public
Health and Human Services
P.O. Box 8005
Helena, MT 59604
Tel: (406) 444-5919

NEBRASKA
Nebraska Department of Health
and Human Services
P.O. Box 95044
Lincoln, NE 68509
Tel: (402) 471-9138

NEVADA
Division of Children & Family
Services
6171 W. Charleston Boulevard,
Bldg. 5
Las Vegas, NV 89102
Tel: (702) 486-7626

NEW HAMPSHIRE
New Hampshire Division for
Children, Youth, and Family
Services
129 Pleasant Street
Concord, NH 03301
Tel: (603) 271-4729

NEW JERSEY
New Jersey Division of Youth and
Family Services
50 E. State St., C.N. 719
Trenton, NJ 08625
Tel: (609) 292-8255

NEW MEXICO
New Mexico Children, Youth and
Families
Drawer 5160
Santa Fe, NM 87502
Tel: (505) 827-8480

NEW YORK
New York State Office
Department of Children and Family
Service
40 N. Pearl St., Mezzanine
Albany, NY 12243
Tel: (518) 474-9447

NORTH CAROLINA
Department of Health and Human
Services
North Carolina Division of Social
Services
325 N. Salisbury Street
Raleigh, NC 27603-5905
Tel: (919) 733-9464

NORTH DAKOTA
600 E. Boulevard
State Capitol Building
Bismark, ND 58505
Tel: (701) 328-4805

OHIO
Office of Child and Adult
Protection
Ohio Department of Human
Services
Bureau of Children's Services
65 East State Street
Columbus, OH 43266
Tel: (614) 466-3438

OKLAHOMA
Oklahoma Department of Human
Services
P.O. Box 25352
Oklahoma City, OK 73125
Tel: (405) 521-3561

OREGON
Oregon State Office for Services to
Children and Families
HRB 2nd Floor South
500 Summer Street, N.E.
Salem, OR 97310-1017
Tel: (503) 945-6687

PENNSYLVANIA
Pennsylvania Department of Public
Welfare
P.O. Box 2675
Harrisburg, PA 17105
Tel: (717) 787-3984

RHODE ISLAND
Rhode Island Department for
Children and Their Families
610 Mt. Pleasant Avenue
Providence, RI 02908
Tel: (401) 457-4763

SOUTH CAROLINA
Office of Children, Family and
Adult Services
South Carolina Department of
Social Services
P.O. Box 1520
Columbia, SC 29202
Tel: (803) 734-5670

SOUTH DAKOTA
South Dakota Department of Social
Services
Children, Youth and Family
Services
Richard F. Kneip Bldg.
700 Governor's Drive
Pierre, SD 57501-2291
Tel: (605) 773-3227

TENNESSEE
Tennessee Department of Human
Services
Social Services Division
Citizens Plaza
400 Deaderick St., 14th Floor
Nashville, TN 37248
Tel: (615) 313-4744

TEXAS
Texas Department of Protective and
Regulatory Services
P.O. Box 149030
M.C. E-557
Austin, TX 78751
Tel: (512) 438-3245

UTAH
Utah Department of Human
Services
Office of Licensing
120 N. 200 West, 3rd Floor
Salt Lake City, UT 84103
Tel: (801) 538-8222

VERMONT
Vermont Department of Social and
Rehabilitative Services
103 S. Main St.
Waterbury, VT 05671
Tel: (802) 241-2159

VIRGINIA
Virginia Department of Social
Services
730 E. Broad Street
Richmond, VA 23219-1849
Tel: (804) 692-1787

WASHINGTON
Division of Licensed Resources
P.O. Box 45700
Olympia, WA 98504
Tel: (206) 902-8009

WEST VIRGINIA
West Virginia Department of Health
and Human Services
P.O. Box 6165
Wheeling, WV 26003
Tel: (304) 232-4411

WISONSIN
Wisconsin Department of Health
and Family Services
P.O. Box 8916
Madison, WI 53707-8916
Tel: (608) 266-0415

WYOMING
Wyoming Department of Family
Services
2300 Capitol Avenue
Hathaway Bldg., Room 319
Cheyenne, WY 82002-0710
Tel: (307) 777-6479

PUERTO RICO
Puerto Rico Department of the
Families
P.O. Box 11398
Santurce, PR
Tel: (787) 724-0771

VIRGIN ISLANDS
Virgin Islands Department of
Human Services
20A Strand Street and 58B Smith
Street
Christiansted, St. Croix, VI 00820
Tel: (304) 774-0939 ext. 4181

Bibliography
Recommended Reading

Adoption Agency Listings

Adoptive Families of America. *A Guide to Adoption*. Place orders through AFA at 2309 Como Avenue, St. Paul, MN, 55108.

International Concerns Committee for Children (ICCC). *Report on Foreign Adoption*. Boulder, CO: ICCC, 2000.

National Adoption Information Clearinghouse. *National Adoption Directory, Revised Edition*. Rockville, MD: NAIC, 1992.

Adoption — General Information

Adamec, Christine. *There ARE Babies to Adopt: A Resource Guide for Prospective Parents*. Kensington Publishing Corporation, 1996.

Adamec, Christine. *Is Adoption for You? The Information You Need to Make the Right Choice*. John Wiley & Sons, 1998.

Adamec, Christine. *The Adoption Option Complete Handbook, 2000-20001*. Prima Publishing, 2000.

Adamec, Christine and William Pierce. *The Encyclopedia of Adoption*. New York: Facts on File, 2000.

Adamec, Christine and William Pierce. *The Complete Idiot's Guide to Adoption*. Macmillan, 1998.

Bartholet, Elizabeth. *Family Bonds: Adoption and the Politics of Parenting*. Houghton Mifflin, 1999.

Gilman, Lois, *The Adoption Resource Book*. Bongo Press, 1998.

Joint Council on International Children's Services. *The Adoptive Parent Preparation Manual*. Order from JCICS at 7 Cheverly Circle, Cheverly, MD 20785-3040.

National Committee for Adoption. *Adoption Factbook*: United States Data, Issues, Regulations and Resources. Washington, D.C.: National Committee for Adoption, 1999.

Schooler, Jayne. *The Whole Life Adoption Book: Realistic Advice for Building a Healthy Adoptive Family*. Pinon Press, 1993.

Adoption of Older Children and Children with Special Needs

Cox, Caroline, ed. *Trajectories of Despair: Misdiagnosis and Maltreatment of Soviet Orphans*. Available as a photocopy. Send $10.00 to Parent Network for the Post-Institutionalized Child, Box 613, Meadow Lands, PA 15247.

Jarratt, Claudia Jewett. *Helping Children Cope With Separation and Loss*. Boston: Harvard Common Press, 1994.

Leof, Joan. "Adopting Children with Developmental Disabilities." Rockville, Maryland: National Adoption Information Clearinghouse.

Maskew, Trish. *Adopting and Parenting the Older Child*. Snowcap Press, 1999.

Welch, Martha. *Holding Time*. Order through Heartland Catalog, P.O. Box 1974, La Porte, TX 77572-1974.

Adoption Support and Awareness (for Family and Friends)

Bloom S. *A Family for Jaime: An Adoption Story*. New York: Potter, 1991.

Children's Books

Kindersley, Barnabas and Anabel Kindersley. *Celebrations*! UNICEF, DK Publishing, Inc., 1999.

Brodzinsky, Anne. *The Mulberry Bird: An Adoption Story, Revised*. Ft. Wayne, Indiana: Perspectives Press, 1996.

Bunin, Sherry and Catherine Bunin. *Is that Your Sister? A True Story of Adoption*. Wayne, PA: Our Child Press, 1992.

Dorow, Sara and Stephen Wunrow. *When You Were Born In China: A Memory Book for Children Adopted from China*. Yeong & Yeong, 1997.

Freudber, J. and T. Geiss. *Susan and Gordon Adopt a Baby*. New York: Random House, 1992.

Copsey, Susan Elizabeth and Barnabas Kindersley, et. al. *Children Just Like Me*. UNICEF, DK Publishing, Inc., 1995.

Koehler, Phoebe. *The Day We Met You*. Aladdin Paperbacks, 1997.

Livingston, Carole and Arthur Robinson. *Why Was I Adopted?* Carol Publishing Group, 1997.

Lowe, Darla. *Story of Adoption: Why Do I Look Different?* Minneapolis, Minnesota: East West Press, 1987.

Petertyl, Mary Ebejer and Jill Chambers. *Seeds of Love: For Brothers and Sisters of International Adoption*. Folio One Publishing, 1997.

Rosenberg, Maxine B. *Being Adopted*. New York: Lathrop, Lee, Shepard Books, 1984.

Schwartz, Perry. *Carolyn's Story: A Book About an Adopted Girl*. Lerner Publications, 1996.

Schnitter, Jane T. *William Is My Brother*. Indianapolis, Indiana: Perspectives Press, 1991.

Stein, Stephanie and Kathryn A. Imlor. *Lucy's Feet*. Indianapolis, Indiana: Perspectives Press, 1992.

Tax, Meredith and Marilyn Haffner. *Families*. Feminist Press, 1996.

Wasson, Valentina. *The Chosen Baby*. Philadelphia: J.B. Lippincott, 1977.

Welch, Sheila Kelly. *Don't Call Me Marda*. Wayne, Pennsylvania: Our Child Press, 1999.

Wickstrom, Lois and Priscilla Marden. *Oliver: A Story about Adoption*. Wayne, Pennsylvania: Our Child Press, 1991.

Walvoord-Girard, Linda and Linda Shute. *We Adopted You, Benjamin Koo*. Morton Grove, Illinois: Albert Whiteman and Company, 1992.

Waybill, Majorie Ann. *Chinese Eyes*. Scottdale, Pennsylvania: Herald Press, 1974.

Cultural Enrichment

D'Aluisio, Faith. *Women in the Material World*. Sierra Book Club, 1998.

Menzel, Peter. *Material World*. Sierra Book Club, 1995.

Home Studies

O'Rourke, Lisa and Ruth Hubbell. "Adopting a Foreign Child through an Agency." Rockville, Maryland: National Adoption Information Clearinghouse.

Smith, Debra. *The Adoption Home Study Process*. Rockville, Maryland: National Adoption Information Clearinghouse.

Infertility and Adoption

Johnston, Patricia Irwin. *Adopting After Infertility*. Indianapolis: Perspectives Press, 1996.

Johnston, Patricia Irwin. *Taking Charge of Infertility*. Indianapolis: Perspectives Press, 1995.

RESOLVE, The National Infertility Association. *Resolving Infertility: Understanding the Options and Choosing Solutions When You Want to Have a Baby*. Harper Resource, 1999.

International Adoption

Dey, Carol and LeAnn Theiman. *This Must Be My Brother*. Victor Brooks, 1995.

F.A.C.E. *F.A.C.E. Resource Manual*. Provides a listing of regional and extraregional programs in the regional and international fields of adoption. Order from Families Adopting Children Everywhere, Inc., PO Box 28058, Northwood Station, Baltimore, Maryland 21239.

International Concerns Committee for Children (I.C.C.C.). *Report on Foreign Adoption*. Boulder, Colorado: ICCC, 1997.

Register, Cheri. *Are Those Kids Yours? American Families with Children Adopted from Other Countries*. New York: The Free Press, 1991.

Van Loon, J.H.A. *Report on Intercountry Adoption*. Social and legal history of international adoption leading toward a convention on international cooperation for the protection of children in connection with intercountry adoption. Order from: Permanent Bureau of the Conference, Scheveingseweg 6, The Hague, Netherlands.

Interracial Adoption

Alstein, Howard and Rita Simon. *Intercountry Adoption*. Praeger Publishers, 1991.

Aldridge, Jane (ed.) and Ivor Gabor. *In the Best Interests of the Child: Culture, Identity and Transracial Adoption*. Free Association Books, 1995.

Simon, Rita J. *Adoption, Race, and Identity: From Infancy Through Adolescence*. Praeger Publishers, 1992.

Simon, Rita J., Howard Alstein and Marygold S. Melli. *The Case for Transracial Adoption*. American University Press, 1993.

Learning Disabilities, ADHD, and Adopted Children

Alexander-Roberts, Colleen. *The ADHD Parenting Handbook*. Dallas, Texas: Taylor Publishing, 1994.

Parenting Adopted Children

Boyd, Brian. *When You Were Born In Korea: A Memory Book for Children Adopted from Korea*. Yeong & Yeong, 1983.

Brazelton, M.D. T. Barry. *Touchpoints: Your Child's Emotional and Behavioral Development*. Addison Wesley Publishing Company, 1994.

Dawson, Connie and Jean Illsley Clark. *Growing Up Again: Parenting Ourselves, Parenting Our Children*. Hazelden Information Education, 1998.

Greenspan, MD, Stanley and Nancy Thorndike Greenspan. *First Feelings: Milestones of the Emotional Development of Your Baby and Child*. Penguin USA, 1994.

Hopkins-Best, Mary. *Toddler Adoption*. Perspectives Press, 1997.

Jarratt, Claudia Jewett. *Helping Children Cope with Separation and Loss*. Harvard Common Press, revised 1994.

Komar, Marian. *Communicating with the Adopted Child*. New York: Walker and Company, 1991.

Leach, Penelope. *Your Baby and Child from Birth to Age Five*. New York: Alfred A. Knopf. 1997.

Melina, Lois R. *Raising Adopted Children: Practical Reassuring Advice for Every Adoptive Parent*. New York: Harper Perennial Library, 1998.

Miller, Margi and Nancy Ward. *With Eyes Wide Open: A Workbook for Parents Adopting International Children Over Age One*. Available from Children's Home Society of Minnesota, 2230 Como Ave, St. Paul, MN 55108.

Schaffer, Judith and Christina Lindstrom. *How to Raise an Adopted Child: A Guide to Help Your Child Flourish from Infancy to Adolescence*. Plume, 1991.

Silber, Kathleen and Speedlin, Phylis. *Dear Birthmother: Thank You For Our Baby*. Using actual correspondence between birth parents and adoptive parents, this book proves that most birth parents care a lot about their children and think about them later. It also helps adoptive parents and adopted persons understand birth parents. Order from: Corona Publishers, 1037 South Alamo, San Antonio, Texas 78210.

Van Gulden, Holly and Lisa Bartles-Rabb. *Real Parents, Real Children: Parenting the Adopted Child*. New York: Crossroad Publishing Company, 1995.

Watkins, Mary and Susan Fisher. *Talking with Young Children About Adoption*. Yale University Press, 1995.

Personal Adoption Experiences (Adoptive Parents)

Bialosky, Jill and Helen Schulman. *Wanting a Child*. Farrar, Straus and Giroux, 1998.

Ciccarelli, Dave. "Children: Gifts from Mother Russia," *F.A.C.E. F.A.C.T.S.*, July/Aug, 1996.

Pohl, Constance. *Transracial Adoption: Children and Parents Speak*. Franklin Watts, 1992.

Sheehy, Gail. *Spirit of Survival*. New York: William Morrow, 1986.

Psychological Issues

Brodzinsky, David and Marshall Schechter, eds. *The Psychology of Adoption*. New York: Oxford University Press, 1993.

Brodzinsky, David M., Ph.D., Marshall D. Schecter, M.D., and Robin Marantz Henig. *Being Adopted: The Lifelong Search for Self*. New York: Doubleday, 1992.

Da, Frank, et al. "Infants and Young Children in Orphanages: One View from Pediatrics and Child Psychiatry." *Pediatrics*, Vol. 97 no.4, pp.569-578, 1996.

Fahlberg, M.D., Vera. *A Child's Journey Through Placement*. Indiana: Perspectives Press, 1996.

Single Adoptive Parents

Doughtery, Sharon Ann. "Single Adoptive Mothers and Their Children." *The Philadelphia Inquirer*, June 13, 1990.

Groze, Victor K. and James A. Rosenthal. "Single Parents and Their Adopted Children: A Psychosocial Analysis." *Families in Society* 72, no.2 (Februrary 1991): 67-77.

Marindian, Hope. *The Handbook for Single Adoptive Parents*. National Council for Single Adoptive Parents, 1998.

Mattes, C.S.W., Jane. *Single Mothers by Choice: A Guidebook for Single Women Who are Considering or Have Chosen Motherhood*. New York: Times Books, 1997.

Oliver, Stephanie Stokes. "Single Adoptive Fathers." *Essence* 12 (1988) 114-116, 146.

Prowler, Mady. "Single Parent Adoption: What You Need To Know." Rockville, Maryland: National Adoption Information Clearinghouse.

State Laws

National Adoption Information Clearinghouse. "Adoption Laws: Answers to the Most Asked Questions." Rockville, Maryland: NAIC.

Other Resources

Films

Erichsen, Jean. How to Adopt Internationally. Distributed by Los Ninos International.

Goodwins. Visible Differences. North Bay Adoption, 9068 Brooks Road South, Windsor, CA 95492.

Tai Kai Productions. Tai Li Comes Homes. 1340 W. Irving Park, #348, Chicago, IL 60613-1901.

Rashad, Phyllis. Baby Alive. Action Films & Video LTD.

Magazines and Newsletters

Adoptive Families. Bi-monthly color magazine. $24.95. Contact Adoptive Families of America, 2309 Como Avenue, St. Paul, MN 55108.

Adopted Child. Published monthly. U.S. subscriptions $22.00 for 1 year, $38.00 for 2; foreign subscribers add $10.00 per year. Order from Lois R. Medina, PO Box 9362, Moscow, ID 83843.

Adoption Medical News. Edited by Jeri Jennista, M.D., International Pediatric Specialist. Order from Adoption Advocates Press, 1921 Ohio Street NE, Palm Bay, FL, 32907.

Adoption Today. Published quarterly. $15.00 annually. 32 pages; information on all aspects of adoption. Order from WACAP, PO Box 88948, Seattle, WA 98138.

Buenas Noticias. Order from Latin American Parents Association (LAPA), PO Box 4403, Silver Springs, MD 20914-4403.

Chosen Child. Bi-monthly color magazine. 246 S. Cleveland Ave., Loveland, CO 80537. Tel: (970) 663-1185.

Connections. For families with children from India and Indian Subcontinent. $14.00 annually for 4 issues. Order from Address: 1417 E. Miner, Arlington Heights, IL 60004.

F.A.C.E. F.A.C.T.S. Published bi-monthly. Newsletter and membership, $20.00 annually. Order from Families Adopting Children Everywhere. PO Box 28058, Northwood Station, Baltimore, MD 21239.

FAIR Newsletter. Published 6 times a year; membership and newsletter, $20.00 annually. Address: PO Box 51436, Palo Alto, CA 94303.

Families with Children from China. 255 W. 90th St., Apt. 11C, New York, NY 10024. Similar groups exist in nearly every major city.

Families for Russian and Ukranian Adoption. Box 2944, Merrifield, VA 22116-2944. Telephone: (202) 429-3385.

News of Los Ninos. Edited by Jean Nelsen-Erichsen. Bi-monthly color magazine. $30.00 per year. P.O. Box 9617, The Woodlands, TX 77387.

Romanian Children's Connection. 5180 Huntclift Trail. Winston-Salem, NC 27104.

The African Connection. $20.00/yr. Focuses on Africa. Order from Americans for African Adoptions, Inc., 8910 Timberwood Dr., Indianapolis, IN 46234.

The Children's Voice. Family/individual = $10.00 yearly. Organizations = $25.00 yearly. Order from National Coalition to End Racism (in America's Child Care System), 22075 Koths, Taylor, MI 48180.

The Communique. For interracial marriages and interracial families. Order form Interracial Family Alliance, PO Box 16248, Houston, TX 77222.

Health Care for Travelers

International Association of Medical Assistance to Travelers. A free directory (donationa appreciated) of English-speaking doctors abroad who charge set fees. Order from: International Association of Medical Assistance to Travelers, 735 Center St., Lewiston, NY 14092. Telephone: (716) 754-4883.

Other Publications

UNICEF: A beautiful catalog which reports on the needs of children in developing countries and offers an outstanding array of international cards, books, games, stationary as well as a growth chart. Order from: UNICEF, United Nations Children's Fund, 475 Oberlin Ave. South, CN 2110, Lakewood, NJ 08701.

World Travel Directory. Vol.8. New York, Ziff-Davis. Published annually. A library reference book which is a source of addresses to write to for free information provided by the U.S.-based tourist information services.

Local Ethnic Organizations

Consult the History Department of the Public Library in large cities. Their "Club File" holds cards for local ethnic group organizations. Names of the organizations as well as current presidents are listed.

Glossary

abandonment	Term used to define a child as an orphan by his or her government's setting a specific time limit, such as three months, in which a relative may reclaim the child. If not, a decree of abandonment is issued.
adoptee	Person who is adopted.
adopter	Adult who adopts a child.
adoption	Consummation, or finalization of a child's placement with a couple or single in the child's native country or in the new country of residence.
adoption agency, U.S.	Performs social work and home study as required by state licensing standards.
agency-initiated adoption	A placement and/or adoption facilitated or processed by an agency.
ambassador	The highest ranking representative appointed by one country or government to represent it in another.
Americans	All the citizens of the Americas. Latin Americans consider themselves Americans, as do Canadians.
apgar score	Health check of a newborn at birth and five minutes later for the quality of the heartbeat, respiratory effort, muscle tone, and reflex action. A perfect score is 10, which is rare. An eight or nine is considered excellent. A low Apgar score is usually found in infants whose mothers had complicated pregnancies or deliveries.
apostille	A form from the state verifying a notary's date of commission.
authentication	There are two types of authentication. The consul of the country from which you wish to adopt attests to the authenticity of your certificate and original documents by his or her seal or signature. The U.S Department of state attests to the authenticity of your documents with red seals and ribbons.
biological parent	Birth mother and birth father.
bonding	The loving, caring, emotional attachment for a successful parent-child relationship.
certification	Issued by the department of vital statistics in the country where the birth, marriage, divorce or death took place.
closed adoption	No exchange of information is agreed upon by both parties.
consulate	Office or residence of a consul.
consul	Citizen appointed by his government to live in a certain city in a foreign country to look after his country's citizens and business interests there.
cooperative adoption	Information is exchanged between birth parents and adoptive parents. Usually, pictures and letters are sent once a month until adoption, then once a year on the child's birthday.
consummation	An adoption decree, issued after the documents have been reviewed by a judge.

custody transfer	When an orphan is escorted from one state or country to another for the purpose of adoption, the government of the agency in authority formally transfers custody of the child to the adoption agency or DPW at the child's destination.
DHS or DPW	Department of Human Services or Department of Public Welfare, or similarly named agencies in each U.S. state where adoption of out-of-state and foreign-born children are approved. DPW studies and records the orphan's documents before the INS gives approval.
disruption	Adoptive placement is interrupted prior to consummation. (Nationally, this accounts for ten to fifteen percent of placements.)
dossier	Envelope containing the application, pictures, legalized documents, and so forth, required by a foreign adoption source.
embassy	Official office or residence of an ambassador in a foreign country; foreign embassies are in Washington, D.C., and U.S. Embassies are usually located in the capital cities of foreign countries with which we have diplomatic relations.
emigration	The act of leaving a country legally.
escort	A child already adopted or to be adopted is brought to the United States by an authorized adult.
ethnicity	A minority within an existing racial group.
finalization	Adoption is complete and the adoption decree is issued.
guardianship	A formal paper is issued by the judge in court which grants legal guardianship of a child to a prospective adoptive couple with the understanding (in foreign countries) that they will adopt the child under the laws of the country in which the child will reside.
hard-to-place children	Children over five, large sibling groups, older sibling groups, babies or children with a correctable or noncorrectable handicap.
home study	An evaluation by a social worker with at least a bachelor's degree in social science.
I-600	Orphan visa petition form.
immigration	The act of entering a country legally.
INS	Immigration and Naturalization Services, a federal agency in each state and in Washington, D.C.
invitation	A letter from the ministry of a foreign country granting permission to obtain a visa.
locating fee	Fee from an unlicensed U.S. individual for finding a foreign orphan for an adopter. Unnecessary and, in some states, illegal.
managing conservator	The legal guardian of the child.
nationality	Nation or colony in which a person is born. (Nationality and race are not the same thing, although, this mistake is often made.)
natural child	English expression for a child of birth-parents, wed or unwed.
natural parents	English expression for birth parents.
networking	Formal or informal agreements between adoption agencies and U.S.-based international agencies to cooperate with home studies for international placements.
notarization	A notary public verifies that the signatures on your original documents are valid.
open adoption	Personal visits between birth parents and child continue after placement with the adoptive parents. This is impractical in foreign adoptions.
original document	Documents generated on your behalf, such as letters of reference.
orphan	Child released for adoption by an immediate relative, or abandoned for a legally prescribed time.
passport	A document required by most countries for entry.

parent-initiated adoption	Direct or independent adoption of a foreign child without the use of a U.S. based international adoption agency.
permission to leave	A form required for orphans in some countries which must be signed by a child-placing authority.
placement	Physical placing of orphan with adoptive parent(s).
postplacement study	A report of a supervisory study in an adoptive home.
power of attorney	A form signed by adopters for use by foreign attorney to initiate the adoption before the adopter arrives, or to arrange an adoption by proxy of a child to be escorted to the United States.
pro se **adoption**	Adoption without a lawyer.
proxy adoption	Child adopted through power of attorney and escorted to the United States; an arrangement usually made by agencies or liaisons.
publication	Information on an abandoned or relinquished child is published in local newspapers, court gazettes, or a central adoption data base for a specific period of time as specified by national or regional law in order to give relatives the opportunity to claim a child prior to termination of the birth parents' rights.
readoption	A second adoption in the United States, under the laws of the child's new county of residence.
referral	Assignment of a child to an adopter, either by phone call or letter, and followed up with medical and social reports and photos.
release/ relinquishment	A release form signed by the orphan's mother or orphanage, and necessary, along with a birth certificate, or the orphan's visa petition and visa issuance.
replacement	Child relinquished by adoptive parents and placed again in a new home.
semi-open adoption	Adoptive and birth parents meet at the child's placement or in court, then proceed as in cooperative adoption.
siblings	Brothers and/or sisters.
social worker	An individual with a bachelor of science, or master of science from an accredited college of social work. Most social workers obtain certification form the state board.
street child	Two types: 1. Child who lives in the street who does not have a caretaker or a home. 2. Child who lives mainly in the streets, but who does have a caretaker of sorts.
Third World	Developing countries, as opposed to First World, (the U.S.A. and other industrially developed nations.)
U.S.-based international adoption agencies	Hold legal contracts with foreign adoption sources to make child placements.
verification	A form from the state verifying the notary's commission.
visa	For adults, an endorsement granting entry into a particular country for a specified length of stay. Adopted orphans are an exception.
waiting children	Children over five, large sibling groups, older sibling groups, babies or children with a correctable or noncorrectable handicap.
waiting pool	A group of prospective adoptive parents who have completed their preadoption requirements for the foreign court and have INS clearance.

Index